D1716074

Black and Brown Planets

BLACK AND BROWN PLANETS

. . .

The Politics of Race in Science Fiction

Edited by Isiah Lavender III

University Press of Mississippi / Jackson

www.upress.state.ms.us

The University Press of Mississippi is a member
of the Association of American University Presses.

Frontis image by Jaz C. Alexander

Edward James, "Yellow, Black, Metal, and Tentacled: The Race Question in American
Science Fiction" was originally published in *Science Fiction, Social Conflict, and War*,
edited by Philip John Davies. Used by permission of Manchester University Press.

First printing 2014

∞

Library of Congress Cataloging-in-Publication Data

Black and brown planets : the politics of race in science fiction / edited by Isiah Lavender III.
    pages cm
Includes bibliographical references and index.
ISBN 978-1-62846-123-7 (hardback) — ISBN 978-1-62846-124-4 (ebook) 1. Science fiction,
American—History and criticism. 2. Race in literature. 3. Minorities in literature. I. Lavender,
Isiah, editor.
    PS374.S35B55 2014
813'.08762093529—dc23   2014010170

British Library Cataloging-in-Publication Data available

Contents

Contents

CODA

Acknowledgments

First and foremost, I must thank God for providing me with the ambition and requisite skills to see this collection to fruition. Second, I thank my wife, Heather, for all of her love, support, prayer, and sacrifice; my sons, Kingsley and Frazier; and my sister, Melissa, for their patience with me. Though I have certainly learned that editing a collection is not at all easy, I am grateful to all of the contributors for the trust they placed in me, for their willingness to revise, and for taking this journey with me. I especially appreciate the advice and additional help offered by Gerry Canavan and Lisa Yaszek.

The idea for this collection originated at the 2010 International Conference of the Fantastic in the Arts, where I moderated a panel, "Black and/or Brown Planets: Politics and Race in Science Fiction," that featured Grace Dillon, David Higgins, De Witt Kilgore, and Patrick Sharp. I am very grateful to these panelists as well as to the audience members who came to listen to their erudition. Likewise, I am indebted to Rachel Haywood Ferreira for spreading the word about the call for papers. I deeply regret not being able to include several more essays by Henri-Simon Blanc-Hoang, Biling Chen, Wei Ming Dariotis, Sharon DeGraw, Uppinder Mehan, and Takayuki Tatsumi. I can only hope they accept my heartfelt apology and perhaps a meal when our paths next cross.

I am also grateful to Brian Attebery for helping me refine my own Butler essay as well as to Dale Knickerbocker and Jen Parrack for pointing out the obvious regarding Butler's character, Beatrice Alcantara. I would be remiss not to express my thanks to my old UCA colleagues—Chuck Bane, Dwayne Coleman, Sonya Fritz, Lori Leavell, David O'Hara, and Wayne Stengel—for listening to me drone on and on about the challenges of editing. I must also thank UCA for providing the time necessary to complete the first draft of this project with a Fall 2012 sabbatical.

Likewise, I have nothing but gratitude toward my new LSU colleagues—Chris Barrett, Michael Bibler, Lauren Coats, Brannon Costello, Jennifer Davis, Daren Dean, Angeletta Gourdine, Benjy Kahan, Gerry Kennedy, Phillip Maciak, Michelle Massé, Elsie Mitchie, Rick Moreland, Anna Nardo, Daniel Novak, Lisi Oliver, and Irina Shport—for showing an immediate interest in my work.

I am also thankful to Manchester University Press for giving Edward James permission to reprint his foundational essay, "Yellow, Black, Metal, and Tentacled: The Race Question in American Science Fiction," which first appeared in Philip John Davies, ed., *Science Fiction, Social Conflict, and War* (1990): 26–49. His essay appears here in virtually identical form.

Finally, I am particularly grateful to the University Press of Mississippi. Walter Biggins believed in the project, Vijay Shah helped me see it through, Katie Keene kept me on schedule, and Ellen Goldlust was an amazing copyeditor.

Black and Brown Planets

INTRODUCTION

Coloring Science Fiction

• • •

ISIAH LAVENDER III

As long as I can remember, science fiction (SF) and race have been tangled together in my thoughts.

• • •

My earliest memory is waking up in my father's arms, a light rain falling on my face, as he carried me into the house. At some point in the summer of 1977, I fell asleep during the trash compactor scene of *Star Wars* at the Grandview Drive-In located in Angola, New York. I had missed the epic light-saber duel between Obi-Wan Kenobi and Darth Vader, though I saw Han Solo shoot the green-skinned Greedo first! I remembered the strange greenness of Greedo's skin and the thrill it gave me. I was three years old.

• • •

I remember my mother's adoration of SF in 1982. I remember her excitement about her birthday present, a subscription to *OMNI* magazine.[1] The magazine's covers were cool, and I loved flipping through the pages. I also remember seeing *Blade Runner* in the middle of June. My sister was at a sleepover, my father was working a weekend night shift, and the babysitting fell through at the last moment. So my mother decided to take me to an R-rated movie at the Holiday 6 Theater, somewhere in suburban Buffalo. I remember the grittiness of the film's opening and the voice of Deckard, the main character, talking about the tolerance his boss, Bryant, showed for difference: "Skin jobs.

That's what Bryant called Replicants. In history books he's the kind of cop who used to call black men niggers." Of course, I did not comprehend the meaning of the comparison and soon forgot about it as the film overwhelmed my barely eight-year-old senses. I do vividly recall Rutger Hauer's very blond head slamming through a wall, though.

• • •

The first time the N-bomb was dropped on me was 1983, but I survived to share this most intimate of memories with the world. I wish that I could have said that the year was 1984, one of the most iconic years in SF fandom thanks to George Orwell's classic *Nineteen Eighty-Four* (1949), but then I would be lying. "Nigger, you're dead!" exploded in my ears as the fists and feet stomped me into the ice-encrusted snowdrifts of a February afternoon in the suburbs of Buffalo, New York. I was eight and three-quarters years old. My world was forever changed. My soul was reorganized on an atomic level. I was made aware of my difference, of my red-toned brown skin, not unlike W. E. B. Du Bois's experience in a schoolyard in Great Barrington, Massachusetts.[2] *Nigger.* The racial epithet was dropped on my eight-year-old self by a pack of fourth-graders that day, and I was consciously exposed to the radiation of racial hatred. I survived the detonation of that nuclear blast in my heart, unlike the Africans in Philip K. Dick's counterfactual history *The Man in the High Castle* (1962).[3] I remember stumbling in the front door with a torn coat, missing one of my blue moon boots, cold, wet, bloody, and exposed to the toxicity of racism. My mother had an incredulous look of anger on her face, and I asked her, "What does nigger mean, Mom?"

With fast feet and a faster mouth, I had decided to jabberjaw at these fourth-graders that morning at the bus stop and had forgotten about it during the school day at Highland Elementary. When I disembarked from the school bus at my street corner that afternoon instead of in front of my house, I made a fateful decision that would shape the rest of my life. I wanted to race the school bus home in my red-rimmed blue moon boots about a quarter mile through the two feet of snow covering the sidewalk. I actually thought I could win. I thought I could fly like the space shuttle *Columbia*, but I lost the race that afternoon. I lost the race, I lost my seat on the bus, and I lost my racial innocence (color-blindness), too.

Those fourth-graders had not forgotten my verbal assault, and they were waiting for me at my driveway. Six of them pounded me into the icy snowbanks. They were shouting "Nigger!" at me when I made it to my driveway. I remember the crash of their fists and weight of their kicks as they trampled me into the snow. I remember the bright redness of the blood I left in the snow that afternoon. I remember the freezing sensation of winter and its paradoxical warmness as my clothes were torn and my left moon boot and its liner were ripped away. I will never forget that day. I was called a bad word because of the color of my skin, because I was different, because I was something Other. Thank God my bus driver, Jonie, stopped when she came back down the court, or I could have been killed. I knew I had been insulted along with the beating, but I did not know what the word *nigger* meant, though I now recalled hearing it the summer before in *Blade Runner*.

After cleaning me up and warming my body with a cup of hot chocolate, my parents tried to explain the implications of the word. They were successful. I understood the power of racism, and the N-bomb in particular, at eight years of age. It is an explosive term with highly negative connotations. It is a painful word, a sad word, a disturbing word, and a word that has not lost its sting over time. It is embedded in the fabric of American society despite the era of political correctness in which we live. It is a hurtful word, a loaded word, a heart-rending word, but it is out there every day. It is the language of racism—of terrorism, in fact. It is meant to harm or kill the spirit of a person, no matter how innocuous the situation in which the word is spoken. It is incendiary! It burns with hatred and masks fear toward those who are different in any context. And I got the meaning of it that night.

My furious parents confronted the school district's superintendent and my principal the next morning as well as the PTA the following week. I had to sit in the front seat on the bus for the rest of third grade. Shortly thereafter, my mother gave me a copy of Ray Bradbury's *The Martian Chronicles* (1950) and I came across the story "June 2003: Way in the Middle of the Air." I distinctly remember blacks leaving the South en masse for Mars on rockets and the main character, Samuel Teece, calling them niggers. I often wonder why my mother gave me that book, but it left another indelible impression on me.

• • •

Thinking on these particular memories and impressions leads to a specific question at the crux of all that I hope to do professionally: why study race in science fiction? My academic curiosity regarding the intersections of race and SF is resolute, and my partial knowledge of other racial binaries in SF demands further investigations. So then, why gather these scholars, and why put together this collection?

Elisabeth Leonard's pioneering 1997 anthology, *Into Darkness Peering: Race and Color in the Fantastic*, was the first text of consequence to undertake a discussion of race in the speculative genre and consequently will always be important because it began the shared dialogue on race and SF. *Black and Brown Planets* continues the conversation that Leonard started. Reexamining SF's background has a significant cultural effect for the twenty-first century because it can assist our understanding of the social changes occurring as the Western world ceases to be dominated by the white majority. SF has charted a few of the alternatives for this unknown territory, and the change presents both opportunities and challenges for society to establish new values.

In short, skin color matters in our visions of the future. Though Du Bois articulated "the color line" as "the problem of the twentieth century" well over a hundred years ago (41), it still remains a fearsome and complicated twenty-first-century problem. This problem challenges and compromises if not corrupts all endeavors to build a better, more progressive world. Even if race and the color line are the work of humans, they are political realities given value by SF writers that must now be reconsidered and reinterpreted by present generations of SF scholars. To transcend various repetitions of the color line—black, red, and brown—we must be conscious of these repetitions. Such a consciousness can be acquired only by exploring the possible worlds of SF and lifting blacks, indigenous peoples, and Latinos out from the background of this historically white genre.

The link between race and politics in SF is always evident but is most often confined to explorations of how racial identity inflects or challenges conventional narrative expectations. However, any evaluation of race should include its overlaps with what could be termed high politics. This collection considers the role that race and ethnicity plays in science fictional scenarios on the design and direction of alternate or futurist high-tech societies. Part 1 emphasizes the political elements of black identity portrayed in SF, from black America to the vast reaches of interstellar space framed by racial history, Afrofuturism, and the postcolonial moment, among other things. Analysis of indigenous SF in part 2 addresses the effects of colonization, assists in discarding the emotional and psychological baggage carried from its impact, and recovers ancestral traditions to adapt in a post-native-apocalyptic world. Likewise, part 2 explores the affinity between SF and subjectivity in Latin American cultures from the role of science and industrialization to the effects of being and moving between two cultures, effectively alienated as a response to political repression. While all of the essays in part 2 in some way address issues of science and technology studies, thus connecting the "brown planets" of North American indigenous SF and Latin American SF, clear contrasts are also addressed, not the least of which is a complex internal racism within Latin American countries and their ambiguous position as both colonized and colonizing nations. For that reason, John Rieder's influential *Colonialism and the Emergence of Science Fiction* (2008) is a touchstone for anyone interested in the issues explored in this volume. This collection briefly (too briefly, some critics would rightly argue) turns to a discussion of techno-Orientalism in the representation of Asian characters in SF before concluding with a critique of online SF fan culture.

Considerations of science fiction concerning the continents of Africa and Asia are beyond the scope of this collection, although it does include one essay on political representations of Asian identity. The roles (political, social, and historical) that skin color, ethnic ancestry, and cultural identity play in one's ability to succeed in future visions of these regions are certainly worthy of further study. For example, South African writer Lauren Beukes's debut novel, *Moxyland* (2008), explores the politics of oppression when a national government, determined to control its citizens, creates its own terrorists with the help of a global technology company. Censoring all lines of communication, infecting protesters and innocent bystanders alike with a lab-controlled Marburg virus, corporate branding of citizens, and rewarding the guilty with higher public status does not seem terribly far-fetched in today's shaky global economy. Nonetheless, I wonder at the meaning of having the only black viewpoint character, Tendeka, a native of Zimbabwe, die a horrible death with his insides liquefying, viewed by some as "a terrorist" and by others as "a martyr" (367).

Another brief illustration involves the inhuman slave status of "New People" in Paolo Bacigalupi's multiple-award-winning novel *The Windup Girl* (2009) (35). Emiko is a "Japanese windup" (36), a bio-engineered human being with superior physical and mental abilities as well as the built in fail-safe identifier, "stutter-stop flash-bulb strange" physical movements (35). The windups are a pop-locking technologically derived ethnicity, a technicity designed to "serve" the whims of their owners, with other uses as soldiers, courtesans, and translators, among other things, in a dystopian Bangkok (36). Readers dare not ignore the racial implications as well as other important issues presented in this disturbing possible future. Bacigalupi surely gets at a deep human truth—our desire to elevate humankind beyond nature through technology, to be something more, something posthuman, yet also to retain old mechanisms of control such as race and ethnicity on our creations, making us spectacularly unsuccessful at transcending our problems of difference. Though we certainly like to think that scientific progress pushes prejudice and discrimination to the side, SF and history suggest otherwise.

This collection offers a timely exploration of the Western obsession with color in analyzing the sometimes contrary intersections of racial politics in

SF. The authors consider how alternate racial futurisms, such as Afrofuturism and indigenous futurism, reconfigure our sense of viable political futures in which people of color determine human destiny. This collection is particularly relevant given the Obama presidency and the increasing stature of postcolonial nations as global powers. How does or can SF respond to this new world, this emerging history?

Black and Brown Planets shows what SF criticism means when joined with critical race theories and histories of oppression. To date, it is the most complete study of SF's color lines. Various race binaries along the color line remain because common prejudices wrongly established by pseudoscientific applications of social Darwinism endure, granting racism a kind of immovability. Perhaps this feeling of permanence is why such an important critical race theorist as Derrick Bell seems to have little hope for the condition of blacks and other perceived minorities, particularly in the United States. He declares, "The fact is that, despite what [blacks] designate as progress wrought through struggle over many generations, we remain what we were in the beginning: a dark and foreign presence, always the designated 'other'" (10). Applying his thinking on a global scale, we can at the very least perceive the many forms of racial oppression around the world that are continually fostered by Euro-American interests without misjudging the importance of their political implications in SF. In this respect, *Black and Brown Planets* has been put together to address these very issues.

· · ·

The Black Planets section opens with Lisa Yaszek's "The Bannekerade: Genius, Madness, and Magic in Black Science Fiction," which demonstrates how artists working both alongside and within genre SF have used a story type she calls "the Bannekerade" to think about science, society, and race in unusual ways by exploring the centrality of SF's two oldest character types, the creative engineer and the mad scientist, in black SF. In "The Best Is Yet to Come"; or, Saving the Future: *Star Trek: Deep Space Nine* as Reform Afrofuturism," De Witt Douglas Kilgore dissects *Star Trek*'s projection of an endless white future by directly challenging the intent of *Star Trek*'s racial politics with its practice of reinstating customary racial traditions. Kilgore argues that a *DS9* episode, "Far beyond the Stars," allows the series to confront African American history as a root of the Federation's utopian future as a reform Afrofuturism. In "Far beyond the Star Pit: Samuel R. Delany," Gerry Canavan approaches the same episode of *DS9* as a frame for analyzing Delany's experiences in science fiction by focusing most directly on his early novella, "The Star Pit," as an allegory for life under segregation. In my contribution, "Digging Deep: Ailments of Difference in Octavia Butler's 'The Evening and the Morning and the Night,'" I demonstrate how Butler's critically neglected story is a race story, with disease functioning as a race metaphor, and how those suffering from the fictional genetic illness Duryea-Gode Disease (DGD) are in fact victims of cultural racism, figurative blackness, and racial Othering. In "The Laugh of Anansi: Why Science Fiction Is Pertinent to Black Children's Literature Pedagogy," Marleen S. Barr illustrates why during the postcolonial moment, the political elements of black identity portrayed in black SF are important for empowering black children.

Shifting the collection's focus to indigenous populations and Latin America in the Brown Planets section, Grace L. Dillon's "Haint Stories Rooted in Conjure Science: Indigenous Scientific Literacies in Andrea Hairston's *Redwood and Wildfire*" emphasizes how this novel deconstructs the excessive capitalism and empire tactics of the Victorian period. In so doing, it creates a renewed form of the speculative novel that emphasizes both the agency and presence of native and African American sciences intertwined with art via the use of indigenous methodologies and epistemologies. In "Questing for an Indigenous Future: Leslie Marmon Silko's *Ceremony* as Indigenous Science Fiction," Patrick B. Sharp critiques the colonial imagination that produced both modern science and the "grammar of race" that codes all nonwhites as incapable of contributing to the futures promised by science fiction. In "Monteiro Lobato's *O presidente negro* (The Black President): Eugenics and the Corporate State in Brazil," M. Elizabeth Ginway investigates Lobato's portrait of American society and Anglo-Saxon culture in the year 2228, influenced by neo-Lamarckian eugenics and the belief in a genetic basis for inherited characteristics. Lysa M. Rivera's "*Mestizaje* and Heterotopia in Ernest Hogan's *High Aztech*" traces the ways in which Hogan embeds Mesoamerican indigenous mythologies in high-tech, technophilic science fictionalized futures and comments on the synergistic affinities between experiences of alienation under colonialism in the Americas (specifically Mexico) and experiences of posthuman, decentered technologies. In "Virtual Reality at the Border of Migration, Race, and Labor," Matthew Goodwin discusses how Latin American writers and artists have shown that virtual reality reproduces colonialism's dystopian construction of race and exploitation of labor, generating not a utopia but just another world to be colonized.

Malisa Kurtz's "A Dis-(Orient)ation: Race, Technoscience, and *The Windup Girl*" examines Bacigalupi's portrayal of a future Bangkok seething with racial tensions and prejudices despite technoscientific advancements. Kurtz's implication that such progress masks imperial and racist ideologies leads perfectly into Edward James's reflections on his classic 1990 essay, "Yellow, Black, Metal, and Tentacled: The Race Question in American Science Fiction," which is reprinted here. Accepting the idea that racial science, written almost exclusively by white men, has created social conflict for people of color in the United States, James argues that racist attitudes and widespread prejudices have shaped SF in the twentieth century. Bridging the twentieth and twenty-first centuries and bridging racial binaries, James's essay is one of the barometers measuring how far race criticism of SF has come in the past twenty-four years—and how far it has left to go.

In the Coda, Robin Anne Reid's "'The Wild Unicorn Herd Check-In': The Politics of Race in Science Fiction Fandom," analyzes work done by fans of color to increase racial and other types of diversity in the science fiction community, which includes not only readers but also editors, publishers, and authors, as a means of increasing diversity in the science fiction narratives themselves.

. . .

Black and Brown Planets begins amending some of the shortcomings in my book, *Race in American Science Fiction* (2011), by tackling race from multifold viewpoints. Here, then, are twelve further reasons why I am compelled to study race in SF. Invoking race and racism in an outwardly white genre is necessary. Coloring science fiction *is* an absolute and radical commitment.

Notes

1. *OMNI* published articles on science and science fiction stories from Oct. 1978 through late 1995 and survived on the Internet until 1998.

2. Du Bois revealed his emerging awareness of racial difference as a New England schoolboy when a white girl imperiously refused to accept his "visiting-card" and "it dawned upon [him] with a certain suddenness that [he] was different from the others; or like, mayhap, in heart and life and longing, but shut out from their world by a vast veil" (44).

3. Dick writes, "But Africa. [Nazi Germany] had simply let their enthusiasm get the better of them there, and you had to admire that, although more thoughtful advice would have cautioned them to perhaps let it wait a bit.... *As to the Final Solution of the African Problem, we have almost achieved our objectives*" (24–25). Though the text does not indicate what this final solution is, inferring that nuclear devices were used on the African population is possible because of "Operation Dandelion," a planned "nuclear attack on the Home Islands" of Japan (189).

Works Cited

Bacigalupi, Paolo. *The Windup Girl*. San Francisco: Night Shade, 2009. Print.

Bell, Derrick. *Faces at the Bottom of the Well: The Permanence of Racism*. New York: Basic, 1992. Print.

Beukes, Lauren. *Moxyland*. Nottingham: Angry Robot, 2008. Print.

Blade Runner. Dir. Ridley Scott. Sir-Run Run Shaw/Warner, 1982. DVD.

Bradbury, Ray. "June 2003: Way in the Middle of the Air." 1950. *The Martian Chronicles*. New York: Bantam, 1950. 89–102. Print.

Dick, Philip K. *The Man in the High Castle*. 1962. New York: Vintage, 1992. Print.

Du Bois, W. E. B. *The Souls of Black Folk*. 1903. New York: Signet Classic, 1995. Print.

Lavender, Isiah, III. *Race in American Science Fiction*. Bloomington: Indiana UP, 2011. Print.

Leonard, Elisabeth A., ed. *Into Darkness Peering: Race and Color in the Fantastic*. Westport: Greenwood, 1997. Print.

Orwell, George. *Nineteen Eighty-Four*. 1949. New York: Plume, 2003. Print.

Rieder, John. *Colonialism and the Emergence of Science Fiction*. Middletown: Wesleyan UP, 2008. Print.

PART ONE

— — — • • • — —

Black Planets

THE BANNEKERADE

Genius, Madness, and Magic in Black Science Fiction

• • •

LISA YASZEK

We need to figure out, as a society, how to portray the work of an intellectual or inventor like Thomas Edison as really exciting. . . . Every now and then, in one of these science fiction films, there is a problem or something breaks down and the guy who is the computer nerd . . . is called. . . . He just seems like this jerk, but in the last twenty minutes of the movie . . . he helps them figure out how to get rid of the beast of whatever. We need to do better than that, and I think we can.

—**Stanley Crouch,** "Straighten Up and Fly Right"

Over the past decade, Afrodiasporic intellectuals have called for new images of black genius in relation to science and technology. Given science fiction's status as the premier narrative of technoscientific modernity, it is perhaps no surprise that these same intellectuals have consistently turned to the genre for stories of black genius. For example, while African American artist and cultural critic Stanley Crouch suggests that black artists can capitalize and improve on the images of genius already found in SF film, his scholarly counterpart, Ron Eglash, shows that at least one such artist is already doing just that: "The development of technological expertise requires not only financial resources but also cultural capital. Nerd identity has been a critical gateway to this technocultural access. . . . The career of African American actor Samuel L. Jackson . . . illuminates the figure of the black nerd in popular media. During the 1980s Jackson played a series of drug dealers and junkies, but . . . he quickly switched to playing black nerds. . . . After confessing his geek love for the *Star Wars* films to producer George Lucas, he achieved the ultimate nerd fantasy of playing a Jedi Knight" (49, 55, 57). This essay provides greater context for the dreams of public intellectuals such as Crouch and Eglash by mapping the nearly two-hundred-year history of black genius in print SF. In particular, artists working both alongside and within genre SF have used a story type I call "the Bannekerade" to think about science, society, and race in novel and sometimes startling ways.

Stories about the technoscientific genius are central to SF and as old as the genre itself. There is even a specific story type dedicated to the adventures of the technoscientific genius: the Edisonade. Named after wildly popular nineteenth-century inventor Thomas Alva Edison, this kind of story "features a young US male inventor hero who uses his ingenuity to extricate himself from tight spots and who, by so doing, saves himself . . . his friends and [his] nation from foreign oppressors" (Clute). While the invention that saves the day is likely to be a weapon, it is also, more often than not, a "means of transportation" and a "certificate of ownership" that enables the boy inventor to claim the foreign oppressors' territory for himself and for Earth as a whole (Clute). Tales in this vein include print SF stories such as Garrett P. Serviss's "Edison's Conquest of Mars" (1898), where the titular character responds to a Martian invasion by inventing a disintegration ray and an antigravity device that enables him to travel to the red planet, beat the Martians at their own game, and then take Mars as a colonial holding for the United States. Traces of the Edisonade also appear in the popular *Flash Gordon* film serials of the 1930s, as polo star turned quasi-military hero Flash uses devices created by his scientist father and the friendly Russian, Dr. Zarkov, to do battle with Ming the Merciless on the planet Mongo.

When Afrodiasporic authors write this kind of story, they follow the same general outlines but extrapolate from the life of a different scientist-inventor, revolutionary-era free black Benjamin Banneker. Born in 1731, Banneker is remembered for creating the first wooden clock in America and for working on the team that surveyed what would become the District of Columbia. In 1792, Banneker—who was also a self-taught astronomer—began publishing his own *Almanac and Ephermis*, which competed successfully with Benjamin Franklin's *Almanac*.[1] Perhaps not surprisingly, Banneker used his technoscientific genius to fight what he perceived as the greatest evil of his own day: slavery. All proceeds from his publications went to abolitionist causes, and Banneker sent Thomas Jefferson copies of his almanac as "tangible proof of the mental equality of the races" (Bedini xx). Banneker spent his entire life studying, conducting scientific experiments, and hosting salons that brought together intellectuals from all races and walks of life.[2] Although Banneker was all but forgotten in the years immediately following his death in 1806, in 1844, abolitionists published "the first relatively comprehensive account of his accomplishments," and in 1853, the Banneker Institute, "a large library and instruction society for young African Americans" opened its doors to the public (Russell loc 7292).

Appropriately enough, in Afrodiasporic versions of the Edisonade—what I call the Bannekerade—the hero is generally a young black male scientist-inventor who uses the products of his genius to save himself, his friends, and his community from domestic oppressors who either are white Westerners or use the machinery of Western institutions as tools for black oppression. Either way, racial tension is an explicit force shaping the narrative at hand. This sustained interest in race leads to two other differences between the Edisonade and the Bannekerade. The Edisonade is usually cast in nationalistic terms, but the international scope of Western imperialism and the various attendant African diasporas lead black authors to cast the Bannekerade in global terms. Furthermore, while the Edisonadian hero usually completely eliminates the threat of foreign oppressors altogether by destroying enemies and appropriating their lands, the Bannekeradian protagonist more often wins a series of immediate battles only to find he is still in enemy territory and faces a drawn-out race war with an uncertain ending.

Key elements of the Bannekerade first appear in what is generally considered to be the first African American SF story, Martin R. Delany's alternate history *Blake; or, The Huts of America.* Initially serialized in the *Anglo-African Magazine* (Jan.–July 1859) and then published in its entirety in the *Weekly Anglo-African* (Nov. 1861–May 1862), *Blake* revolves around the adventures of Henry Holland, a "handsome, manly, and intelligent" free black from the West Indies who is kidnapped and sold into slavery under the name Henry Blake (16). Blake suffers his fate in silence until his owners sell his wife, Maggie, to a Cuban slaveholder. Blake then devises a series of ingenious plans that allow him to escape captivity and travel through the American South to Cuba to rescue his beloved. Along the way, he liberates his immediate family, sows the seeds of revolution among other enslaved blacks, and gathers a group of like-minded men and women who dream of building a global black empire. In its broadest dimensions, then, *Blake* is very much the story of a young black male who uses his genius to liberate himself, his friends, and his community from domestic oppressors.

Delany does not cast his protagonist as an inventor but insists that scientific knowledge and technical ability are central to Blake's emancipatory project. Early in his story, Delany describes Blake as "a man of good literary attainments" (17). Later, it becomes evident that Blake is also a man of good scientific attainments when he teaches Maggie's family astronomy and compass navigation, explaining that this kind of knowledge is "all that's necessary to guide you from a land of slavery and long suffering, to a land of liberty and future happiness" (134). In this respect, Blake functions much like a "creative engineer," using his scientific and technical knowledge "for the good of all people, rather than the benefit of any individual person, business or nation" (Yaszek 387).

What is perhaps most interesting about Delany's story as a proto-Bannekerade is his vision of a global black future built by collective technoscientific action. As one member of Blake's Grand Council explains, "The African race is now the principal producer of the greater part of the luxuries of the enlightened countries.... They are among the most industrious people in the world.... [E]re long they and their country must hold the balance of commercial power by supplying ... the greatest staple commodities in demand[:] rice, coffee, sugar, and especially cotton" (260). Furthermore, "Africans in all parts of the world readily and willingly [mingle] among and [adopt] all the usages of civilized life, attaining wherever practicable every position in society" (262). Working together, the Council dreams, Africans and Afrodiasporic people might leverage their native agricultural skills and acquired technocultural expertise to build a transcontinental empire that supplants the West—and especially the American South—as the engine of futurity.[3]

Although Delany's heroes dream of a utopian black future, *Blake* ends on a rather different note, with members of the Great Council preparing for an all-out race war they seem unlikely to win. Despite his misgivings, the most vocal advocate of military action is Blake himself. As he tells the Council, "You know my errand among you; you know my sentiments. I am for war—war against the whites.... May God forgive me for the wickedness, as my conscience admonished and rebuked me.... But my determination is fixed, I will never leave you" (290–91). Thus Delany insists that black people have both the resources and talent to compete in a high-tech global economy. To deny them this opportunity is to halt the natural progression of capitalism, turning nonviolent economic and technocultural competition into apocalyptic military battle.

The themes that first emerge in *Blake* come together most forcefully in a group of texts published between 1880 and 1945, a period that saw consolidation of SF as a distinct popular genre and that marks peak popularity of both the Edisonade and the Bannekerade. Stories including Sutton E. Griggs's *Imperium in Imperio* (1899), Pauline Hopkins's *Of One Blood; or, The Hidden Self* (1903), Edward A. Johnson's *Light ahead for the Negro* (1904), Roger Sherman Tracy's *The White Man's Burden: A Satirical Forecast* (1915), and George S. Schuyler's *Black No More* (1931) and *Black Empire* (1936–38) all celebrate black technoscientific genius. Johnson and Sherman do so in a general way, treating black genius as the birthright of all black people; Griggs, Hopkins, and Schuyler express their ideas about the promise and perils of black genius through individual characters who are recognizable scientist-inventors. Furthermore, while these authors imagine that black geniuses might fight domestic oppression with a wide range of tools—including everything from scientific discoveries about the dangers of miscegenation and the possibility of raising people from the dead to the invention of new communication technologies and biological weapons—they agree that the systemic oppression of such genius can lead only to the devastation of the entire human race.

Griggs's *Imperium in Imperio*, for example, revolves around an African American shadow empire that has existed within the United States since the nation's birth. Griggs creates a deep history for the Imperium that would have been familiar to turn-of-the-century African American readers. While the Imperium includes hundreds of thousands of African Americans at the time the story unfolds, it is actually the creation of a single technoscientific genius: "There lived, in the early days of the American Republic, a negro scientist who won an international reputation by his skill and erudition. . . . Because of his learning and consequent usefulness, this negro enjoyed the association of the moving spirits of the revolutionary period. By the publication of a book of science which outranked any other book of the day that treated of the same subject, this negro became a very wealthy man. . . . [He] secretly gathered other free negroes together and organized a society that had a twofold object. The first object was to secure for the free negroes all the rights and privileges of men, according to the teachings of Thomas Jefferson. Its other object was to secure the freedom of the enslaved negroes the world over" (94). Griggs extrapolates from what is clearly Benjamin Banneker's life story to imagine an alternate world where the great scientist uses the profits of his genius to ensure the liberation of his free friends, his enslaved African American counterparts, and the global Afrodiasporic community. Banneker himself thus becomes the first fully developed Bannekeradian hero in speculative fiction.

While Griggs creates a powerful history of black technoscientific genius, he is less sanguine about the possibility of such genius in either the present or the future. *Imperium* follows the adventures of two childhood friends who have very different experiences of America but who both end up as leaders in the Imperium. Belton Piedmont is a poor, dark-skinned educator who encourages African Americans to gain mastery over the mass media and the industrial arts so they will be recognized as the technocultural equals of their white counterparts. When he is almost lynched for these activities, Belton leaves his wife and child to go into hiding with the Imperium, where he quickly rises to the rank of Congressional Speaker. By way of contrast, Bernard Belgrave is a rich, light-skinned Yale graduate determined to make a name for himself as a lawyer. When Bernard's fiancée discovers a scientific study suggesting that miscegenation causes black sterility and will eventually destroy the black race, she kills herself to avoid marrying Bernard. Half-crazed with grief, a newly militant Bernard joins the Imperium and eventually, as president, advocates violent action against the United States. When Belton protests, Bernard orders his friend's death. As the novel draws to a close, Bernard stands poised to lead the Imperium into a full-blown race war.

By way of contrast, Schuyler's *Black Empire* locates black technoscientific genius squarely in the present. Published as two interlocking serials in the *Pittsburgh Courier* between 1936 and 1938, *Black Empire* relates the tale of a global revolution masterminded by the brilliant Dr. Henry Belsidus and carried out by the cadre of equally brilliant Afrodiasporic men and women he has gathered from around the world. As Belsidus explains, white people might have all the money and power, but they "haven't got all the brains. We are going to out-think and out-scheme the white people. . . . I have the organization already . . . scattered all over the world; young Negroes [who are] intellectuals, scientists, engineers. They are mentally the equal of the whites. They possess superior energy, superior vitality, they have superior, or perhaps I should say more intense, hatred and resentment, that fuel which operates the juggernaut of conquest. . . . You will see in your time a great Negro nation in Africa, all-powerful, dictating to the white world" (15). Belsidus's plan is, in essence, the narrative trajectory of the Edisonade reversed and writ large. In the conventional story of technoscientific genius, one heroic young white man uses his talents to do battle against the dark foreign oppressor. Here, Schuyler revises that story to show how a heroic collective of young black people might use their talents to do battle against the white homegrown oppressor.

And that is precisely what these Bannerkeradian heroes do. First, the Black Internationale, as they call themselves, perfect hydroponic farming, solar energy, and international communication systems to ensure the self-sufficiency of their future black empire. Then they go to war. After decimating the United States with biological warfare, the Black Internationale liberates Africa from its European colonial oppressors and announces the birth of the Black Empire. When the Europeans protest, Belsidus's second in command, air force general Patricia Givens, masterminds a complex series of air raids that quickly brings Europe to its collective knees.

Despite the war's amazing pyrotechnics, Schuyler, like Griggs and Delany before him, does not ultimately endorse violent black revolution. Instead, all three write cautionary tales—what members of the SF community call the "if this goes on" story.[4] In this case, early African American SF authors insist that if systemic racial oppression goes on, black technoscientific genius will not be squashed; rather, it will be perverted by hate into something that threatens the entire human race.

While Delany dramatizes this possibility through the evolution of Blake from man of learning to man of arms, Griggs and Schuyler do so by casting their protagonists as one of the most popular science fictional character types in America at the turn of the century: the mad scientist. Generally speaking, the mad scientist is not literally mad but a "rash or hubristic" creator who works outside the boundaries of the scientific community for personal rather than altruistic reasons (Langford). In Griggs's novel, Bernard Belgrave is cast both as mentally unstable and as a bad scientist. In her suicide note, Bernard's fiancée admits that she has never verified those scientific studies connecting interracial reproduction to the death of the black race, so she begs Bernard to do that. Crazed by grief, Bernard skips over that step and rushes into militant political action.

Meanwhile, Schuyler depicts Henry Belsidus as both utterly brilliant and completely amoral from the very start. As Schuyler's readers learn early on, Belsidus acquires start-up funds for the Black Internationale by mesmerizing, swindling, and then murdering rich white women. Schuyler's protagonist defends himself to his peers with the argument that a few white lives are nothing compared to the millions of black men and women who have been murdered by slavery and subsequent racial oppression. But for readers, it is difficult to ignore the fact that both sections of *Black Empire* end with the image of Belsidus's girlfriend, the good-hearted European countess Martha Gaskins, weeping for all the lives lost in the creation of a new world order. And thus, these early stories serve as both celebrations of black technoscientific genius and warnings about what might happen if that genius is denied its rightful place in the modern world.

By the mid-1950s, the Edisonade had all but vanished from SF storytelling. This disappearance occurred in large part as a consequence of internal aesthetic developments within the genre. Early science fictional representations of genius in the Edisonade both anticipated and reflected the technocratic ideals of early twentieth-century America. These ideals—to create a more egalitarian and efficient society by replacing economic and political governance with its scientific counterpart—were embodied in stories such as Hugo Gernsback's 1911 serial *Ralph 124C+*, where the titular character's inventions win him the accolades of an adoring public, the love of a beautiful woman, and even the grudging respect of his enemies. Such characters seemed very much to be "nonpolitical and in service of a national ideal" (Huntington

4). However, as subsequent generations of SF authors strove to write more complex, character-driven stories, they found themselves grappling with the possibility that the technoscientific genius might also be monstrously selfish, recklessly competitive, and ruthlessly driven to master the world rather than save it (Huntington 55). As such, figures like the self-taught genius-inventor Kidder from Theodore Sturgeon's 1941 novelette "Microcosmic God," who creates a race of synthetic beings and the forces them to evolve through systematic abuse and whose secret nearly triggers World War III, became characters to envy and fear rather than love and admire.

Midcentury political events also conspired to make the Edisonade an increasingly irrelevant story form. Over the course of the atomic age, people became increasingly skeptical about the wholesale benevolence of science and technology. With the encouragement of SF magazine editor and taste-maker John W. Campbell Jr., authors replaced the naive optimism of Edison-ade with more culturally relevant story types such as dystopic nuclear war narrative and the cautionary "if this goes on" tale (Westfahl 184). By the time the New Wave—with its mandate to make the genre new—took center stage in the 1960s, many SF writers had abandoned the notion of technoscientific genius altogether, linking technocultural progress to brilliance within the soft sciences and arts instead.

While the Edisonade has all but vanished from speculative writing, the Bannekerade remains popular with Afrodiasporic authors. From its inception, black authors have used the Bannekerade to critically assess the politics of technoscientific genius as it pertains to racial, national, and global communities. As such, it was—and still is—better equipped to explore political and cultural change than its Edisonian counterpart. But modern authors update this story form in strategic ways. Like earlier Bannekerades, stories including Walter Mosley's *Futureland* (2001), Steve Barnes's *Charisma* (2002), Minister Faust's *Coyote Kings of the Space Age Bachelor Pad* (2004), Amiri Baraka's *Tales of the Out and Gone* (2006), and Andrea Hairston's *Mindscape* (2006) relate the adventures of young black geniuses battling oppressive forces on behalf of themselves, their friends, and their various communities. However, all these authors insist that the geniuses in question may be male or female and that whatever their sex, they are likely to use both traditional and novel forms of technoscience to save the day. Furthermore, while more established authors such as Mosley, Barnes, and Baraka identify racism as the primary force thwarting true scientific and social progress, newer ones such as Faust and Hairston treat racism as a side effect or tool of much larger natural and supernatural forces.

To a certain extent, Mosley's story most closely resembles but also most clearly marks the limits of the classic Bannekerade. *Futureland* is a series of nine interlocking short stories set in a dystopic corporate-run future where workers oscillate between meaningless jobs and the half-life of subsistence-level unemployment. Constitutional rights are taken away from anyone who challenges the system, and prison inmates are used as experimental subjects. While the media claim that racism is dead, people of color bear the brunt of *Futureland*'s bad social and scientific practices and white people flock to hate groups like the revived National Socialist Party. The avatar of this bad future is Dr. Ivan Kismet, CEO of MicroCode and the richest man in the world. More than mere profiteer, Mosley casts Kismet—whom he describes as having "the second highest IQ in the history of such things"—as the classic mad scientist, a man who casually exploits workers and prisoners alike in his quest to develop a biomedical technology that will enslave the entire human race (loc 969).

But all is not lost. Mosley's collection revolves around the exploits of various black scientists, inventors, and computer hackers as they use the products of their genius to fight for a better future. These efforts are led by Ptolemy Bent, a young black man from rural Alabama who is the purest soul and greatest genius in history. Bent's family fiercely protects the brilliant boy, gladly selling body parts on the black market so they can afford in-home educational technologies that will teach him to "find his own way an' make up his own mind" rather than sending him to a state institution where "them white people and them people wanna be white [will] turn him into some cash cow or bomb builder or prison maker" (loc 264). Bent flourishes in this environment. At the age of four, he invents a device to communicate with the benign Gaia-like alien that has wrapped itself around the Earth; at sixteen he uses a modified version of this device to release the minds of his uncle and grandmother from their dying bodies so they can merge with the Gaia being. As the avatar of the Bannekeradian hero, Bent uses his inventions quite literally to reduce suffering and increase knowledge for his people.

Not surprisingly, *Futureland* revolves around the struggle between Kismet and Bent to influence the shape of things to come. Terrified by the potential he sees in Bent, Kismet imprisons the boy inventor on his private island. Mosley's hero turns the situation to his advantage by using all the resources available in Kismet's lab to reestablish contact with the Gaia alien and create the first truly autonomous artificial intelligence, which names itself Un Fitt. Together, Bent, the alien, and Un Fitt identify six thousand men and women with "undiscovered brilliance and the power to dream of something other than their minds locked into this world"—including all of *Futureland*'s other protagonists—and set up the conditions by which they can act on their dreams of revolution (loc 4145). At the same time, Bent works tirelessly to develop a biotechnology that will render Kismet's biocontroller useless by changing "the capacity and nature of the brain [thereby pulling] us out of the darkness of technology" (loc 4166). Thus, Bent dreams a future where his best and final invention will liberate all humans from the dangerous tendencies of technoscientific capitalism by literally enlarging their minds.

But this amazing future is put on indefinite hold by two events: Kismet's discovery of Un Fitt and Bent's discovery that the National Socialist Party has created a plague designed to "target racial indicators" and kill all black people (loc 4303). In response, Bent devises a plan that saves the AI and most of the other geniuses who have been arrested by Kismet's people, frees himself from jail to reunite with his remaining family members, and then "rig[s] something like a flashlight to emit the correct band of radiation," thereby rendering the virus inert (loc 4318). Unfortunately, one plague canister is mutated rather than destroyed and the virus kills "everybody but people with at least 12.5 percent African Negro DNA" (loc 4835). This mutation, in turn, triggers precisely the race war Bent hopes to prevent, with radical black activists raising a global army to claim the Earth as their own and swarthy survivors who still identify as white banding together to kill their obviously black counterparts. And so while Mosley departs from earlier authors such as Griggs and Schuyler with his depiction of a truly benevolent black genius, he nonetheless comes to the same conclusion: one man working alone within Western paradigms cannot save humanity from its deeply entrenched habits of domination and destruction.

So what is the black genius to do? Minister Faust's *Coyote Kings of the Space Age Bachelor Pad* offers one possible solution: ally the Afrodiasporic inventor with his non-Western counterpart. Faust's novel follows the story of the titular Coyote Kings, two African Canadian friends who are drafted into a seven-thousand-year-old battle between good and evil originating in Africa and spanning the entire globe. The Bannekerian hero of Faust's novel is Yehat Gerbles, a video store clerk, science fiction fan, and all-around "genius with gadgets" (10) who has spent the past two years of his life building "a giant, mechanical, exoskeletal anime [machine]" he calls his R-Mer (57). Yehat's best friend is Hamza Senesert, a dishwasher, comic book fan, and would-be poet who learns that his talent for discovering lost things is part of his heritage as an African *sekht-en-cha*, or desert hunter (407). Together, the Coyote Kings embody two character types familiar to science fiction and comic book fans the world over: the brilliant boy inventor and the genetically superior human—what early members of the SF community called "the slan" and what contemporary audiences may recognize as "the X-Man."

In good Bannekeradian fashion, Yehat uses his inventions to get himself and Hamza out of tight spots. Faust's novel revolves around the revelation that Hamza is destined to find an ancient artifact that can be used to create either universal enlightenment or universal slavery. Hamza vows to give the artifact to the representatives of goodness, but when two agents of evil follow him to the artifact's hiding place, Yehat and his R-Mer must save the day (497). As it turns out, Yehat's actions have profound effects far beyond the immediate battle. When the Coyote Kings kill the agents of evil, they kill the masterminds behind a series of drug epidemics that have decimated poor black societies around the globe, turning their victims into murderers and cannibals. So, in the course of saving himself and Hamza, Yehat ultimately saves the larger Afrodiasporic community from a fate worse than death.

As even this brief discussion of *The Coyote Kings* makes clear, the Bannekerade continues to resonate with modern readers because authors such as Faust use it not just to celebrate Western modes of technoscientific ingenuity but also to put Western technoscientific traditions in dialogue with their counterparts from around the globe. A good deal of the narrative force driving Faust's novel comes from the tension between Yehat's investment in Western engineering practices and Hamza's willingness to believe in what seems to be African magic. In fact, when Yehat learns the story behind the artifact, he abandons Hamza because "you're saying that every rational thing in the world isn't worth two kumquats. . . . This is all bullshit!" (486–87).

But if telepathic desert hunters and unstoppable forces of evil are bullshit, then why does Yehat come back in the end to save the day? The easy answer is that Coyote Kings don't abandon one another. While that is true, Faust offers another answer as well: African magic is really another mode of science. Every time something that seems supernatural happens, there turns out to be a perfectly plausible explanation for it: desert hunters are created either genetically or chemically; agents of evil are unstoppable because they consume natural and synthetic physical enhancers. What seems like magic turns out to be "an advanced science the world hasn't seen in thousands of years" (496).

And that is how Yehat—and perhaps many of Faust's readers—make their peace with this situation. From the very beginning of *Coyote Kings*, Yehat is described as a "hard SF" fan in "genre alignment" with Arthur C. Clarke (13). As Clarke himself famously noted, "Any sufficiently advanced technology is indistinguishable from magic" (36). Yehat returns to Hamza in the end because he realizes that while his "whole understanding of the world has been turned upside down," he does not have to choose between science and magic (523). Instead, he takes it "on faith" that it is possible to put African and Western modes of science in dialogue to become a real "protector of the world" (523). This is perhaps why the Bannekerade still speaks to SF authors and readers today. Even if Western modes of technoscientific genius are not the only means by which people can save the world, they can take it on faith that they are still useful and very much compatible with other ways of knowing and creating a better world.

Finally, Andrea Hairston's *Mindscape* offers the most dramatic and most optimistic rewriting of the Bannekerade to date. Like other SF authors working in this tradition, Hairston celebrates the possibility that brilliant black individuals might bring about a new world order. But, she insists, if that new world order is truly to be more equitable, it must be the product of the individual genius collaborating with a community of equally talented men and women who represent different kinds of science and the arts. *Mindscape* is set on a near-future Earth that has been irrevocably changed by the Barrier, a "blood red cloud of unknown material" that erupts from another dimension, denying humans access to the stars and carving the world up into three distinct zones (loc 66). These zones include the corporate-run technoscientific realm of Paradigma, the gang-run film empire of Los Santos, and the democratic territory of New Ouagadougou, where people mix high art with scientific, religious, and magical traditions from around the world to perfect biomedicine and genetic manipulation. Despite their literal divorce from history, the leaders of each zone ultimately repeat historical precedence, publicly embracing the free trade of goods and ideas while privately scheming to bring each other down.

The leaders of each zone also and more specifically repeat the bad practices of racism found throughout human history. Thanks to the gene art of New Ouagadougou, the zones are all technically postrace and postgender societies, where anyone can look like anything. Yet each zone continues to distinguish Self from Other in brutal ways. For example, the rulers of Los Santos march "dusky Extras" into the Barrier in times of famine, while Paradigma officials promote light-skinned geniuses to positions of power while their dark-skinned "ethnic throwback" counterparts "be languishin' back in . . . impoverished settlement[s]" (loc 2155, 2140). Meanwhile, New Ouagadougou—a country that defines itself against the bad practices of the other zones—wages genocide against the Vermittler, a hybrid race of people comprised of human and Barrier DNA created by a renegade gene artist to serve as "go-betweens" with direct control over the Barrier (loc 91). Thus, Hairston brings together elements of both the classic Edisonade and the classic Bannekerade, creating a world threatened by alien and domestic forces alike.

Hairston also picks up on a theme raised by Mosley and Faust: the need to create better futures by exchanging technoscientific paradigms for their bioscientific counterparts. This is particularly apparent in her depiction of Paradigma. In classic SF technocracies such as Gernsback's *Ralph 124C+*, brilliant scientists and engineers replace "capitalism mismanagement of industrial production" with a scientifically derived system that encourages "industrial democracy, production for use and not profit, and the non-utopian horizon of a post-scarcity culture"—and, more often than not, receive great accolades from an adoring, well-educated public for their efforts (Ross 118–19). While Paradigma claims to fulfill this ideal, its leaders are actually corporate executives who encourage "monopoly, not diversity," profiting from semilegal weapon sales to the other zones and systematically persecuting scientists interested in any kind of science or art other than those that have made their nation's fortune (loc 3244). To protect themselves and the system they have created, Paradigma officials surround themselves with military experts who are "chemical dependents," programmed to protect the status quo even at the expense of their own lives (loc 3483). Thus Hairston teases out the protofascist tendencies of the classic technocratic utopia, showing how easily such a utopia might become its own nightmarish double.

By way of contrast, Hairston presents New Ouagadougou, with its emphasis on democratically elected Council leaders and globally derived biosciences, as the most viable source of utopian change. New Ouagadougouian healers draw on both indigenous botanical practices and Western technical procedures to combat deadly post-Barrier viruses, while New Ouagadougouian scientists use insights about the illusory nature of reality drawn from various systems of art and magic in tandem with Western technology to create objects (and people such as the Vermittler) that tunnel safe new passages through the Barrier. Even so, the leaders of New Ouagadougou are nearly as problematic as those of Paradigma, hiding their best discoveries from the other zones and murdering all Vermittler who refuse to work for the Council's vision of national purity: "Maintaining our own humanity is difficult enough. New Ouagadougou certainly can't humanize Paradigma or Los Santos. . . . Imperialists are not the route to our humanity. Europe cannibalized Africa and the Americas, remember? [It is] a waste of spirit to struggle with Paradigma and Los Santos . . . and then they'd define us. [We will not] help technocrats and thugs rape our spirits" (loc 2643). While Hairston clearly celebrates the ideal of a globally produced bioscience over its Western, machine-oriented counterpart, she is careful to show that new kinds of scientific progress do not automatically equal social or political progress.

Given her interest in bioscience, it is no surprise that Hairston also celebrates the possibility of black bioscientific genius. The character that most clearly plays this part is Elleni Xa Celeste, one of the last living Vermittler. Despite her sometimes horrific appearance—Elleni is a rather plain, stocky black woman whose eyes turn inside out when she is manipulating space-time and who sports a head full of multicolored, venom-dripping, semisentient dreadlocks—Hairston's protagonist is dearly loved by the people of New Ouagadougou for her healing talents. Furthermore, while they consider the Vermittler to be "false griots, abominations," the members of the New Oua-gadougouian Council tolerate Elleni because she can sculpt new passages through the Barrier with nothing more than song—and because they believe that the Barrier will eventually demand a "blood sacrifice" on the part of the Vermittler "to make sense of the world" as it has evolved (loc 3999, 5518). If New Ouagadougou is a modern interpretation of the classic SF technocracy, then Elleni is very much a modern interpretation of the classic Bannekera-dian protagonist: a brilliant individual whose invention, the sculpting song, may eventually save the world, but one who confuses the distinction between hero and victim, human and alien, inventor and invention, and scientist and artist in the person of her own body.

While Elleni is both a symbol of and catalyst for change, Hairston insists that she cannot do it alone. Early in *Mindscape*, readers learn that Elleni needs contact with someone completely unlike herself to return home after transdi-mensional travel through the Barrier, and it soon becomes apparent that she also needs contact with an entire cohort of geniuses unlike herself to fulfill New Ouagadougouian prophecy and "shepherd [humanity] into the future" (loc 91). These brilliant men and women include the Major, a cyborg soldier who overcomes his programmed loyalty to Paradigma when he realizes that change is the only logical way to solve the world's problems; Lawanda Kitt, an ethnic throwback ambassador who crusades tirelessly for justice; Aaron Dunklebrot, a transsexual and transraced director who uses considerable sto-rytelling talents to gain public consensus for Elleni's mission; and Ray Vallero, Elleni's lover and Aaron's star actor, an ex-gangster who becomes a real-life hero when he volunteers to sacrifice himself to the Barrier with Elleni. The actions of these various characters eventually inspire two Vermittler to join Elleni's crusade as well: the Wovoka, an apostate citizen of New Ouagadou-gou who releases souls of the dead from the Barrier so the living can make peace with the past, and Sidi, a Council leader who merges with the Barrier in place of Elleni and Ray, using her genetically enhanced persuasive talents to coax the Barrier into opening permanent new passages between the three zones and between Earth and other worlds. And so *Mindscape* ends on a truly hopeful note, with Elleni and Ray embracing each other while those who have sacrificed themselves to the Barrier recite lines from a Yoruba prayer: "Aboru, Aboye, Aboşişe. May what we offer carry, be accepted, may what we offer bring about change" (loc 7956).

Notes

1. Biographers Charles Cerami and Robert M. Silverstein suggest that the success of Banneker's almanac stemmed from an early exposure to both African (specifically Dogon) astronomy at home and Western mathematics at a local Quaker school (17, 26). Whether or not this was the case, it has become a central part of Banneker's mythology. Moreover, this idea resonates well with Bannekerades such as Pauline Hopkins's *Of One Blood: or, The Hidden Self* (1903), where the protagonist's scientific aptitude is revealed to be part of his royal African heritage; Andrea Hairston's *Mindscape* (2006), where one faction of humanity builds a bioscience empire by combining Western and African ways of knowing the world; and Minister Faust's *Coyote Kings of the Space Age Bachelor Pad* (2004), where a thoroughly Westernized young black engineer must team up with representatives of African "magical" traditions to save the world.

2. For a fascinating discussion of Banneker's correspondence with Jefferson, see Andrews.

3. As Mark Bould points out, this fictional vision of black industrial and commercial dominance reiterates many of the "Heinleinian 'engineering' solutions" that Delany proposed in his political writing (55). For further discussion, see Bould.

4. The "if this goes on. . ." tale is named after a Robert Heinlein story of the same title that first appeared in *Astounding Science-Fiction* in 1940 and has been reprinted numerous times since then.

Works Cited

Andrews, William. "Benjamin Banneker's Revision of Thomas Jefferson: Conscience versus Science in the Early American Antislavery Debate." *Genius in Bondage: Literature of the Early Black Atlantic.* Eds. Vincent Carretta and Philip Gould. Lexington: UP of Kentucky, 2001. Print.

Baraka, Amiri. *Tales of the Out and Gone.* New York: Akashic, 2006. Print.

Barnes, Steven. *Charisma.* New York: Tor, 2002. Print.

Bedini, Silvio A. *The Life of Benjamin Banneker.* New York: Scribner, 1972. Print.

Bould, Mark. "Revolutionary African-American Sf before Black Power Sf." *Extrapolation* 51.1 (2010): 53–81. Print.

Cerami, Charles A., and Robert M. Silverstein. *Benjamin Banneker: Surveyor, Astronomer, Publisher, Patriot.* New York: Wiley, 2002. Print.

Clarke, Arthur C. *Profiles of the Future: An Inquiry into the Limits of the Possible.* Rev. ed. New York: Harper and Row, 1973. Print.

Clute, John. "Edisonade." *The Encyclopedia of Science Fiction.* Eds. John Clute and Peter Nichols. 6 Oct. 2012. Web. 12 Oct. 2012.

Crouch, Stanley. "Straighten Up and Fly Right." *Black Genius: African American Solutions to African American Problems.* Eds. Walter Mosley et al. New York: Norton, 1999. 248–68. Print.

Delany, Martin R. *Blake; or, The Huts of America.* 1859–62. Boston: Beacon, 2000. Print.

Eglash, Ron. "Race, Sex, and Nerds: from Black Geeks to Asian-American Hipsters." *Social Text* 20.2 (2002): 49–64. Print.

Faust, Minister. *Coyote Kings of the Space Age Bachelor Pad.* New York: Del Ray, 2004. Print.

Flash Gordon. 1936. Dir. Frederick Stephani. Universal Pictures, 2000. DVD.

Gernsback, Hugo. *Ralph 124C+.* 1911. Lincoln: Bison, 2000. Print.

Griggs, Sutton E. *Imperium in Imperio.* 1899. New York: AMS, 1969. Print.

Hairston, Andrea. *Mindscape.* 2006. Seattle: Aqueduct, 2011. Kindle.

Heinlein, Robert A. "If This Goes On. . ." 1940. *Revolt in 2100 and Methuselah's Children.* New York: Baen, 1998. 7–175. Print.

Hopkins, Pauline E. *Of One Blood; or, The Hidden Self.* 1903. New York: Washington Square, 2004. Print.

Huntington, John. *Rationalizing Genius: Ideological Strategies in the American Science Fiction Short Story.* New Brunswick: Rutgers UP, 1989. Print.

Johnson, Edward A. *Light ahead for the Negro.* 1904. Whitefish: Kessinger, 2007. Print.

Langford, David. "Mad Scientist." *The Encyclopedia of Science Fiction.* Eds. John Clute and Peter Nichols. 1 Oct. 2012. Web. 29 Oct. 2012.

Mosley, Walter. *Futureland: Nine Stories of an Immanent World.* New York: Warner, 2001. Kindle.

Ross, Andrew. *Strange Weather: Culture, Science, and Technology in the Age of Limits.* New York: Verso, 1991. Print.

Russell, Dick. *Black Genius: Inspirational Portraits of African-American Leaders.* New York: Skyhorse, 2009. Kindle.

Schuyler, George S. *Black Empire.* (Originally published as *Black Internationale* and *Black Empire*, 1936–38). Boston: Northeastern UP, 1991. Print.

———. *Black No More.* 1931. Boston: Northeastern UP, 1989. Print.

Serviss, Garrett P. *Edison's Conquest of Mars.* 1898. Project Gutenberg. 29 Aug. 2006. Web. 29 Oct. 2012.

Sturgeon, Theodore. 1941 "Microcosmic God." *Microcosmic God*, vol. 2, *The Complete Short Stories of Theodore Sturgeon.* Ed. Paul Williams. Berkeley: North Atlantic, 1998. 127–56. Print.

Tracy, Roger S. *The White Man's Burden: A Satirical Forecast.* 1915. Charleston: Nabu, 2010. Print.

Westfahl, Gary. *The Mechanics of Wonder: The Creation of the Idea of Science Fiction.* Liverpool: Liverpool UP, 1999. Print.

Yaszek, Lisa. "Science Fiction." *Routledge Companion to Literature and Science.* Eds. Manuela Rossini and Bruce Clarke. New York: Routledge, 2010. 385–95. Print.

"THE BEST IS YET TO COME"; OR, SAVING THE FUTURE

Star Trek: Deep Space Nine as Reform Astrofuturism

• • •

DE WITT DOUGLAS KILGORE

A strongly skeptical analysis of the *Star Trek* franchise's liberal astrofuturism (the idea that an American advance into a wide-open space frontier might solve social and political problems) uncovers the ways in which it fails to fully realize the political hopes it proclaims.[1] It can be argued that Trek's principal failure is in visualizing a future that is more than merely an extension of Euro-American hegemony into the final frontier. Daniel Bernardi argues that the show's "liberal humanist project is exceedingly inconsistent and at times disturbingly contradictory, often participating in and facilitating racist practice" ("*Star Trek* " 211). The program cannot help but do this because it is produced within a "Hollywood [that] consistently constructs whiteness as the norm in comparison to which all 'Others' necessarily fail" (*Star Trek* 21). David Golumbia agrees, identifying a "hegemonic whiteness" at the core of Trek, an ethic built into the "rational-logical structure of the Federation" (85). *Star Trek* is a regime so powerful that it erases the ability of such famous tokens of space future diversity as Uhura (Nichelle Nichols) and Sulu (George Takei) to remember or even understand the tumultuous history that made their presence necessary (Golumbia 83–84; Bernardi 1997, 217–18). In this postracial future, peoples of African and Asian descent have been uprooted, they cannot speak from a position that is at variance with Gene Roddenberry's universal accord.[2] *Star Trek*'s popular astrofuturism, in other words, leads us to expect what Bernardi identifies as an endless white future. Following this line of reasoning, Roddenberry's liberal humanist ambition to forecast a postracial future constitutes a horizon within which whiteness operates as the determinant of historical memory and the limit condition of any utopian human destiny. Racial Others are tolerated by being swept into a uniform sameness, exchanging their particularities for a political harmony founded in what George Lipsitz has called a "possessive investment in whiteness" (2). Within this regime, any actual claim to human diversity (or contested historical reference) seems to have little room to maneuver. Thus, while Africans, Asians, Native Americans, and others may participate as willing partners in the franchise's particular brand of astrofuturism, their unique experiences may never direct the enterprise.

This argument's thrust rests on the observation that *Star Trek's* science fiction is authored and produced by American whites and functions as an extension of their (un)conscious investment in traditional American racial custom. This critique, naturally, overrides the producers' explicitly stated desire to dramatize a future that breaks radically with contemporary racial politics. What this skeptical chain of reasoning questions, however, is not necessarily intent but a practice that reinstates customary racial mores as it wishes them away.

To fully accept this analysis, we must assume that the white ethnic producers of *Star Trek* are in absolute control of its futurism and how it might be used or interpreted. However, if we define that control as incomplete rather than perfect, then we can chart those moments when minority agents take responsibility within mainstream *Star Trek* continuity. We then must ask at least two questions: are the African/Asian actors, directors, and writers who have helped produce the franchise's fictions simple pawns of the racial politics identified by skeptical critics? Or do they represent the kind of resistance that could modify how we read *Star Trek's* pattern of racial expectation?

This chapter argues that the work of actor-director Avery Brooks represents a significant resistance to the whiteness of *Star Trek*, allowing us to open out our reading of its astrofuturism. In the 1990s, Brooks was prominently involved in the third Trek series, *Star Trek: Deep Space Nine* (1993–99) as the series' lead actor. In concert with the series's creators and producers, Brooks worked to make visible African American history as a root of the Federation's utopian future. By validating African American experience within *Star Trek's* millennium, they produce a reform astrofuturism that revises *Star Trek's* space future and what it could mean as an outcome of contemporary circumstances.

I define reform astrofuturism in relation to that strong Afrofuturist imaginary that seeks an escape from a culture that confines the social and representative (aesthetic) possibilities of African American life and art.[3] Reform astrofuturism seeks neither separation nor assimilation with a white-dominated cultural order but rather a settlement. The resulting contract would allow for free expression of historic racial trauma and unambiguous authority in narratives of national destiny. Even when an African American president stands at the pinnacle of American power, this notion remains contested if not radical. Under the reform rubric, an Afrocentric, postblack imaginary attempts to move *Star Trek*'s popular astrofuturism away from the investment in whiteness that remains a central preoccupation of American culture.[4]

Breaking the White Ceiling Television Drama

In 1993, Paramount Television launched the third series in what would become a five series franchise, *Star Trek: Deep Space Nine* (*DS9*). In *DS9*'s first season, the program served as a spin-off of its predecessor, *Star Trek: The Next Generation* (*TNG*) (1987–94) before finding its footing as the most politically grounded and socially adventurous version of Roddenberry's astrofuturism. This change may be attributed to the fact that Roddenberry, the founder of the franchise, was not involved in the creation and production of the show.

Among the significant changes Rick Berman and Michael Piller, *DS9*'s creators, made was casting Avery Brooks as the program's lead actor. In the context of early 1990s television, the decision to focus a major television series on an African American actor could still be judged as risky. While a handful of network shows from the late 1960s through the 1980s did feature black leads, most of them were situation comedies such as *Julia* (1968–71), *Sanford and Son* (1972–77), and *The Jeffersons* (1975–85). The record for dramatic television that featured black protagonists (as neither part of an ensemble or a salt-and-pepper team) in the same period is one of interesting failure. Shows starring Richard Roundtree (*Shaft*, 1973–74), James Earl Jones (*Paris*, 1979–80), and Lou Gossett Jr. (*Gideon Oliver*, 1989) all appeared and vanished before finding significant audiences. Brooks also played a role in this trend as the title character of ABC's *A Man Called Hawk* (1989). His work in this short-lived series laid the foundation for what he accomplished in *DS9*.

Hawk was a spin-off of the popular Robert Urich crime drama, *Spenser: For Hire* (1985–88), in which Brooks created Hawk, the tough, streetwise enforcer who occasionally works with Spenser. The actor's charismatic performance prompted the development of a series centered on the character. As the central protagonist, Hawk gained dimension as a cultured man with a philosophical view of black life in the show's Washington, D.C., setting. Brooks made the character a man who could both represent African American cultural achievement and project the idealized masculinity required by the crime/action genre. As Donald Bogle notes, the series presented Hawk as both "a man of the people" and "a refined jazz pianist" (307). While the series ran for only thirteen episodes in the fall of 1989, it established a pattern that *DS9* would follow: leverage the success of a white-dominated show designed around ambitious "nontraditional" narrative choices and casting.

During the seven seasons of *DS9*'s original run, Brooks received an opportunity rare for an African American actor in dramatic television: the freedom to develop a fully rounded character over a generous amount of time. The fact that the character both is black and hails from a distinctly African American background and is the point of authority in the show marks the critical difference between *DS9* and the other iterations of the Trek franchise. While black actors have always been part of the *Star Trek* representation of a multiracial future, their roles were almost always subordinate in Roddenberry's idealized military/exploratory command structure, Starfleet. The fleeting presence of various nonwhite captains and admirals in Trek's various shows and films only emphasized that status. Casting Brooks as the Starfleet commander, central to the narrative and in charge of its fictional space station, producers Berman and Piller introduced a significant reform of the kinds of stories Trek's writers were authorized to tell. In other words, the producers set a challenge to see whether Roddenberry's 1960s promise of a future in which command was no longer the exclusive right of white (human) males (from Iowa) could be represented and sustained on television. This reform produced a character designed both to continue the masculinist traditions of the Starfleet command narrative and to fulfill its promised break with white investment.

Starfleet's Middle-Class Negro

Brooks's character, Benjamin Sisko, begins his narrative journey as an individual who seems quite different from his actor's previous network persona. His family background is resolutely middle class (his father is the owner/chef of a famous New Orleans restaurant); he is a Starfleet Academy graduate, an engineer who specializes in starship design, and a career officer who is proud of the uniform he wears. His work ethic and leadership skills allow him to rise through the ranks of a highly competitive meritocracy. By the time we meet him in the pilot episode of the series, "Emissary" (3 Jan. 1993), Sisko is offered as a substantial break from Hawk in terms of approach, social position, and style: he is a clean-shaven, middle-class professional with a full head of hair.

He is also presented as something unusual for the male lead of an action adventure. In the pilot episode of *DS9*, he becomes a grieving widower and a single parent responsible for raising a son. The character, in other words, has a number of traits that invite audience sympathy. Sisko is not presented as a particularly happy man, but he also lacks the brooding menace that is so much a part of Hawk's roguish charm.[5]

As originally conceived, Sisko is well suited to the presumptively white (if we ignore all of the alien prosthetics) professional world of the narrative and of the show's production environment. He is designed to appeal to viewers who are theoretically liberal or at least nonracist but are usually not directly challenged by the social arrangements of the entertainment they consume. It is fair to say that while Hawk without Spenser operates as a provocation within the protocols of television drama, Ben Sisko enters center stage in as nonthreatening a manner as possible.

If the character had remained where he was in *DS9*'s first season, we would be forced to accept that *Star Trek*'s astrofuturism is only a variety of liberal pluralism that projects a Eurocentric whiteness unto the final frontier. This position, after all, makes a great deal of sense. Despite the best intentions of its producers, the franchise has always been vulnerable to the racial invest-ments of its industry and the society it serves. The institutional realities of social representation and reproduction have also made a hegemonic white masculinity a pillar of the franchise's energetic space future. However, while the inclusion of African Americans and other nonwhites may normally be only an enlightened tokenism, placeholders for potentials that we may imag-ine are fulfilled off-screen, they also create the potential for moving the hori-zon of expectation such that the broadcast of white patriarchy is shifted from narrative centrality. As Ben Sisko's character evolves over the series, we see what happens when that potential is taken seriously and exploited.

As a cultural artifact, *Star Trek*, despite its institutional/ideological limi-tations, is open to this line of reasoning *because* of its liberal pluralism and the way that its space future has been perceived as a solution to contempo-rary social problems. Micheal Pounds argues that Roddenberry's adventurous casting initiatives made direct representation of racial and ethnic diversity a necessary sign of *Star Trek*'s future vision and its difference from the segre-gationist ethos that dominated American life.[6] As Bernardi claims, the cre-ation of this ethnoscape[7] is merely a front for a future that is "depressingly Western and painfully white" (*Star Trek* 180). However, Roddenberry's desire to telecast a postracist future helped make *Star Trek* a repository for popular hope that such is achievable. The original show's central social conceit is that a nation currently riven by race and gender, class and culture, politics and religion would find communion in the grand adventure of space exploration. Roddenberry's risky but opportune appeal to this sentiment opened a narrative space for women and people of color that could be exploited. This is the piece of the *Star Trek* legacy that *DS9* exploited by forcefully thematizing the complexity of a multicultural community that can remember and speak to the rights and wrongs of the past. Therefore, if the producers of *DS9* may be said to have had a particular vision for the direction of the franchise following Roddenberry's retirement and death, it was to fulfill the political hope that the first two series compromised. Pounds notes that Berman and Piller paid homage to Roddenberry's original progressive social intent by establishing a new *Star Trek* in which the "themes of race, gender, ethnic difference, religion, imperialism and liberation" could find a more complete realization ("Explorers" 211–12). This gesture was authorized, as Bernardi observes, by "fans' passion for Trek's multicultural future," which in turn "prompted Paramount . . . to continue casting an increasingly diverse group of actors in *Deep Space Nine* and *Voyager*" (*Star Trek* 6).

Given the ensemble nature of a television program that follows its several characters through different personal arcs, different approaches to this point are possible. However, the evolution of Benjamin Sisko, as Brooks exerts control over the character, best makes my case that *DS9* projected a reform astrofuturism that represents a break from the Eurocentric future assumed by its predecessors.

Though Sisko is introduced into *Star Trek* continuity as a fairly standard issue officer, his tonsorial difference from Hawk signals that twentieth-century racial politics have been posted. The production staff may also have sought to ease Brooks's introduction by making his character a commander instead of a captain. Unlike the commanding officers who preceded him, Sisko has to prove himself worthy of the most coveted title in *Star Trek*'s fictive hierarchy; he is on trial. In the pilot episode, "Emissary," Captain Jean-Luc Picard (Patrick Stewart) holds this title and takes on the task of fostering his promising but troubled subordinate. We should not miss the symbolism in the transfer of authority that occurs in this instance. Picard not only represents a leveraging of the successful previous series for the next but also functions as the stern but just authority who leads a grieving Sisko to a higher calling. Unpacking the meaning of Picard's cultured European whiteness in this instance and how it relates to Sisko's African American blackness helps delineate what is at stake.

As originally conceived, Picard, the captain of *TNG*'s USS *Enterprise* (*NCC-1701-D*), was envisioned to move beyond the brash white, heterosexual masculinity of James T. Kirk (William Shatner). Picard is French rather than American, deeply cultured and academically inclined, and at least initially averse to rousing adventures either on the battlefield or in the bedroom. Middle-aged instead of young, Picard is a stern father to his crew, not the virile older brother. These traits position the character as a patriarch who represents the best of the terrestrial (mostly Anglo-American) culture that his actor champions during *TNG*'s seven-year run. His whiteness is constructed around great books and art as well as the advanced science and engineering that allow him to carry that tradition into extraterrestrial space. Picard is, in essence, a cultural ideal, a hero of the utopian technocracy he represents and defends. This cultural baggage authorizes the senior officer's position as he chastises Sisko for nurturing his grievances and prompts the junior officer to pursue a higher goal. What the Sisko character can mean is thus established by Picard's initial sponsorship.

This reading naturally supports the critique offered by Bernardi and Golumbia: Sisko is a client rather than a designer of the future he inhabits. The dominant culture, through its narrative emissaries, imposes a racialized social discipline that discounts or diminishes perspectives or possibilities emerging from outside the grand tradition represented by the French captain and the English actor who portrays him. Such a legacy leads us to ask whether Brooks is a simple pawn in a hegemonic Eurocentric futurism or whether he takes the tools that *Star Trek* offers to create a fiction that does more than simply reinforce white dominance. I argue that as *DS9* established itself as a credible iteration of the franchise, Brooks exploited the opportunity to create an authoritatively African American presence within *Star Trek*'s ostensibly rootless future. In so doing, he helped craft narratives that seek to escape a liberal pluralism that makes the shedding of historical or cultural particularity a desirable social goal. Brooks's work helps remind us why *Star Trek*'s imagined futurity might seem attractive to people who belong to communities often denied representation or agency in mainstream commercial narratives.

The Starfleet Captain as Black Hero

During his tenure on the show, Brooks demonstrated an interest in using his work to change the representational options open to African Americans in late-twentieth-century media. In a 1989 *Essence* magazine interview, Brooks expanded on this point by remarking, "I cannot speak for all Black people, so I'm availing myself of every resource at my disposal so we have a chance to look at the world through brown eyes for at least a few minutes every week on prime-time television" (Southgate 114). Any actor aware of what J. Fred MacDonald calls "the social implications of black performance" could do no less (126). On *DS9*, this aspect of the actor's work gains prominence when

Sisko is, with some fanfare, promoted to captain in the final episode of the program's third season, "The Adversary." The character's elevation makes him an authoritative presence within the Federation's fictive history. Sisko's promotion also gave the actor and the production staff the cultural capital they needed to mount a credible reform of *Star Trek*'s racial norms.

Brooks's growing status in the production and his creative control of the Sisko character is further indicated by the reappearance of the shaved head and goatee he popularized as Hawk, a transition that paralleled the character's promotion. According to Ira Steven Behr, Brooks wanted the change, and his producers backed him, although they were concerned about how the studio would react: "We had geared ourselves up for this big fight and there was no fight. Paramount was fine with it. And Avery was very pleased" (Erdmann 257). The styling change produced a visual redefinition of the character as well as a certain freedom for the actor. Brooks made this clear in an exchange with one of the show's directors: "I was shooting ['The Way of the Warrior'] and I happened to look at some of the reruns of the earlier shows and I said to Avery, 'It's like a different actor.' And Avery said, 'I *feel* like a different guy.' And you can see it in his performance. With his head shaved, I think he feels much freer, much more himself" (Erdmann 257). Here, Brooks recovers the "black" or urban style that had made him a recognizable star. Adopting it for Benjamin Sisko moves the character away from uniform blandness and toward a fashion that marks him as an individual with a particular cultural flavor. This physical declaration, echoed in civilian costuming that references African textures, positions the character as a space-born representative of the African diaspora. Through this relatively small change, Brooks signals his desire that Sisko not be seen as a deracinated minority in a white future.

Dismissing this change as a bit of actorly vanity is possible. However, Brooks took pains to make clear that he saw his role in broader terms: "For me, this is as hard-core as it gets: Because I am brown and American and male, it is important for me—and for our brown children everywhere—to be able to think in the long term. Today many of our children, especially males, do not project that they will live past the age of 19 or 20. *Star Trek* allows our children the chance to see something they might not otherwise imagine. My life's work has always been about making a way for succeeding generations" (Logan 10). For him, the Sisko role is a placeholder for the future.

Black History and a Future in Space

The centrality of Benjamin Sisko's character in *DS9*'s futurity is demonstrated in episodes that come in two distinct modes. Time travel teleplays—such as

"Past Tense, Part I" (2 Jan. 1995) and "Past Tense, Part II" (9 Jan. 1995)—present Sisko in the authorizing mode of the Starfleet officer whose decisions maintain history's progressive course.[8] Tales such as "Badda-Bing, Badda-Bang" (24 Feb. 1999) and "Far beyond the Stars" (11 Feb. 1998) cast him as the moral guide who remembers a history that the future tends to forget. In this latter mode (unique to *DS9*), we see the Sisko character's signal contribution to revising our view of Trek continuity as only a white salvation. This revision is achieved in part by the importation of situations that account for the presence of African Americans in the space future and the relevance of their history to its meaning.

The seventh-season episode "Badda-Bing, Badda-Bang," written by showrunner Ira Steven Behr and producer Hans Beimler, offers one of the key moments in *Star Trek* where the pains of the past are shown to have relevance to any living future. The episode begins as a fairly innocuous story in which the crew works to solve a problem on the holodeck. A program patch that changes the venue into a Rat Pack–style casino, complete with gangsters, has reconfigured a popular recreation program set in a Las Vegas nightclub. The crew plans and executes an *Ocean's 11*–style heist to reboot the program.[9] The caper becomes part of a larger entertainment in which the past seems to be an escape from the complexities of the present moment. This release is neither completely innocent nor unproblematic. Captain Sisko questions the sense of an advanced interracial society (one in which the assumption of multispecies harmony is always in dramatic doubt) using this section of American history as a theme park. His dissent is raised in an argument with black freighter captain, Kasidy Yates (Penny Johnson), the woman who will become his second wife. Sisko takes seriously what it meant to be black in the mid-twentieth century and the legacy of that history. The scene is instructive:

> SISKO: Las Vegas, 1962. That's my problem. In 1962, black people weren't very welcome there. Oh sure, they could be performers or janitors, but customers? Never.
> YATES: Maybe that's the way it was in the real Vegas, but that's not the way it is at Vic's. I have never felt uncomfortable there and neither has Jake [Sisko's son].
> SISKO: But don't you see? That's the lie. In 1962, the civil rights movement was still in its infancy. It wasn't an easy time for our people, and I'm not going to pretend that it was.
> YATES: Baby, I know that Vic's isn't a totally accurate representation of the way things were. But it isn't meant to be. It shows us the way things could have been. The way they should have been.
> SISKO: We cannot ignore the truth about the past.
> YATES: Going to Vic's isn't going to make us forget who we are or where we came from. What it does is remind us that we are no longer bound by any limitations except the ones we impose on ourselves.

The situation is remarkable not only as a scene in *Star Trek* but also in the world of commercial television. Sisko is not explaining himself to a white outsider, human or alien, but to a woman from his own background. He includes her in his historical concerns through his use of the possessive pronoun *our*. And Yates responds in kind, putting forth a different perspective from within their shared community of concern. Rank and gender introduce complicating dynamics, but the communal rhetoric renders the debate as internal, indicative of how black people position themselves both in the productive reality of the show and in the fictive future of its narrative. Crucially, these black characters are allowed to remember and to speak in a way that was unavailable to Uhura and Sulu two decades earlier. The production environment for racial representation has changed that much at least.

The episode does not resolve the Sisko/Yates exchange, but a settlement is reached that allows the captain to participate in the adventure, contributing to its success. Sisko's critique of *Star Trek*'s normally deracinated use of history reforms what the franchise's astrofuturism means and refigures whose history matters in its creation. Here, the necessity of the black empowerment that authorizes Sisko's historical recall is drafted into a logic that makes *Star Trek*'s interspecies humanism more credible as something achievable. While the argument's place in the episode underscores what is at stake when the multiracial cast successfully pulls off the caper, it is a future in which interracial teamwork reflects a fusion politics that is proof against the revenants of a racist past.

The meaning of Sisko's participation in the nightclub adventure is underscored by his duet with Vic Fontaine (James Darren), the venue's owner, after the holodeck program has been restored. The captain and the crooner close "Badda-Bing" with a cover of "The Best Is Yet to Come," a song Frank Sinatra popularized in the early 1960s. The tune underscores the show's period nostalgia as it lends a certain cultural endorsement to the message of the series overall. The familiar midcentury liberal image of a black man and a white man singing together in harmony, having overcome a historically segregated space, about a shining future is designed to produce an emotional release for the Sisko/Yates debate. The point is reinforced by reaction shots that include a smiling Yates as the multispecies crew enjoys the performance. To appreciate the full impact of this moment, we must remember that it happens on the stage of a science fiction in which the "yet to come" has been achieved. And that achievement invites us to accept a counterfactual and sentimental evocation of history.

The choice of the song itself may also be read as a canny historical move. "The Best Is Yet to Come" was created in 1959 by composer Cy Coleman and lyricist Carolyn Leigh. Sinatra produced a hit cover of it in a 1964 album, *It*

Might as Well Be Swing, backed by the Count Basie Orchestra with Quincy Jones as arranger and conductor. This collaboration recalls a moment in American popular music when prominent musicians worked to break down racially imposed barriers between popular musical forms. The use of the song as a set piece in *DS9* ties the series' astrofuturism into the problems, ambitions, and achievements of American popular art, thus saving the glamour of an actual past for a future in which its wrongs are righted.

A pessimistic reading of this gesture would be that the episode absolves the past of sin. A reparative reading accepts the narrative's actors as active participants in the historical confrontation and reenactment the episode stages. The historical play of "Badda-Bing, Badda-Bang" renders a multiracial future in which "our people" (the descendants of the African diaspora) occupy a pivotal place that can define the nature and direction of the franchise's fictive future. This moment allows the series to advance Behr's respectful critique of the ease with which Roddenberry's vision might be achieved.

Race-ing the Stars

The willingness of the series producers to confront the relationship of America's racial history to *Star Trek*'s future is demonstrated by another Behr/Beimler teleplay, "Far beyond the Stars." This sixth-season episode predates "Badda-Bing" and was directed by Brooks, who also served as lead actor in two roles—Captain Sisko and 1950s science fiction writer Benny Russell. This episode most clearly models *DS9*'s reform astrofuturism.

"Far beyond the Stars" has Benjamin Sisko walk from his twenty-fourth-century present into the New York City of 1953. *Star Trek* time travel stories almost always have their characters retain knowledge of their future lives: the faults of the past are, therefore, in direct contrast to the glorious future. Most often, the mission is to save or restore that future (so that they may continue to exist). In this tale, however, Sisko loses direct knowledge of his future life and becomes completely embedded in the past. This displacement allows the character to become a part of the historical situation re-created by the episode, avoiding the ironic distance that is a familiar feature of *Star Trek* time travel narratives. This gesture forces Sisko to live in the moment, to take what happens to him as a reality from which there is no easy escape. As a member of Harlem's black community, he must face the ordinary racism of midcentury America at work and on the street.

An account of each of the episode's racial incidents—which progress from slights to full-on violence from the police—would give us the texture of the show's social concerns. Yet noting how the episode handles the hopes of black people, who are told they must not dream of anything better, is more important. The teleplay tells its story from the viewpoint of a community of dreamers who must make their way in a polity that discounts their aspirations: a baseball player (Michael Dorn) works to break his sport's racial barriers; Russell's fiancée (Penny Johnson) hopes to buy a diner and start a family; a young hustler (Cirroc Lofton) pursues a big score; and Russell seeks to have his best work published. All of them live in an America that uses racism to smother their ambition. Sisko does not want this painful legacy papered over in "Badda-Bing, Badda-Bang."

"Far beyond the Stars" revolves around Russell's creation of a story cycle in which a "Negro" is captain of a U.S. Air Force station, Deep Space Nine. Within the narrative, the writer has no idea that his fiction predicts *DS9*'s reality. His principal concern is to publish his best work and in so doing herald a time in which the chains placed on his community are broken. As an effort to confront the nightmare his community experiences, the future that he writes is real.

Set just before the modern civil rights movement, there is no easy resolution for Benny Russell's race-based problems. Russell may write of a future in which "Negroes" are free of the constant humiliation and stifled promise of ordinary life, but that is all he can do. However, as a mysterious street-corner preacher (Brock Peters) tells him, "You are the dreamer and the dream." His ability to imagine a finer world is crucial. This ability defines both Russell/Sisko's present limitations and his real achievement in *Star Trek*'s actual continuity. He writes the truth that will set his people free.[10]

The response to Benny Russell's effort to write a science fiction that does not replicate midcentury racial hierarchy is censorship followed by mental breakdown. The editor (René Auberjonois) of the magazine for which he works, *Incredible Tales*, argues that despite the presumed openness of SF readers to new ideas, they are not ready to imagine a future in which Negroes are deemed equal to whites.[11] Russell resists and resents the editor's advice to make his captain white but accepts a compromise in which his story is revealed to be "only a dream." That settlement (which, as one of Russell's colleagues complains, would "gut" the story) is not enough. The magazine's owner has the entire issue "pulped" to avoid printing the offensively egalitarian tale. This drastic act prompts the writer's dramatic collapse as he shouts, "The future is real. I made it real." Sisko soon wakes from Benny's nightmare, but this moment lingers in the viewer's mind.

"Far beyond the Stars" positions *DS9* as an answer to a very particular American trauma. When Sisko returns to his present, we are relieved that the space future reappears and does not replicate the racist norms of the early 1950s. We move from a segregationist America in which even SF writers labor for a racist and sexist status quo to a yet-to-be in which no single group profits from the work of a subordinate class. In this new-age Sisko's captaincy, his privileged position in Starfleet's hierarchy is presented as remarkable only in light of the history evoked by the episode. Naturally, the story itself would not have been possible absent the creative presence of the multiethnic and international cast headed by Brooks. The multispecies, bigendered ensemble of *DS9*'s main continuity is recast as the black and white ethnic citizens of 1953 New York. There is pleasure in seeing some of these actors out of their alien makeup, playing characters that directly reference their own backgrounds. This interest in engaging the clashes around race and ethnicity that define American history allows Behr to exploit the dramatic potential inherent in *Star Trek*'s imagined future.[12]

Futurism in Black

Given the nature of series television, one could argue that the reform astrofuturism that I have identified here is confined to this handful of episodes. Since the days of 1960s Westerns, there have always been moments when popular television has attempted to confront the nation's racial structure. Such attempts were most often made by casting a black guest star in single episodes of dramas constructed around white casts. Sammy Davis Jr., for example, appeared in *Lawman* (1961), *The Rifleman* (1962), and *The Wild Wild West* (1966). Brook Peters, who played Benjamin Sisko's father in *DS9* as well as the preacher in "Far," appeared as a runaway slave in "Pompey," an episode of *Daniel Boone* (10 Dec. 1964). Whether or not race was an issue in any particular episode, the characters had little or no effect on the central concerns of a show or on the relationships considered normal on a frontier dominated by white heroes and the communities they defended. *DS9* breaks this pattern by offering its viewers a nonwhite hero who both commands and defends a community that is neither racially monochromic nor settled into a postracial consensus. The memory of 1950s racism strengthens Sisko's resolve to remain in Starfleet. This memory also confirms his role as the captain whose actions save *Star Trek*'s multicultural frontier.

Through this motif of heroic salvation, Sisko's role is linked to the conventions of white male leadership that are a staple of popular television. This motif also indicates the difference that *DS9* makes in reforming the racial import of the future the show represents. Ben Sisko's narrative prominence in this world leads the character toward an apotheosis reserved for many of the franchise's male heroes. In the last episode of the series, "What You Leave Behind" (2 June 1999), Sisko helps win the Federation war with an alien empire (the Dominion) and fulfills his destiny as the emissary of the Bajoran religion. The latter distinction means that he joins Bajor's prophets in the atemporal transdimensional space that is their home. He ascends, therefore, into a kind of heaven, gaining the divinity that both previous series established as the final human destiny.

However, Sisko's rise comes at a price: he leaves behind his son and his pregnant wife. This ending could disappoint viewers who expect the character to remain in a human world as an ideal role model. Within *Star Trek*, however, such a satisfyingly ordinary resolution does not justify investment in narratives of individual and species transcendence. *Star Trek: Deep Space Nine* cannot end, like a Victorian novel, with the love and marriage of its principals (though these small advances are included in the ordinary business of the series' transspecies relationships): one if not all of them must move beyond the merely human. The most coveted destiny of *Star Trek*'s heroes is to achieve a celestial transfiguration. *DS9*'s innovation is to have an African American captain occupy this resonant position and to symbolize whatever hopes may be attached to it. Sisko becomes the best of what humanity has to offer.

Having succeeded as a father, a leader in peace and war, a historically informed futurist, and an emissary to a powerful extraterrestrial species, Sisko takes the next step: going beyond what we know. This gesture is a radical act that breaks with the possessive investment in whiteness that would otherwise limit *Star Trek*'s astrofuturism. Going further, we might say that this ending seeks an escape from the discursive limits of contemporary racial politics. This evasion of current custom does not completely satisfy our time-bound political desires because we are not used to imagining a postblack regime that subscribes to a blackness that is more than an obverse of whiteness. We can imagine this transcendence, but we cannot feel it from within the confines of our ordinary culture.

However, like the more familiar ascensions that have been accorded to white male heroes, Sisko's apotheosis is also limited by its presuppositions. The character's commanding masculinity as performed by Brooks is a match for that of his predecessors. *DS9*'s future may not be only white, but it remains patriarchal. Sisko's final divinity is underscored by his status as a good father, a signal difference between this captain and those who precede and follow him. While *DS9* may have complicated the racial meaning of the franchise's astrofuturism, it reinforces the notion that only the hero as father can guarantee human survival and give meaning to it. Here the future is limited to the expectation of a transcendent paternity that can sustain *Star Trek*'s metanar-rative of good social order.

The casting of Brooks as the commanding office of *Star Trek: Deep Space Nine* opened up new narrative possibilities in a popular and long-lived media franchise. The program functions as a logical extension of Roddenberry's orig-inal vision while critiquing its limits through stories centered on a multiethnic (and fictionally multispecies) ensemble. A central component of that critique is a serious and sustained focus on American racial history and a specific inter-est in the relationship of African American experience to a putatively white future. These commitments help humanize *Star Trek*'s astrofuturism, making it less of a simple escape from the racial politics that dominated the late twen-tieth century. The participation of black actors made possible an Afrocentric reform of our expectation of what *Star Trek* must mean as a projection of twentieth-century hopes and fears. Through the lens of this reform, we gain the ethical ground from which to understand what is at stake in a science fic-tion where human variation exists alongside difference with the other human-oid species of *Star Trek*'s fictional universe. Differences have always mattered in this galactic club. The political hope has been that those differences will only be a prelude to some harmonious settlement.[13] The series's African American captain is figured as the locus of that hope. As a cultural product within a national story, *DS9* offers us a way of understanding the millennial upwelling that attended the election of the first black U.S. president in 2008.

Notes

1. For a more complete examination of this phenomenon, see Kilgore 2003.

2. For more on the erasure of historical memory for *Star Trek*'s people of color, see Golumbia 83–86. For direct statements by Nichols and Takei on how they saw the limits of their roles and how they fought to make them fulfill *Star Trek*'s promise of racial equality, see Asherman; Takei.

3. For more on how Afrofuturism has been defined and performed as a robust compo-nent of contemporary science fiction, see Kilgore.

4. Postblack is a term coined by curator Thelma Golden and artist Glenn Ligon to describe a strand of African American art in the 1990s (Golden 14). For a more current assessment, see Touré.

5. Bogle praises Brooks's creation of Hawk and the focus and talent that he put into creating an aggressively unique character (306). However, Bogle also notes that *Spenser* limited the character to a single simple function: to save the show's white hero (123). Thus a character designed to represent a confrontational black autonomy is tamed. Brooks's force-ful argument that he saw Hawk as something more than *Spenser*'s Tonto indicates that the actor was aware of the problem (Bogle 306).

6. Roddenberry's "intent to break new ground on race and gender in *Star Trek*'s cast met strong resistance," according to Pounds (*Race* 51–52). Pounds notes that the character who would eventually become Lieutenant Uhura was originally conceived as the USS *Enterprise*'s executive officer, a position second only to the captain; however, the black female "Number One" was made white in time for the making of the first pilot, "The Cage," and was replaced by the more familiar Mr. Spock when the second pilot, "Where No Man Has Gone Before," was authorized (*Race* 52–53).

7. For more on how ethnoscape may be defined and deployed, see Lavender 157–85.

8. This generic feature of *Star Trek* narrative was pioneered in an original series episode, "Tomorrow Is Yesterday" (26 Jan. 1967).

9. Starring Frank Sinatra, Sammy Davis Jr., Dean Martin, and other members of the Rat Pack, *Ocean's 11* is a 1960 heist film that follows a group of World War II veterans who plan and execute the robbery of five Las Vegas casinos.

10. Deliberately invoking the Gospel of John ("And you will know the truth, and the truth will set you free" [8:32]), Behr and Beimler use religious authority to underwrite the moral as well as political ethnoscape of "Far beyond the Stars."

11. This moment in *DS9* mirrors Samuel R. Delany's *Nova* rejection experience with legendary *Analog* magazine editor John W. Campbell Jr. (Delany)

12. Behr's concern with featuring a racial realism in his stories is a consistent thread in his *DS9* work. In the fourth-season time travel teleplays, "Past Tense, Part I" and "Past Tense, Part II," characters find themselves in a past when race determines their plot position. Behr is clear about why: "The simple fact [is] that a beautiful white woman is always going to get much better treatment than two brown-skinned men. That's the reality of life" (Erdmann 197).

13. The desire for transspecies racial harmony is hardwired into *Star Trek*'s fictive continuity. In "The Chase" (26 Apr. 1993), a *Star Trek: The Next Generation* episode, Klingons, Romulans, and terrestrial humans discover that they are a consanguineous kind, genetically linked to an extinct progenitor race. The episode helps explain why miscegenation is such a marked part of the franchise's attempts to bring its dramatically fractious alien empires together, one couple at a time.

Works Cited

"The Adversary." *Star Trek: Deep Space Nine*. Written by Ira Steven Behr and Robert Hewitt Wolfe. Dir. Alexander Singer. Paramount. 19 June 1995. DVD.
Asherman, Allan. *The Star Trek Interview Book*. New York: Pocket, 1988. 70–72. Print.
"Badda-Bing, Badda-Bang." *Star Trek: Deep Space Nine*. Written by Ira Steven Behr and Hans Beimler. Dir. Mike Vejar. Paramount. 24 Feb. 1999. DVD.
Bernardi, Daniel. *Star Trek and History: Race-ing toward a White Future*. New Brunswick: Rutgers UP, 1998. Print.
———. "*Star Trek* in the 1960s: Liberal-Humanism and the Production of Race." *Science Fiction Studies* 24.2 (1997): 209–25. Print.
Bogle, Donald. *Primetime Blues: African Americans on Network Television*. New York: Farrar, Straus, and Giroux, 2001. Print.

"The Chase." *Star Trek: The Next Generation*. Written by Joe Menosky. Dir. Jonathan Frakes. Paramount. 24 Apr. 1993. DVD.

Delany, Samuel R. "Racism and Science Fiction." 1998. *Dark Matter: A Century of Speculative Fiction from the African Diaspora*. Ed. Sheree R. Thomas. New York: Warner, 2000. 383–97. Print.

"Emissary." *Star Trek: Deep Space Nine*. Written by Michael Piller. Dir. David Carson. CBS. 3 Jan. 1993. Television.

Erdmann, Terry J., with Paula M. Block. *Star Trek: Deep Space Nine Companion*. New York: Pocket, 2000. Print.

"Far beyond the Stars." *Star Trek: Deep Space Nine*. Written by Ira S. Behr and Hans Beimler. Dir. Avery Brooks. Paramount. 11 Feb. 1998. DVD.

Golden, Thelma. "Introduction." *Freestyle*. New York: Studio Museum in Harlem, 2001. Print.

Golumbia, David. "Black and White World: Race, Ideology, and Utopia in *Triton* and *Star Trek*." *Cultural Critique* 32 (1995–96): 75–95. Print.

Kilgore, De Witt Douglas. "Afrofuturism." *The Oxford Handbook of Science Fiction*. Ed. Rob Latham. New York: Oxford UP, forthcoming. Print.

———. *Astrofuturism: Science, Race, and Visions of Utopia*. Philadelphia: U of Pennsylvania P, 2003. Print.

Lavender, Isiah, III. *Race in American Science Fiction*. Bloomington: Indiana UP, 2011. Print.

Lipsitz, George. *The Possessive Investment in Whiteness: How White People Profit from Identity Politics*. Philadelphia: Temple UP, 1998. Print.

Logan, Michael. "Avery Brooks: The Private Commander." *TV Guide*, 15 Jan. 1994, 10. Print.

MacDonald, J. Fred. *Blacks and White TV: African Americans in Television since 1948*. Chicago: Nelson-Hall, 1992. Print

Ocean's 11. Dir. Lewis Milestone. Perf. Frank Sinatra, Dean Martin, and Sammy Davis Jr., et al. Warner Bros., 1960. Film.

"Past Tense, Part I." *Star Trek: Deep Space Nine*. Written by Robert Hewitt Wolfe. Dir. Reza Badiyi. Paramount. 2 Jan. 1995. DVD.

"Past Tense, Part II." *Star Trek: Deep Space Nine*. Written by Ira Steven Behr and René Echevarria. Dir. Jonathan Frakes. Paramount. 9 Jan. 1995. DVD.

Pounds, Micheal C. *Race in Space: The Representation of Ethnicity in Star Trek and Star Trek: The Next Generation*. Lanham: Scarecrow, 1999. Print.

———. "'Explorers'—*Star Trek: Deep Space Nine*." *African Identities* 7.2 (2009): 209–35. Print.

Sinatra, Frank. "The Best Is Yet to Come." *It Might as Well Be Swing*. Reprise, 1964. CD.

Southgate, Martha. "Avery Brooks: Not Just Another Pretty Face." *Essence*, Apr. 1989, 74–76, 114. Print.

Takei, George. *To the Stars: The Autobiography of George Takei, Star Trek's Mr. Sulu*. New York: Pocket, 1994. Print.

Touré. *Who's Afraid of Post-Blackness?: What it Means to Be Black Now*. New York: Free Press, 2011. Print.

"What You Leave Behind." *Star Trek: Deep Space Nine*. Written by Ira Steven Behr and Hans Beimler. Dir. Allen Kroeker. Paramount. 2 June 1999. DVD.

FAR BEYOND THE STAR PIT
Samuel R. Delany

• • •

GERRY CANAVAN

> I am black, I have spent time in a mental hospital, and much of my adult life, for both sexual and social reasons, has been passed on society's margins. My attraction to them as subject matter for fiction, however, is not so much the desire to write autobiography, but the far more parochial desire to set matters straight where, if only one takes the evidence of the written word, all would seem confusion.
> —**Samuel R. Delany,** *The Straits of Messina*

Written in 1965 and published in 1967, Samuel R. Delany's early novella "The Star Pit" presents for its reader an intergalactic narrative landscape in which a final, unbreakable constraint has been imposed on the ability of certain people to achieve. Humanity has expanded off Earth into a thriving network of extrasolar colonies, only to find that travel beyond the limits of the Milky Way galaxy causes insanity and death in nearly any human being who attempts it. Only a select elite have the capacity to transcend this barrier and freely travel the wider universe, in all its unimaginable and indescribable splendor; these privileged travelers are the "goldens," and they are objects of great jealousy for the average people of the galaxy, despite the dangers of their work, their generally unappealing personalities, and the callous and unfeeling demeanor that arises out of their special privilege. For the nongolden characters of "The Star Pit," the arbitrary ceiling on their achievement is confronted as a nightmare, even as an existential horror, the recognition of which permanently scars and deforms their lives. One character, Ratlit, is desperate to see the full splendor of the universe as only a golden can—but, as his friend, Vyme, sadly warns him, "You can't fight reality" (26). The highest heights are open only to a few.

In this chapter, I focus on the way the experience of race in mid-twentieth-century America is reimagined in this often-overlooked early story from Delany. I read "The Star Pit" as an allegory for life under the regime of legal and customary segregation known as white supremacy—that historically fluctuating set of codes, assumptions, and restrictions that greatly affected Delany's development as an author and critic of SF over his long and distinguished career. In "The Star Pit," as in Delany's later critical writings, we find racism—and by extension the related ideological categories of sexism, classism, heteronormativity, and ableism, also important both in this novella and in Delany's work more generally—allegorically figured as overawing symbolic landscapes that we all necessarily and permanently inhabit. These social constructs are framed by Delany as our "total surround[s]," as gravity wells that can never be transcended or escaped, not even in our most cherished dreams ("Racism" 391). And yet Delany does not leave us mired in this unhappy conclusion, either. We recover in the end a vision of hope, just not the doomed hope for liberal cosmopolitanism that has typically dominated SF visions of a "postracial" future. In Delany, raciality can never be "post-"—nor, he would explain, should we want it to be.

The Only Reason They'll Ever Let Us in Space Is If They Need Someone to Shine Their Shoes

In "Far beyond the Stars" (11 Feb. 1998), a sixth-season episode of *Star Trek: Deep Space Nine,* Captain Benjamin Sisko finds himself experiencing an alternate life as Benny Russell, an African American science fiction writer living in New York in the 1950s. In the episode—a fan favorite directed by the actor who plays Sisko, Avery Brooks—Russell's race has been kept secret from his readers on the grounds that the predominantly white audience of *Incredible Tales* would be unwilling to accept a black writer of SF.[1] Inspired by a magazine illustration of a space station that suggests his now-forgotten former life as a Starfleet captain, Sisko-as-Russell begins to compose a story about Captain Sisko, which is rejected by his editor despite its obvious merit on the grounds that an African American astronaut-hero is simply "not believable." (As Russell notes, this appeal to "believability" is a truly astonishing claim from a magazine publishing fantastic stories about robots, dragons, and invaders from Mars.) "I'm sorry, Benny. I wish things were different, but they're not," the editor insists. "Wishing never changed a damn thing," Russell replies. Unexpectedly, Russell faces parallel skepticism from his African American peers, who fail to see the point of "writing stories about a bunch of white people on the moon."² "I'm not doing that any more. I'm writing about *us*," Benny tries to explain. But his friend is unmoved: "A colored captain. The only reason they'll ever let us in space is if they need someone to shine their shoes.... Today or a hundred years from now, don't make a bit of difference—as far as they're concerned, we'll always be niggers."³

In "Racism and Science Fiction," a frequently anthologized essay written in 1998 for the *New York Review of Science Fiction*, Delany notes that at least part of the "Far beyond the Stars" story actually happened to him early in his career.⁴ Legendary editor John W. Campbell rejected Delany's novel *Nova* (1968) for serialization in *Analog* on the grounds "that he didn't feel his readership would be able to relate to a black main character." Delany further notes rumors of letters between Campbell and Dean Koontz in which Campbell argues that "a technologically advanced black civilization is a social and a biological impossibility" (387).⁵

Nova depicts a world at least somewhat like the utopian world of *Star Trek*, in which racial thinking has largely ceased to matter; it similarly echoes the color-blind world of Heinlein's *Starship Troopers* (1959), which Delany has frequently said initially helped draw him to science fiction (see, for example, *Starboard* 8–9).⁶ But even *Nova*'s fraught sense of partial postraciality—already a bridge too far for Campbell—is something of an outlier in the Delany canon. In his most characteristic work (like "The Star Pit"), the liberal fantasy of a postracial future is simply impossible to achieve. Crucially, Delany's lifelong exploration of the consequences of systemized racism has even extended to a startling and unexpected deconstruction of his own lauded and well-deserved place within the science fiction canon. As he writes in "Racism and Science Fiction," with respect to his frequent pairings with other renowned black SF writers such as Nalo Hopkinson and Octavia Butler, "As long a racism functions *as* a system, it is still fueled from aspects of the perfectly laudable desires of interested whites to observe this thing, however dubious its reality, that exists largely by means of its having been named: African-American science fiction" (395). As Delany puts it, writing of an early experience of earning a Nebula Award and feeling the eyes of every white male writer in the room on him, "No one here will ever look at you, read a word you write, or consider you in any situation, no matter whether the roof is falling in or the money is pouring in, without saying to him- or herself (whether in an attempt to count it or to discount it), 'Negro . . .' The racial situation, permeable as it might sometimes seem (and it is, yes, highly permeable), is nevertheless your total surround. Don't you ever forget it . . . ! And I never have" (390–91). In the years since his Nebula victory, society has not become "color-blind," he elaborates in *Shorter Views*, as much as "color-deaf";

these laws of privilege still exist, and are still very powerful, but now cannot even be spoken about (119). Benny Russell's plaintive demands for respect and equality—"I'm a human being, dammit!"—in the name of a better future become, in Delany's hands, permanently forestalled. Benny Russell, in this sense, looks something like *Star Trek's* bad conscience or its hidden truth. It is little wonder, then, that "Far beyond the Stars" ends with a suggestion that Benny may in fact be "real" and Sisko just a fantasy; in a real sense, this is precisely the case.

This diversion into the politics of allegedly color-blind, postracial space operas like *Star Trek* sets the stage for my discussion of "The Star Pit." "The Star Pit," after all, was written in the context of a dominant tradition in SF that "from the 1950s onward . . . postulated and presumed a colorblind future" for humanity (Bould 177).[7] As Carl Freedman has recently noted of Delany's career, "Beginning mainly in a field—space opera—where the glib and pernicious oversimplification has a long, powerful, and inglorious history, Delany has spent nearly his entire career patiently insisting that things are never as simple as we all like to believe they are" (107). In contrast to the genre's typically premature and self-congratulatory pronouncements of postracial triumph, in "The Star Pit" we find the constitutive, oversimplified values of *Star Trek*–style space opera—postraciality and liberal inclusivity, certainly, but also freedom, openness, expansion, adventure—deconstructed to their foundations precisely through the reassertion of racial difference as a limit point for this kind of fantasy. What space operas like *Star Trek* deliberately seek to forget—the actual and ongoing history of difference and oppression on Earth—"The Star Pit" insists we remember.

Welcome to the Star Pit

"The Star Pit" depicts the future of a human race that has expanded off Earth into the many stars of the Milky Way galaxy. Earth itself, while still recognized as the origin of the human species, is now considered a somewhat primitive backwater, far from the important trade routes and with its own peculiar habits and cultural practices (21). Not only do residents of Earth still believe in biological race and practice racism (68), but they still have monogamous marriages (25) and cannot even control the weather (63)! The story's first-person narrator and protagonist, Vyme, explains that he grew up on Earth "in a city called New York" that he does not expect his audience to have ever heard of (21). In fact, he has long since abandoned the planet for a life in outer space, first as a pilot and later as a spaceship handyman.

On the surface, "The Star Pit" mimics many of the familiar tropes of Golden Age space opera, among them Isaac Asimov's Foundation series and Gene Roddenberry's *Star Trek,* which would premiere on CBS the year after "The Star Pit" was composed—most notably the intertwined rhetorics of *expansion* and *progress.* In "The Star Pit," the human race has not only achieved incredible technological wonders as it spread across the galaxy but has also made incredible social progress. Humanity achieves gender equality[8] and eliminates racism while simultaneously abolishing the heteronormative family in favor of egalitarian and flexible plural marriages that (as far as the story depicts) make everyone a lot happier.[9]

Delany's innovation is to introduce into this otherwise utopian situation of galactic exploration a racialized class struggle, in the process deconstructing the logic that equates expansion with progress by questioning what happens when expansion is no longer possible. Despite the wonders of interstellar colonization, the barriers of the galaxy nevertheless represent a hard limit for human expansion. The galaxy, humans find, is enclosed by two cosmic phenomenon, the Psychic and Physiologic "shells." What happens at the Psychic and Physiologic Barriers is quite literally indescribable—no vocabulary exists for the quantum experience of total reality breakdown that occurs at these limits. At the Psychic Barrier, twenty thousand light years from the galactic rim, "some psychic shock" causes insanity in any intelligent being (or computer) that attempts to pass beyond; at twenty-five thousand light years, the Physiologic Barrier causes death in any living organism that attempts to go beyond as well as catastrophic malfunction in any inorganic recording device (22). Reality, it seems, is a side effect of gravity; get too far from the mass of the cluster of stars that make up the Milky Way, and the laws of physics become so unstable and unrecognizable that consciousness itself breaks down. The galaxy, then, is all there is for us; there is no way to ever get beyond.

Until, that is, everything changes during Vyme's young adulthood. Two individuals are able to breech the barriers and go beyond. They are two "psychological freaks with some incredible hormone imbalance in their systems," looking "sullen as hell" as they are presented to the galaxy by the news media as the first harbingers of the new intergalactic exploration regime (22). "'Some few of us,'" the head of the commission assigned to study the phenomenon determines, "'whose sense of reality has been shattered by infantile, childhood, or prenatal trauma, whose physiological orientation makes life in our interstellar society painful or impossible—not all, but a few of these golden . . .' at which point there was static, or the gentleman coughed, 'can make the crossing and return.' The name golden, sans noun, stuck" (23). As one character, Ratlit, remarks in the narrative, the grammatical singularity of *golden* contributes to the sense of unease that surrounds them. An adjective that has become a noun, the word *golden* requires no additional subject, frequently drops definite and indefinite articles, and uses a singular plural (25).

Less than one in thirty-four thousand people is "golden," with the "particular psychosis and endocrine setup" to survive the passage (23). But this slim minority is still enough, in a galaxy of billions, to open up a vast new sphere of exploration and trade with points outside the galaxy—capitalism, as it does, quickly inaugurates a new rush of primitive accumulation to claim and monetize the next new open frontier.[10] "Back then," Vyme remembers, "there was excitement, wonder, anticipation, hope, admiration in the world: admiration for the ones who could get out" (23).

When we meet Vyme, however, that "admiration" has turned sour, becoming fierce resentment. In the first pages of the story, his first plural marriage is in the process of being destroyed in his blinkered, alcoholic fury that others can achieve what he is barred from. At that time, Vyme is living near the galactic center on Sigma-Prime; the children of the group marriage of which he is a part have built a massive "ecologarium" on the sand to watch alien worms and lizards grow behind glass. The ecologarium is the central conceit of "The Star Pit," which both begins on the image and returns to it over and over: animals butting up uselessly against a glass barrier that marks the limits of their freedom, paralleling the inability of the vast majority of humans to explore beyond the limits of the galaxy and allegorizing the experience of nonwhites in a culture whose white majority insists (both ideologically and legally) on white supremacy. Traditional space opera points to a fantasy of expansion and exploration that replicates, sometimes unknowingly and other times quite deliberately, America's frontier history of white-settler colonialism. Delany challenges this fantasy from the first words of the story: "Two glass panes with dirt between and little tunnels from cell to cell: when I was a kid I had an ant colony" (13). The ecologarium is that ant colony's outsized, space opera equivalent, betokening not some wide-open new frontier but rather a horizon of limitation and constraint.

When one of the children of the colony, Antoni, opens up the access door of the ecologarium and is bit by one of the sloths, earning himself a set of puffy blue pinprick bite marks on his wrist, the offending sloth falls to the ground outside the ecologarium and quickly dies in the ultraviolet heat of Sigma-Prime. The child is deeply disturbed by the revelation that the sloths are confined to the ecologarium and asks, "Wouldn't it be nice, Da . . . if some could go outside, just a few?" (17). "'I don't know about that, kid-boy,' Vyme replies. 'It might be pretty bad for the ones who had to stay inside. . . . I mean, after a while'" (17). Life, he explains, in a striking synthesis of pseudo-Darwinist biologism, New Age metaphysics, and the late-capitalist American ideology of the frontier, is necessarily a process of permanent growth. "You have to grow all the time. . . . Not necessarily get bigger. But inside your head you have to grow, kid-boy. For us human-type people that's what's important. And that kind of growing never stops. At least it shouldn't. You can grow, kid-boy, or you can die. That's the choice you've got, and it goes on all your life" (18).

A few nights later, a drunken Vyme, furious beyond reason after a near-miss collision in orbit with a golden returning from a mission outside the galaxy (19), projects his rage onto its most obvious symbol, its concrete manifestation: the terrarium itself. In front of the children, he viciously destroys the terrarium, killing most of the plants and animals inside, except the sloths, who vanish mysteriously and are never found.[11] Utterly humiliated, Vyme leaves the group, eventually winding up running a repair shop at an outpost on the edge of the galaxy, the Star Pit, where (like picking a scab, or nursing a cold sore) he repeatedly confronts his own permanent limitations through constant encounters with the goldens he serves. Even though he is now sober, life on the Star Pit is difficult for him. The repeated confrontation with the knowledge that "this was as far as you could go" does "something to the part that grows I'd once talked about with Antoni" (21). Marked by parentheses— as if the thought comes unbidden—Vyme's narration immediately turns from this melancholic self-reflection to the memory of the children's ecologarium, again figuring the misery of enforced limit: "(And I remember a black-eyed creature pressed against the plastic wall, staring across impassable sands)" (21): This same depressed finality is, of course, registered in the title of the story itself, which transforms the wide-open horizon and endless possibilities of outer space into a hyperspace truck stop—the unparalleled heights of the New Frontier into the yawning depths of a "star pit."

~~White~~ Golden Supremacy

In the theoretical appendix to *Trouble on Triton* (1976), one of Delany's characters notes that "the landscape is always the primary hero of the SF novel, the *épistèmé* is always the secondary one" (333).[12] The close reading of the opening pages of "The Star Pit" should already have made clear the sense in which the situation of "The Star Pit" allegorizes the *épistèmé* of life under a regime of white supremacy should already be clear. The privileges afforded to the golden take the form of a natural law rather than a social one—but, then, ideology always claims that white supremacy is not a social construct but simply an immutable fact of the universe, "just the way things are." Delany's theoretical thoughts on race as an "effect" rather than an essence are quite useful here: race is not an essential category but an impermanent social construct, a system, always in flux; it only looks to be "natural," much less "biological," from the synchronic, unhistoricized perspective of white supremacist ideology.[13] He makes much the same point in "Racism and Science Fiction," noting, "Racism is a system. As such, it is fueled as much by chance as by hostile intentions and equally the best Intentions as well. It is whatever systematically acclimates people, of all colors, to become comfortable with the isolation and segregation of the races, on a visual, social, or economic level—which in turn supports and is supported by socio-economic discrimination" (394). The golden are not racially marked in the traditional sense; both Vyme and the golden with whom he nearly collides are of African descent (19). But the difference dividing the golden from the bulk of humanity *is* both biologized— they are *just different*, at the level of the endocrine system—as well as visually indicated by the wearing of a golden belt (which nongoldens can theoretically steal to "pass" as golden, as two minor characters do). And this new racial difference carries with it a new regime of customary and legal segregation of persons of differing "colors." From the point of view of the nonmarked, nongolden masses of humanity, the golden "live by their own laws and walk their own ways" (23)—totally unencumbered, radically free subjects, not beholden to the everyday constraints of normal folk.

Delany explores here the persistence of racial thinking even after liberal progress will supposedly have transcended the fantasy of biological race. The race-class privilege afforded to the golden—access to the open, expansive frontier of tomorrow—is (as with the ideology of white supremacy more generally) tantamount to ownership of the future itself. Each of the plot threads in "The Star Pit" replays the same horror of limit that appears in Vyme's encounter with the ecologarium: the horror of being told one can go this far and no further. Whether Delany's characters self-destructively test these boundaries or resign themselves stoically to their fate, all are defined by their inability to come to terms with an arbitrary and existentially *unfair* cap on the possibilities for their lives. On the one hand, Ratlit decides to impersonate a golden and attempts to leave the galaxy despite knowing it will only kill him horribly, in the process abandoning his lover, Alegra, to a miserable death alone. On the other hand, Vyme and Sandy seem to have accepted their destiny by the end of the story.

The relationship between being golden and contemporary white privilege is made fully explicit in Delany's unexpected and explosive use of the word *nigger* near the end of the story, an effect even more shocking for today's readers than for his contemporaneous ones. For a golden to suggest that the nongolden might have things better, Vyme suggests, is tantamount to the kind of ugly racist condescension that would only be possible on a world as primitive as Earth: "Even if you *are* crazy, don't go around telling people who are not golden how they've trapped you. That's like going to Earth and complimenting a nigger on how well he sings and dances and his great sense of rhythm. He may be able to tap seven with one hand against thirteen with the other while whistling a tone row. It still shows a remarkable naïveté about the way things are" (68). Accordingly, golden attract the same sorts of adjectives that the privileged always attract in communities of the disprivileged. When one character steals a golden's belt and passes as golden, he learns this from both directions: "And wearing that belt, I learned just how much I hated golden. Because I could suddenly see, in almost everybody who came by, how much they hated me while I had that metal belt on." Mischievously, he soon adds, "Maybe I'll steal another one." (27)

Rhetoric around golden in "The Star Pit" would not be out of place in the heated discussions about "white people" and "white privilege" that are increasingly common on Internet forums and in college classrooms today: Golden are "unsettling" (24); haughty, arrogant, "proud proud proud" (35). "There's only two types of golden," Ratlit tells Vyme, "Mean ones and stupid ones.... When a golden isn't being outright mean, he exhibits the sort of nonthinkingness that gets other people hurt" (38).

Simultaneously "cruel" and "free" (50), goldenness is best read as whiteness. Privilege thereby becomes revealed as a form of monstrousness—echoing Frantz Fanon's psychoanalytic case notes about colonizer and colonized in *The Wretched of the Earth* (1961), the psyches of both golden and nongolden are utterly deformed by this power differential.[14] We might likewise think of Aimé Césaire, who writes in *Discourses on Colonialism* (1955) of the way that "colonization works to decivilize the colonizer, to brutalize him in the true sense of the word, to degrade him, to awake him to buried instincts, to covetousness, violence, race hatred, and moral relativism" (35).

The monstrousness of privilege is a crucial theme in early Delany—this relationship of psychic deformation caused by racial difference is closely paralleled, for example, in the relationship between the Spacers and the *frelks* they abuse in Delany's well-known "Aye, and Gomorrah" (1967), published the same year as "The Star Pit" in Harlan Ellison's New Wave anthology, *Dangerous Visions* (1967) and appearing alongside it in *Driftglass*.[15] To be privileged when others are not—and to embrace that privilege without compunction or regret—is, in some basic sense, to be fundamentally inhuman.

What Delany accomplishes over the course of "The Star Pit," then, is a reversal of the ordinary logic of privilege and power. In keeping with the observations of the Afrofuturist tendency in SF more generally,[16] white supremacy's ideological claim on the future becomes entirely deconstructed, and the subaltern, not the hegemon, is revealed as the true human subject. Benny Russell's insistence on his own humanity—"I am a human being, damnit!"—is here reversed; *he* is a human being, surely, but perhaps his racist editor is not.

There Is No Outside

But true to form, Delany goes further still, finally deconstructing his own deconstruction. In a dialectical reversal, the golden themselves are revealed near the end of the story to be figures for racialized oppression as well. The visit of a young golden, An—who could almost be Vyme's lost son, Antoni (52), if he had not been killed in one of the galaxy's many cataclysmic wars (21)—reveals that much has changed since Vyme was young; the golden are no longer found but are *made* with brutal psychological intervention from childhood on golden-potential youth. As the young golden rants, "The psycho-technician who made sure I was properly psychotic *wasn't* a golden, *brother!* You *pay* us to bring back the weapons, dad. *We* don't fight your damn wars, *grampa! You're* the ones who take us away from our groups, say we're *too* valuable to submit to *your* laws, then deny us our heredity because we don't *breed* true, no-relative-of-mine!" (58). From this perspective, the goldens are marked both by their "color" and by their mental illness/cognitive difference. (The constant assertions of golden "psychosis" never really manifest in the story proper; generally speaking, they do not behave much differently than anyone else.) Again like the Spacers of Delany's "Aye, and Gomorrah," who are sexually mutilated as the price for their participation in and ownership of humanity's interplanetary future, the golden are themselves figures for the racialized hyperexploitation native to biopolitical capitalism. And perhaps we should have seen this all along—the exploitation of their shared mental illness points us toward any number of similar fictional and real-world exploitations of the deprivileged, the precarious, and the dispossessed. Both parties in this biopolitical circuit, in essence, believe the other has reduced them to a kind of Agambenian *bare life*—and both have a pretty good case.[17]

Worst of all, the golden's encounter with cosmic transcendence is itself ultimately incomplete—on the other side of the galactic barrier is simply a larger, universal barrier that even the golden are incapable of crossing. The only thing known that can cross universes is something even smaller, less agential, less human than the golden—a tiny sloth whose bite leaves puffy blue pinprick bite marks on the skin. Yes, the same sloths Vyme seemingly murdered at the story's beginning turn out to be universe-hoppers—their leaps are powered by fear, and when they slip the bonds of our cosmos, they never come back. "Privilege" and "power" are thus in the final moment of the sloth abstracted into utter nonsense; the strongest is revealed to also be the weakest, and the weakest as also the strongest. Race fantasy, this is to say, like any power fantasy, is deeply unstable, necessarily creating the conditions for its own negation.

What Delany suggests in this unexpected final punchline to "The Star Pit" is an alternative strategy for understanding and confronting power—an understanding (straight out of Fanon, W. E. B. Du Bois, or even Hegel's master and slave) that disprivilege carries its own kind of authority.[18] This final suggestion is of race as a condition that is borne by all; no one is unmarked either by racial difference or by the limits it creates, no matter what one may fantasize about oneself. "There are certain directions in which you cannot go," Vyme says to his reader at the end of "The Star Pit," a "you" who might conceivably occupy any number of intersecting positions of race, class, sex, sexuality, ability, and so on. We might therefore restate the point: no one can go in *all* directions, not even golden. In the fact of this situation of universal limit, which is applied unevenly but applied to all, only one choice is left to the individual: "Choose one in which you can move as far as you want" (70). This choice is a call to live within the reality of race rather than focusing on the unachievable fantasy of a world without it.

This is not to say that Delany's SF is anti-utopian; far from it. As Delany himself puts it, "In most of my futures the racial situation has changed and changed for the better. As a young writer I thought it very important to keep an image of such a possibility before people" (Peplow 120). But this possibility is not the same as obliterating race, which is a hopeless act of fantasy. Delany continues, "I don't ever remember subscribing to the idea that 'being black doesn't matter.' I wanted to write about worlds where being black mattered in *different* ways from the ways it matters now" (qtd. in Govan 46; emphasis added). More directly, however, it might be better to say that Delany does not understand his work to be about the future at all; in an interview with Adam Roberts, Delany notes that both *Nova* and "The Star Pit" were "concerned with describing, in heightened form, things I saw about me at the time," with "the science fictional elements there largely to foreground some of those things with particular vividness" (107). If these are stories about the future, then, they are about the future in only one very particular sense: they argue that the future belongs to everyone, not to just one sliver of the human race. If this gesture is radical, Delany says, it is only because Europe has historically sought to completely deny all other cultural histories as well as non-European futurities (Tatsumi 204).

Here we see the sharp contrast between Delany's work and the narrative of cosmopolitan liberal progress promoted by *Star Trek* and metafictionally critiqued by the Benny Russell episode. The Captain Sisko fantasy Russell constructs is that *someday race will not matter*; Delany's answer is that such a day—"the game in which the white-male-heterosexual position is assumed to be the particular dream outside of history in which, today, everyone could, of course, live comfortably . . . if only we'd all leap ever so lightly into it" (Tatsumi 212–13)—is quite literally inconceivable from the perspective of the present we inhabit. There is in fact nothing outside the ecologarium. The liberal fantasy of a world of unencumbered, radically unmarked, universally white subjects makes the world safe for difference only by squashing it. "Are you a specific human being," he challenges the reader of an interview in *American Literary History*, "or are you some sort of generalized abstraction without a body and of wholly homogenized catholic sympathies?" ("Situation" 294).

The specificity of difference is inescapable, particularly in a historical moment in which we have only just begun to unravel these categories. The fantasy that there might exist (even in theory) a "place to stand outside" these "hegemonic discourses" is precisely what Delany denies through his insistence on the lived reality of his characters across his fiction: "If we didn't inhabit the same discourse, we couldn't understand racist jokes when we heard them nor could we find others' use of them offensive when the contradiction with our own situation is too painful to allow us to laugh. While the part of us that we consider our 'self' may each be positioned differently within it, none of us is outside it. That is *particularly* true for those of us who are black, or disabled, or overweight, or Asian, or women, or gay, or part of whatever group we have been socially assigned to, because if we didn't know that discourse deep down in our bones, we'd be dead" (Luskin 170–71). Those who inhabit the margins know better than to imagine that a stance outside history is possible—and science fiction, he suggests, as a marginal literature, also ought to know better (McCaffery and Gregory 41–42). Indeed, this is exactly what initially struck Delany when he first read *Starship Troopers*—the sudden discovery that the hero is not some unmarked abstraction but a specific person with a specific life and a specific body that ties into a specific and inescapable set of historical structures. No matter what the political future may hold, on some far-off star pit in some unimaginably distant time, the felt and visceral history of difference in the here and now cannot be erased. Nor should we want it to be.

With considerable self-awareness, Delany has equally applied this observation to his own (pardon the pun) "authority" in his career as a writer. In

"Racism and Science Fiction," he offered further thoughts on winning the Nebula and on his place in the literary canon more generally:

> The concept of race informed everything about me, so that it could surface—
> and did surface—precisely at those moments of highest anxiety, a manifest-
> ing brought about precisely by the white gaze, if you will, whenever it turned,
> discommoded for whatever reason, in my direction. Some have asked if I per-
> ceived my entrance into science fiction as a transgression.
>
> Certainly not at the entrance point, in any way. But it's clear from my story,
> I hope (and I have told many others about that fraught evening), transgression
> inheres, however unarticulated, in every aspect of the black writer's career in
> America. That it emerged in such a charged moment is, if anything, only to be
> expected in such a society as ours. How could it be otherwise? (392)

Notes

1. "It's not personal, Benny," the editor says while explaining why the magazine will not run Russell's photo, "but as far as our readers are concerned, Benny Russell is as white as they are. Let's just leave it that way." The editor even intimates that the publication of the story could spark a "race riot." A female author, Kay Eaton, who writes under the pseudonym K. C. Hunter—an homage to Catherine "C. L." Moore and the original *Star Trek*'s own Dorothy Catherine "D. C." Fontana, whose genders were similarly obscured—is likewise told to "sleep late" the day author photos are to be taken.

2. The dialogue's echo of the famous Gil Scott-Heron protest song, "Whitey on the Moon" (1970), is undoubtedly intentional.

3. According to the Star Trek Memory Alpha Wiki, a fan encyclopedia of the show, the sole use of the word "nigger" anywhere in the franchise's fifty-year history occurs in the "Far Beyond the Stars" episode.

4. In a 2001 interview with Jayme Lynn Blaschke, however, Delany said he had never seen the episode.

5. The Asimov archive at Boston University contains heated exchanges between Campbell and Isaac Asimov on the subject of segregation that make this claim seem quite plausible. For more on this aspect of Campbell's thought, especially his belief in a progressivist theory of history that places only certain ethnicities at the apex of human development, see Berger, especially chapter 10, "The Editor as Elitist."

6. In particular, Delany describes a scene midway through the novel in which the hero, Johnny Rico, looks into a mirror and is revealed to have black skin. As Lavender has noted, Delany's memory of the book's inclusivity seems to have shifted significantly in the retelling; some of the most radically inclusive gestures he describes are not actually in *Starship Troopers* but appear to exist only in his memory of it (159).

7. Additional discussion of this shared vision of a color-blind future can be found in James; Kilgore; Lavender, "Critical." For more on "Far beyond the Stars," see Kilgore, this volume.

8. Indeed, one of the jokes of the story is the late revelation that Vyme's friend and lover, the mechanic Poloscki, is a woman (67). No gender tags are provided for the character before a final conversation near the end of the story, presumably encouraging readers to assume that an unmarked character in a masculine profession is a man. In his "Notes on 'The Star Pit'" (1998), Delany regrets that the surprise of this "gender-skewing" could not be retained in the radio play version of the novella—though a similar effect is achieved elsewhere in the piece when a letter from Sandy's plural marriage is read in the voice of a woman, only to be signed "Joseph."

9. The only comparison point provided to the stable system of communal marriage is to Vyme's own unhappy childhood on Earth; Vyme's mother "ran off with a salesman," abandoning Vyme and his four siblings and leaving them in the care of "an alcoholic aunt" (25).

10. In his "Progress vs. Utopia; or, Can We Imagine the Future?" (1982), Fredric Jameson calls our attention to SF's failure to imagine genuine historical difference outside the cultural assumptions of capitalism, using terms that directly evoke the narrative situation of the "The Star Pit": "On the contrary, [SF's] deepest vocation is over and over again to demonstrate and to dramatize our incapacity to imagine the future . . . to serve as unwitting and even unwilling vehicles for a meditation, which, setting forth for the unknown, finds itself irrevocably mired in the all-too-familiar, and thereby becomes unexpectedly transformed into a contemplation of our own absolute limits" (28).

11. Late in the story, we discover that this moment is a near-exact replication of a childhood tantrum; then, Vyme's worried mother would not allow her sickly child to go see the spaceships arrive in the rain, so he spitefully destroyed his ant colony, strewing sand and ants and shards of broken glass across the family's living room (62–63). Another moment in the story suggests itself as a kind of primal scene for Vyme: his memory of the harness in which his parents placed him when he was a baby (28).

12. The piece was later published in revised and expanded form as "Shadows" and then in still longer form as "Shadow and Ash."

13. See, for example, "Race and *Star Trek* with Samuel Delany and Avery Brooks."

14. The psychic effects of colonialism on the colonizer, as identified by Fanon, are often overlooked in favor of a perfectly understandable focus on the effects on the colonized subject. The case Fanon calls A-4 describes the posttraumatic stress disorder of an otherwise happy European police officer working in Algeria: "What troubled him was having difficulty sleeping at night because he kept hearing screams" (194). A-5 describes "a European police inspector [who] tortures his wife and children" (196) out of guilt for the work he does; he comes to Fanon looking for a way to "torture Algerian patriots without having a guilty conscience, without any behavioural problems, and with a total peace of mind" (198–99).

15. This passage from "Aye, and Gomorrah" would not be out of place in "The Star Pit": "'You have your glorious, soaring life, *and* you have us.' Her face came up. She glowed. 'You spin in the sky, the world spins under you, and you step from land to land, while we . . .' She

turned her head right, left, and her black hair curled and uncurled on the shoulder of her coat. 'We have our dull, circled lives, bound in gravity, *worshipping* you!'" (117).

16. Afrofuturism denotes an approach to SF that recognizes that stories of technologically advanced aliens who kidnap, rape, and enslave human beings are not fantasies but are, rather, retellings of the actual history of contact between Europe and Africa. As Greg Tate has memorably put it, "Black people live the estrangement that science fiction writers imagine" (qtd. in Dery 208).

17. In *Homo Sacer* (1995), Giorgio Agamben describes the division between "political life" and "bare life" as the constitutive gesture of politics. Those with political life are full citizens of the polis; those who are merely bare life are exiled from participation in civic life and exist only to be exploited.

18. We might look, for example, to Du Bois's treatment of double consciousness in *The Souls of Black Folk* (1903), wherein African Americans are "gifted with second-sight" that not only allows them to see both America and themselves more clearly than their white peers but that also ennobles their spirits, "for he knows that Negro blood has a message for the world" (364–65).

Works Cited

Agamben, Giorgio. *Homo Sacer: Sovereign Power and Bare Life.* 1995. Trans. Daniel Heller-Roazen. Stanford: Stanford UP, 1998. Print.

Berger, Albert I. *The Magic That Works: John W. Campbell and the American Response to Technology.* San Bernardino: Borgo, 1993. Print.

Blaschke, Jayme Lynn. "A Conversation with Samuel R. Delany." *Conversations with Samuel R. Delany.* Ed. Carl Freedman. Jackson: UP of Mississippi, 2009. Print.

Bould, Mark. "The Ships Landed Long Ago: Afrofuturism and Black SF." *Science Fiction Studies* 34.2 (2007): 177–86. Print.

Césaire, Aimé. *Discourse on Colonialism.* 1955. Trans. Robin D. G. Kelley. New York: Monthly Review Press, 2000. Print.

Delany, Samuel R. "Aye, and Gomorrah." 1967. *Driftglass.* New York: Signet, 1971.

———. "Notes on *The Star Pit*." Pseudopodium.org. 1998. Web. Accessed 25 Aug. 2012.

———. *Nova.* New York: Doubleday, 1968. Print.

———. "Racism and Science Fiction." 1998. *Dark Matter: A Century of Speculative Fiction from the African Diaspora.* Ed. Sheree R. Thomas. New York: Warner, 2000. 383–97. Print.

———. "Shadow and Ash." *Longer Views: Extended Essays.* Hanover: UP of New England, 1996. Print.

———. "Shadows." *The Jewel-Hinged Jaw: Notes on the Language of Science Fiction.* New York: Berkley Windhover, 1977. Print.

———. *Shorter Views: Queer Thoughts and the Politics of the Paraliterary.*" Hanover: UP of New England for Wesleyan UP, 1999. Print.

———. "The Situation of American Writing Today: An *American Literary History* Interview." *About Writing: Seven Essays, Four Letters, and Five Interviews*. Middletown: Wesleyan UP, 2005. Print.

———. *Starboard Wine: More Notes on the Language of Science Fiction*. 1984. Middletown: Wesleyan UP, 2012. Print.

———. "The Star Pit." 1967. *Driftglass*. New York: Signet, 1971. Print.

———. *Trouble on Triton*. 1976. Hanover: Wesleyan UP, 1996. Print.

Dery, Mark. "Black to the Future: Interviews with Samuel R. Delany, Greg Tate, and Tricia Rose." *Flame Wars: The Discourse of Cyberculture*. Ed. Mark Dery. Durham: Duke UP, 1995. 179–222. Print.

Du Bois, W. E. B. *The Souls of Black Folk*. 1903. New York: Library of America, 1987. Print.

Ellison, Harlan. *Dangerous Visions*. New York: Doubleday, 1967. Print.

Fanon, Frantz. *The Wretched of the Earth*. 1961. Trans. Richard Philcox. New York: Grove, 2004. Print.

"Far beyond the Stars." *Star Trek: Deep Space Nine: The Complete Sixth Season*. Written by Ira Steven Behr and Hans Beimler. Dir. Avery Brooks. Paramount, 1998. DVD.

"Far beyond the Stars." Star Trek Memory Alpha. Web. Accessed 25 Aug. 2012.

Freedman, Carl. "Adventures of the Dialectic; or, On Delany as Critic." *Science Fiction Studies* 28.1 (2001): 107–18. Print.

Govan, Sandra Y. "The Insistent Presence of Black Folk in the Novels of Samuel R. Delany." *Black American Literature Forum* 18.2 (1984): 43–48. Print.

Hegel, G. W. F. "Lordship and Bondage." *Hegel's Phenomenology of Spirit*. 1807. Trans. A. V. Miller. New York: Oxford UP, 1977. Print.

Heinlein, Robert. *Starship Troopers*. New York: Putnam's, 1959. Print.

James, Edward. "Yellow, Black, Metal, and Tentacled: The Race Question in American Science Fiction." *Science Fiction, Social Conflict, and War*. Ed. Philip J. Davies. Manchester: Manchester UP, 1990. 26–49. Print.

Jameson, Frederic. "Progress vs. Utopia; or, Can We Imagine the Future?" 1982. *Archaeologies of the Future: The Desire Called Utopia and Other Science Fictions*. New York: Verso, 2005. Print.

Kilgore, De Witt D. *Astrofuturism: Science, Race, and Visions of Utopia*. Philadelphia: U of Pennsylvania P, 2003. Print.

Lavender, Isiah, III. "Critical Race Theory." *The Routledge Companion to Science Fiction*. Eds. Mark Bould et al. New York: Routledge, 2009. 185–93. Print.

———. *Race in American Science Fiction*. Bloomington: Indiana UP, 2011. Print.

Luskin, Josh. "The Wiggle Room of Theory: An Interview with Samuel R. Delany." *Conversations with Samuel R. Delany*. Ed. Carl Freedman. Jackson: UP of Mississippi, 2009. Print.

McCaffery, Larry, and Sinda Gregory. "The Semiology of Science: The *Science Fiction Studies* Interview." *Silent Interviews: On Language, Race, Sex, Science Fiction, and Some Comics*. Hanover: Wesleyan UP, 1994. 21–58. Print.

Peplow, Michael W. "Meet Samuel R. Delany, Black Science Fiction Writer." *The Crisis*, Apr. 1979, 115–21. Print.

"Race and *Star Trek* with Samuel Delany and Avery Brooks." starlady.dreamwidth.org. 1 Aug. 2009. Web. Accessed 25 Aug. 2012.

Roberts, Adam. "An Interview with Samuel Delany." *Conversations with Samuel R. Delany.* Ed. Carl Freedman. Jackson: UP of Mississippi, 2009. Print.

Scott-Heron, Gil. "Whitey on the Moon." *Small Talk at 125th and Lenox.* 1970. Flying Dutchman/RCA, 2001. CD.

Tatsumi, Takayuki. "Science Fiction and Criticism: The Diacritics Interview." *Silent Interviews: On Language, Race, Sex, Science Fiction, and Some Comics.* Hanover: Wesleyan UP, 1994. Print.

DIGGING DEEP

Ailments of Difference in Octavia Butler's
"The Evening and the Morning and the Night"

• • •

ISIAH LAVENDER III

Society often fears diseased bodies. Victims are marked as Other and made to suffer by healthy citizens, who often degrade and stereotype these people in ways that have similar social impacts to race and racism because hale citizens dread contamination. Octavia E. Butler's story "The Evening and the Morning and the Night" (1987) investigates societal responses to genetic disease and fears of the Other. Set in the near future, the story, which has not received the critical attention it merits, depicts people suffering with a hereditary disease who are forced to live apart from society in protective wards and are subject to discriminatory treatment because of a fearful populace influenced by the mass media. The protagonist, Lynn Mortimer, gives a first-person account of her life as a sufferer of Duryea-Gode Disease (DGD), a latent genetic disorder that will end with self-mutilation and death. This story ostensibly concerns medical science. However, what if this story were also about race and the disease as a literalized metaphor for race? How would an audience respond to a main character who is not racially marked in a narrative where the default setting is clearly not white?

Social experience itself becomes questionable because science fiction's characteristic "literalization of metaphor" makes us conscious of how we construct and perceive identity (Le Guin 30). Samuel R. Delany famously illustrates an example of a literalized metaphor with the sentence "the red sun is high, the blue low" in his classic essay, "About 5,175 Words," by examining each word of a sentence in his line-by-line corrective reading process called subjunctivity (*Jewel* 7). As Delany states, "The particular verbal freedom of SF, coupled with the corrective process that allows the whole range of the physically explainable universe, can produce the most violent leaps of imagery. For not only does it throw us worlds away, it specifies how we got there" (12).

Drawing on Delany as a theorist, I believe racial identity is a key component of Butler's story. Her storytelling dexterity in raising "made invisible" racialized issues to light is especially praiseworthy. For example, the meaning of a sentence such as "Hell, *they* should pass a law to sterilize the lot of *us*," is unmistakably racial when examined through the lens of subjunctivity (42; emphasis added). The subjunctive tension of this sentence is generated through the binary opposition of *they* and *us* revised by the intent of *should*, the meaning of *law*, and the menace behind the wish of the word *sterilize*. The desire to destroy a person's ability to reproduce generates fear, forcing the reader to ask who is meant by *they* and who is meant by *us*. The subjunctive tension of the story is clearly racial; ending an inferior race is surely the stuff of science fiction. SF's ability to literalize metaphor heightens what is often in our societies submerged as invisible yet trenchantly remains, like divisive racial binaries, a strong feature in the histories of race and disease.

Not surprisingly, thirty-one states had eugenic laws on the books at one time, and African American women, particularly in the South, had well-grounded fears of sterilization by the predominantly white medical establishment. Disproportionately large numbers of black women delivered babies and came out of hospitals with their tubes tied, unable to have any more children.[1] As Edward J. Larson writes, some twentieth-century eugenicists thought that blacks from the South bred "carelessly and disastrously," while African Americans believed that sterilization was "a plan for extermination" and looked on such programs with "distrust and hostility" (156). Moreover, Johanna Schoen demonstrates a link between the targeting of blacks for sterilization and the exponential growth of black welfare recipients in North Carolina between 1950 and 1961 (108–9). Such controversy continued in the 1990s, when David Duke, "a former Grand Wizard of the Ku Klux Klan," introduced legislation requiring Louisiana's female welfare recipients to use Norplant because "a large number of African Americans received welfare in the state" (Larson 165). In fact, eugenics repackaged as contemporary genomics raised its ugly head in media coverage about insurance coverage for birth control during the 2012 presidential race.

Returning to Butler's story, another layer of meaning becomes apparent when considering exactly who says, "Hell, they should pass a law to sterilize the lot of us" (42). Somewhat oddly, the story's only racially marked character, Alan Chi, Lynn's black double-DGD fiancé, makes this declaration. Alan has had himself sterilized long before he met Lynn, and he wishes that his parents "would have had [him] aborted the minute [his] mother realized she was pregnant" (41–42). His self-hatred is the result of internalizing racism. This idea of internalization is a reminder of double consciousness, at least in that having this disease clearly causes psychological problems that rise solely out of society's view of the disease rather than the afflicted's day-to-day experience of the illness.[2] In effect, the disease has become a metaphorical extension of race, disguising "the forces, events, classes and expressions of social decay . . . far more threatening to the body politic than biological 'race' ever was" (Morrison 63). Thus, Butler comments on how racial constructs operate through the disease itself.

Readers do not know Lynn's racial identity, creating even more anxiety in this story. Racial imagery is in play here. The thread of meaning that runs between our referential world and SF depends on DGDs struggling "to overcome the prejudices and barriers of race" in this particular story, "but it is never not a factor, never not in play" (Dyer 1). This subjunctive juncture models the precise form between SF and reality.

The near absence of race in this story and of discussions of race in scholarship on this story are notable since Butler is a race writer par excellence. Existing scholarship on this story has thus far concentrated on feminist readings of the text (see, for example, DeGraw). However, Butler utilizes DGD as a metaphor for both race and racist responses to DGD, consequently drawing attention away from how readers normally think of race in terms of biology. Lynn is literally marked as a racial Other by this disease regardless of her actual race, though she has been extended the privilege of whiteness, designated as a member of "a social group" representing "the human ordinary" by readers and critics alike (Dyer 47). This literalized metaphor is so powerful that critics assume that the character is white by default. These critics overlook the racial tension in the story because Lynn's race is "not mentioned." She is "assumed to be white or [her race is assumed to be] irrelevant to the events of the story" (Leonard 254). In my view, gender functions as a symptom of the story's engagement with racial dynamics. Butler asks her readers to challenge this "white" default position by not identifying Lynn's biological makeup. She is digging at her readers' embedded assumptions of her readers.

No textual evidence of Lynn's race exists: no racially suggestive bodily, cultural, or linguistic characteristics, no possibly race-tied name. Lynn is neither a white woman nor a woman of color. She is of no identifiable race because Butler specifically does not want her readers to know (especially after making clear that Lynn's fiancé is black). Butler offers all her readers the option of "guessing" Lynn's race, though Butler's refusal to mark Lynn racially has been employed as a strategy in some of her other works where learning the race of her female protagonists is seemingly coincidental. Thus, the open-ended nature of Butler's story defies simplistic, essentialist, reductionist readings that conclude that because Butler is a black writer, her stories are about racism.

In fact, Butler had profoundly mixed feelings about people reading her fiction as a metaphor for race. She spoke often, even compulsively about how much it upset her that people read "Bloodchild" as a story about masters and slaves, even though that particular story is obviously at least about masters and slaves and certainly can be read as something else, too—"a love story," "a coming-of-age story," or her "pregnant man story" (*Bloodchild* 30). Sometimes Butler's stories are explicitly and overtly (among other things) about race and racism (*Kindred*); sometimes Butler features people of color and mixed communities (*Wild Seed, Dawn,* and *Parable of the Sower,* among others); and sometimes strong claims can be made that a story is implicitly about racism, even when, on the surface, it is about something else ("Speech Sounds"). The underlying tensions of racial dynamics in her stories speak to this express negotiation, potential conflict, and rearranging of intersectionalities. "The Evening and the Morning and the Night" is no different. Lynn's fiancé is Nigerian, yes, but Lynn and Beatrice, a pivotal character, are not puzzled out as raced characters. Though Butler's intentions for this story are guided by "wondering" about the "board game" of genetics and "disease as one way to explore answers" (*Bloodchild* 69), critics should also consider the possibility that this story is a race story and that those suffering from the fictional genetic illness called DGD are in fact victims of cultural racism, figurative blackness, and racial Othering, which represent the rules of this board game.

Racing DGD

While there is no specific textual detail, like a quotation, that bolsters the idea that DGD is a racial metaphor, bits of tangential evidence indicate that we can read the story this way, even if these bits are inconclusive and speak to other kinds of oppression: the segregation and isolation of DGD victims, the violence and self-destruction of those infected with the disease, DGD's hereditary elements, prejudice, Lynn's attempts to pass as an unafflicted individual, and the portrayal of black matriarchal households. When linking race and disease, there are things in this story that are relevant to race, likely to be race metaphors. Disease and fear combine with the racial Other to produce a striking critique of social power. Such a reading is possible only when considering the problematic idea of cultural racism.

When racial definitions shift focus from fixed biological markers such as skin color or hair texture to measures such as lifestyle, beliefs, traditions, artistic sensibilities, and languages, they become cultural. Attempting to debunk the "link between race and biology," legal scholar Taunya L. Banks uses misconceptions about sickle-cell disease as an example (584). Banks outlines how medical professionals, linking biology with race, often miss detecting sickle-cell disease in patients because it is so prevalent in black Americans, though this particular disease is more accurately determined by "ancestral geographic origins" not just in Africa but also in the Mediterranean, Middle East, Near East, and Central America (582). For this reason, "the Executive Committee of the American Anthropological Association (AAA) concluded: 'present-day inequalities between so-called 'racial' groups are not consequences of their biological inheritance but products of historical and contemporary social, economic, educational, and political circumstances'" (584).

Butler explores race as a cultural construction rather than as a biological inevitability. Physical characteristics have been replaced by cultural ones as the focal point of discrimination. Butler provides an example of this cultural racism in her Hugo Award–winning short story "Speech Sounds" (1983), where a worldwide epidemic destroys humanity's ability to communicate in words. Left-handed people face discrimination because they retain a bit more of their mental faculties, such as rudimentary speech or the ability to read. These types of people are "raced" in a different manner because race must be understood on grounds that diverge from conventional features such as skin color and hair texture and focus instead on other physical characteristics. Hence, left-handed people are defined as a race. The same biases apply, although this kind of racism goes beyond that based on biology and the color line. The "earlier forms" of racism "have been powerfully transformed by what people normally call a new form of 'cultural racism,'" according to cultural theorist Stuart Hall (339). Substitute cultural racism as disease, with disease symbolizing blackness, and Butler breaks fixed and acquired biological features of race. Race as we think of it becomes invisible as illness is made visible through a new racial structure.

Consequently, Butler does not have a biological model of race in mind for "The Evening and the Morning and the Night." With race "situated at the crossroads of identity and social structure," the disease "frames inequality," and "political processes operate" in creating new racisms where health matters (Winant ix). The diseased versus the healthy is the primary difference that organizes the life possibilities for the characters, creating new ethnic groups. As race theorist Howard Winant claims, "Any 'ethnic' group can be racialized": for example, "the British racialized the Irish" (35). Butler does a similar thing, where the healthy racialize DGD sufferers because the healthy are afraid of "what different genes (even those we would agree produce 'disease') might offer" (Kalbian and Shepherd W18). Yet the social construction of DGD ultimately limits the lives of characters, not the disease itself. Though illness is the foundational difference here, Butler is talking about race and racism through disease metaphors.

As a result of this metaphoric leap, visible signs of disease have such scale and power that they can affect the human imagination. In *The Birth of the Clinic* (1963), Michel Foucault writes, "The 'glance' has simply to exercise its right of origin over truth" when "illness is articulated on the body" (4). Foucault means that a difference exists between seeing a thing and knowing a thing, that quickly interpreting what is merely visible prevents a full disclosure of the illness itself. Fear of illness exists between seeing and knowing something about the illness's effect on the body. In this sense, fear and eyesight are connected because of possible harmful contact with a DGD. As an exclusionary rationale develops, to be diseased is to be feared as Other. Panic results because the threat posed by this idea and its ability to spread quickly far exceeds the capacity of any government's ability to contain it. Real diseases are used to encourage "authoritarian ideologies . . . vested . . . in promoting fear" (Sontag 61–62). The same ideology is true of Butler's story when the media promotes fear of the DGD populace, causing a realignment of social boundaries to safeguard healthy people. Nobody wants to see "act[s] of self-mutilation," where people rend themselves bloody (50).

Racial Ailments

A segregation system, much like Jim Crow, is one particular behavioral response to fear of this disease,[3] where the rights of the DGD sufferers are curtailed by the discriminatory policies of the health care industry. Practically deprived of their citizenship, active DGDs are mandatorily removed and placed out of sight in government-backed hospitals by a society that considers the DGDs a problem. They are placed in separate, underfunded state facilities, where they cannibalize themselves and where especially troublesome patients are placed in "a bare room" and are allowed "to finish themselves" off by digging (56). Public pressure to separate people with DGD means that the deprivations of these wards are essentially undisclosed. No wonder society thinks of them as being a problem. This feeling of being a problem in the story is ironically reminiscent of one of W. E. B. Du Bois's musings on the black condition in America: "Being a problem is a strange experience" (44). Healthy and diseased humans are separated from each other through political means and social norms. Both groups seem to prefer associating with their own members, though hierarchical situations arise through close contact and controlled DGDs cope with discrimination on a daily basis.

Whether this separation is racist rationalization or justified containment, Butler likes to work at the uneasy border between the two. This government treatment strategy may seem logical, if extreme, in terms of protecting healthy citizens, but it also reflects intolerance for an afflicted population of citizens. Butler's construction of race is made real because it *is* a construct, a construct with power where the idea of containment or quarantine mirrors segregation. Through extrapolation, we make the metaphoric connection between racism and disease in this story, where inequality is maintained by social institutions like hospitals in society's attempts to halt potentially lethal outbreaks. Thus, the hospital is a segregation metaphor. While the public expects and even justifies containment of infectious diseases such as Ebola or Marburg since the entire human species is potentially at stake, there are few if any circumstances where carriers of genetic diseases should be isolated. Public hysteria to segregate and racialize the afflicted becomes an obsession.

DGD as a race metaphor thus offers a perspective on racist thinking with all the same signs, including social visibility and the fear of living with difference. The idea of racism operates in part according to a fear of contact with the other. Though racism may not be catching itself at this contact point, the stigma of race, an outsider status, can be caught because some people fear race mixing as well as racial myths. When the elements of racism and illness are placed together as a metaphor, Butler implicitly compares illness to racism to suggest a similarity based on difference while exchanging skin color for disease to make her examination of race and racism less obvious and more ironic. Butler's *Clay's Ark* (1984) highlights these superimposed fears when an extraterrestrial virus forces a branch of humanity into its next evolutionary step. Put simply, a fundamental fear of catching this disease drives the fear of the racial Other. The binary of healthy (white) versus unhealthy (black) contributes to this fear and has ominous similarities with racism. In "The Evening and the Morning and the Night," such fear results in reactionary measures to social, environmental, and cultural change, such as violence or attempts at isolation because unhealthy people have been made alien.

The social response to DGD is infectious in every sense of the word on the level of the individual as well as of the total population. In addition to being hereditary, Butler's disease features the need for a special diet, mental impairment, and self-mutilation as well as "particular twists" such as scenting abilities and delusions of corporeal self-entrapment (69–70). The fear of DGD is that it turns its victims into frightening self-mutilating monsters who might attack unafflicted persons on the street without provocation. Though this fear of attack seems unjustified, there is the example of Lynn's DGD father attacking her DGD mother, so some fear is warranted because such attacks, though rare, do exist. Fear for personal safety causes prejudice against those afflicted in public social settings, which in turn generates a powerful sense of cultural racism.

With this notion in mind, the idea of DGD attacking DGD mirrors the problem of black-on-black violence that emerged in the Reagan era. According to prominent sociologist Patricia Hill Collins, "The use of the phrase 'black-on-black' violence to describe violence within African American urban neighborhoods" is exploited by "print and broadcast media ... to install a racial frame of interethnic violence" (164). In the story, the government and the media use fear of DGD violence to promote communal policies that envision DGDs as a blot on society. Instead of considering the responsibility of the drug and medical industries for creating this problem, society emphasizes the perceived defective citizens of this new black subculture "by revealing their fall from normal states" (Wilson 86). Violence is attributed to the sense of futility that DGDs experience. For example, Lynn describes "a kind of driving hopelessness" that cause some DGDs to go "bad and bec[o]me destructive," producing "more than our share of criminals" (37). Such a discourse places blame squarely on the afflicted, and the public then begins to perceive the discourse as reality. The DGDs have been racially demonized as well as marginalized. "Much more consumable than its more traditional variety, biological determinism," cultural racism blames lifestyle and morality, which that are easy to suspect (Wilson 125). Butler must have been aware of the black-on-black violence social construction at the time she was writing and disputed its assumptions through this story. In fact, her 1994 *Crisis* interview lends support: "One of the horrifying things I'm noticing is that the younger kids, especially the ones who are raised in poverty, they're raised with a great contempt for caring. My God, look how they have to live. By the time they're old enough to get a gun and shoot somebody with it, they've seen enough so that's nothing" (Jackson 47). Society marginalizes DGDs because of the fear that they will attack and kill people. Clearly, such fear is justified when Lynn explains how her parents died. Without warning, Lynn's father "skinned her [mother] completely" to death before killing himself by "digging" through his own flesh and bone, managing "to reach his own heart before" dying (36). Paranoia and prejudice are further stoked by her father's actions. This murder/ suicide should be interpreted as another instance of black-on-black violence, and white people are right in fearing the possibility that this violence will spill over into their living spaces. Her parents' ignominious ending is precisely "the kind of thing that makes people afraid of [DGDs, though the] Duryea-Gode Disease Foundation has spent millions telling the world that people like [Lynn's] father don't exist" (36). Reactionary legislation has "created problems with jobs, housing, [and] schools" for DGDs because no healthy person really knows when a nonsymptomatic DGD will go off (36). Society has created a racist outlook for DGDs via fears of attack and of a contaminated gene pool.

When Butler associates "bad genes" with DGD victims, she engages notions of genetic purity (43). Healthy people must have good genes, while the unhealthy have bad genes. While DGD is the disastrous consequence of a rushed cancer treatment drug, Hedeonco, understanding why a segment of the population is outcast as undesirable relates to the racial paradigm of miscegenation (46). Healthy people desire uncorrupted offspring and consequently fear the possibility of sexual contact, mixing with the diseased Other in most circumstances, even if DGD is a genetic ailment. The desire to safeguard "pure" society from contamination enflames public opinion against the afflicted and symbolically involves the one-drop rule, since any descendants of a person treated with Hedeonco suffer from the disease and from discrimination. The rule's social influence is derived from the white concern about the contamination of the gene pool through racial intermarriage, and anyone with black lineage, no matter how remote, cannot be white. Separation and categorization maintain white power based on the genetics of a pure blood system. Nonetheless, if we reject "the possibility that humans might actually *choose* to engage in unprotected sex," we discount "the complexity of social and circumstantial factors informing our behavior" (Fink 420). Such denial leads to the development of "restrictive laws" in the story and "gets some [DGDs] into trouble for picking at a pimple or even for daydreaming" (36). Yet some afflicted and some healthy people possess enough "courage to have children" together because of advances in medical science and the development of the DGD diet (38). Human curiosity dictates contact despite the opposition and critical attitudes of the vast majority against the blending of the fit and the afflicted.

As long as they have not "drifted," controlled DGDs face prejudice while living in the non-DGD world. The fundamental structures of racism and segregation are transformed by the disease but remain wholly intact, where stereotypes, fears, marginalization, and admonishment daily occur. Lynn's time in college is a case in point. Earning "top grades" while majoring in biology, Lynn experiences moments of intolerance from the healthy student body, although she has no "particular hope" for the future from going to school (37). The minute she enters a "public space," her "body becomes marked with meaning" because people "fail to see a shared humanity" (Alsultany 107). For example, she does not eat in public because she "didn't like the way people stared at [her] biscuits—cleverly dubbed 'dog biscuits' in every school [she'd] ever attended" (38). Depending on the Foucaultian "glance," race is being performed in this social setting because healthy students disparage Lynn's DGD

identity by simply taking note of her diet and subjecting her to racial discrimination.[4] "Racial identity is not merely an instrument of rule; it is also an
arena and medium of social practice" as Winant claims (36).

Lynn's DGD emblem presents another racial issue: passing as healthy.
The nasty stares and ugly murmurings drawn by her public DGD identification emblem compel Lynn to wear "it on a chain around [her] neck" and
place "it down inside [her] blouse," though people spot it anyway (38). Lynn
may wear her emblem, but she hides it in an attempt to appear like an average college student. In this context, she is making a small effort "to pass as
normal" (38), but only a small one. If an emergency occurred and her emblem
were not visible, she could receive the wrong medication and die. Butler signifies American race history here; many light-skinned blacks have disappeared
within the white world—passed for white—in response to discrimination, at
a heavy cost to their positive self-identity. Passing individuals must by necessity disown any links to their colored past. With respect to mixed heritage as
it is presented in *Kindred* (1979), Butler stated that "it was very inconvenient
to be black and if you could pass, well, there was a time when that was a good
idea" (DiChario 208). Similarly, Lynn's desire to seem normal provides the
necessary "linkage between culture and structure which is at the core of the
racial formation process" for DGD identity (Winant 40). The need for com-
panionship prompts Lynn and several other DGDs to rent a house together,
where she eventually meets Alan Chi.

Black Matriarchies

At the halfway point in the story, Lynn and Alan visit Dilg, an exclusive private DGD facility, where every resident is an uncontrolled DGD under the
direction of a matriarchy headed by Dr. Beatrice Alcantara. I believe this
matriarchy is a black one, designed by Butler to counter perceptions of overly
aggressive black mothers as failures socially propagated by the 1965 release
of the Moynihan Report, since the author was raised by a single, widowed
black mother. Andrea Hairston puts it better: "The stereotype of the evil-tem-
pered, ball-busting black woman with weapons grade attitude and machine
gun mouth has been anxiously performed throughout the twentieth and into
the twenty-first century" (303). Likewise, I think this black matriarchal myth
has been intensified in the post-civil-rights period, when Butler wrote this
story, by the investment of the Reagan and Bush presidencies in promoting
images of "crack mothers" and "welfare queens" to countermand perceived
abuses of the welfare system by black people. "A Black family dependent upon

the welfare system is perceived as a dangerous scenario" because "Black women's children are in danger of growing uncontrollable" (Rousseau 51–52). The obvious parallel between uncontrolled DGDs and uncontrolled black children creates a racial subtext, where fear of this disease leads to attacks on its victims and outbursts by healthy citizens. "It is not news that racism derives much of its energy from sexism, from the efforts of men to possess and control women's bodies," declares Winant (128).

Beatrice is empowered as a healer fighting against segregation, violence, and discrimination through her own difference, providing a healthy living environment for metaphorically black people who have been denied their humanity. Jenny Wolmark sees "strong, black female characters who struggle against repressive power structures" as the hallmark of Butler's fiction (28–29). This characterization is a strategy Butler uses throughout her writing, and it makes a strong feminist statement on how Butler views gendered power and utopian, alternative ways of power. Beatrice as a medical doctor has the training to restore DGDs to health, and she can nurture this ability in Lynn. Skill coupled with nurturing is a way to bring to an end the cultural racism that DGDs face in their daily lives. Of course, the only problem with such a race reading is that Butler does not identify the race of Beatrice Alcantara.

Despite Butler's disinclination to show Beatrice as race-specific, aside from being a DGD, there is something else Other about Beatrice. Butler provides a couple of important clues. First, Beatrice is from Southern California. She and "a group of controlled DGDs in L.A." set up a DGD ward "in an old frame house with a leaky roof" "to prove" themselves "to the Dilg family" (56). The kind of neighborhood this DGD group could realistically afford is a deteriorated urban one, the inner city, because banks would certainly place a restrictive covenant on the afflicted. Second, and more important, Alcantara is a Spanish surname. It is not too far-fetched to believe that Beatrice Alcantara might have Anglicized her last name to help secure a loan for the Los Angeles property. If her name is spelled Beatriz Alcántara, one might reasonably assume a Latin American ethnicity of some kind at the very least. Butler does have a well-known predilection for peopling her fiction with multiethnic characters, and who better to guide Lynn through the inferno of memories regarding her first visit to a DGD ward than Beatrice? Who better to help Lynn recognize the benefits of DGD?

Lynn is like Beatrice in that both women are double afflicted (both parents were carriers) and can actually bring about change, however temporary. Their double DGD bodies emit "sex-linked" pheromones, allowing them to control DGD outbreaks through their scent, and they "can really do some good in a place like" Dilg (61). With a scent strong enough to gain the

attention of a drifting DGD, Beatrice is able to block destructive impulses
as well as return a feeling of dignity to these DGDs who "know they need
help, but . . . have minds of their own" (66). Michelle Green notes, "Dilg is
feminist by necessity" because women "simply handle certain aspects of the
disease better than" men (180). Importantly, female double DGDs as nurtur-
ers have a calming influence on single DGDs, which goes against the racist
perceptions of their society. As such, Lynn is startled by the revelation that
she is "a rare commodity" among DGDs, with this "pheromone that allows
her to command [their] attention" (Kalbian and Shepherd W17). In fact,
Lynn struggles to accept this thought until Alan reveals to Beatrice that they
already live in a DGD household at college and that their house is controlled
because Lynn puts all of them at ease by leaving her scent all over the house.
Lynn begins to understand that her role in society is that of a healer in her
own separate facility.

The disease has enabled women such as Beatrice and Lynn to transform
their domestic space (that is, Dilg and the rental house) in ways that are
viewed as stereotypically female yet in this context are not because they "offer
DGDs a chance to live and do whatever they decide is important to them"
(66). Beatrice is unquestionably advocating a policy of tolerance that might
lead to acceptance of difference among DGDs at least. By embracing their
own difference, metaphorical blackness, DGDs can anticipate the outside
world learning to live with them, though Butler's ending is more pessimistic
because humans who project their internalized doubts as fear of the other are
attempting to preserve a healthy sense of self.

At Dilg, the health crisis resulting from the fear of DGD has been transformed by the shared sense of autonomy, but only because of Beatrice's use
of pheromones to control behavior among the DGD population. In fact, Alan
seems a bit incredulous to learn that "out-of-control DGDs create art and
invent things" (48). This carefully fostered independence allows the ward to
escape the well-founded rumors of atrocities committed at the public institutions as well as prevent them. Butler uses the notion of pheromones to transform the diseased into a healthy social group as well as to counteract the
cultural transmission of racism from the outside world. DGDs use their difference to create art as therapy and to become a family.

Beatrice also challenges the young couple's preconceived notions about
DGD. The first erroneous belief is the destructive nature of all DGD sufferers. For example, the DGD invention of palm voice locks for doors in this
alternate world indicates that people who are characterized as Other can offer
something beneficial to the world; in effect, proof of their genius sanctions
tolerance from a racist society. Likewise, DGDs also "create art"—sculptures

and paintings that are "even sold . . . to galleries in the Bay Area or down around L.A." despite their tainted genetic material (48). The Dilg residents are industrious and creative as scientists and artists because they embrace the disease's "peculiar manifestation of specially elevated powers of concentration and creativity" (Kalbian and Shepherd W17). As Marty M. Fink believes, "Illness and difference" are being used "as potential sites of creation and community development" (425). DGDs may be born with a horrifying affliction, but they must demand change from a world that sees them as second-class citizens at best.

The second fallacy relates to the affirmation of the DGDs' powers of concentration. Like many others, Beatrice believes that "no ordinary person can concentrate on work the way our people can," but Lynn replies, "It's what people say whenever one of us does well at something. It's their way of denying us credit for our work" (55). Just as harmful as negative stereotypes, beneficial ones encourage faulty opinions based on preconceptions. In this respect, the stereotype of single-minded focus represents a functioning inequality where the entire group is scrutinized. "Ordinary" people often mean the praise as a backhanded compliment. Such an inversion rectifies a compromised sense of racial purity as an "outcome of nonracial dynamics" (Bonilla-Silva 2). The ability to focus takes on a racist connotation in Lynn's mind because she feels that society holds her DGD capacity to concentrate against her. This particular genetic ability become symbolic of *racial* identity because interactions between the healthy (white) and the afflicted (black) in the story are informed by a segregationist past based on false notions of racial purity. Beatrice does not help by calling DGDs "our people" several times throughout the tour in perceptible racial contexts. Nonetheless, Lynn begins to learn that her genetic disorder accentuates her personal value.

This education scares Alan because he realizes that he is powerless against the pheromone. He is, in fact, an objectified black man, only doubly so, since he is marginalized by the non-DGD world. Collins states, "Black men, *by definition*, cannot be real men, *because they are Black*" (193). Alan begins to understand the psychological effects of gender difference when he is made malleable by pheromones. He feels emasculated, made effeminate in his impotence to withstand the calming effect of the scent. Alan calls Lynn's newly realized desire to run a facility like Dilg an attempt to "play queen bee," though he has no "ambition to be a drone" (64). He sees a future where he is not in control, where he is subservient if not irrelevant. While Beatrice values her role as the leader of her household, meaning all of Dilg, Alan is disturbed by the idea that Lynn will one day commit him to such a life. Alan seemingly wants power and privilege more than survival, so he shifts blame for his sense of castrated manhood from the social world in which he lives to double DGD women. He has yet to realize that racism and sexism are interlocking oppressions: "Racism can *never* be solved without seeing and challenging sexism" (Collins 5).

Lynn will become what Beatrice already is, a strong DGD woman who cares for her household (that is, all of the DGDs under her roof) and provides some sort of discipline in the unstable and abused lives of DGDs everywhere. By creating her own independent DGD community, Lynn will work against a reactionary society that generates the oppressive conditions DGDs encounter every day. With a refreshed sense of value, purpose, and identity gained from Beatrice, Lynn has found her life's vocation as a leader of the afflicted, understanding that "power can be seen as an interdependence between the leader and those accepting that leadership, each accepting those limits on freedom that still allow for survival of the self" (Shinn 214).

Deep Digging

At some levels, Butler is "digging" at issues related to racism in her story about disease. Disease seems to be "raced" in the story—that is, made into race by cultural perceptions, whereby Butler is purposefully tangling together the symbolic and the literal, the victim and the society. Standard connotations of race suggest that clearly marked racial characters must be present in a story, yet Butler presents a more complex story that requires a more difficult argument and gives readers the option of "racializing" the disease when considering how society treats DGD victims.

Through Dilg, Butler draws another racial analogy. Dilg is "an elaborate old mansion," a "big, cumbersome estate" in a pastoral setting reminiscent of the big house (46). The racial association is unmistakable. The expression "big house" has a dual meaning: first, "it meant the master's house" during slavery (Winant 90); second, "it means the prison" (91). Dilg is simultaneously a quarantine site and a prison, where people who suffer from a deadly disease are locked away like criminals. Early in the story, Lynn suggests that the disease itself is a prison sentence when she thinks, "I knew what I was in for. . . . Whatever I did was just marking time" (37). Lynn also comments that "a maximum security prison wouldn't have been as potentially dangerous" (45). Butler's analogy works only in light of the possibility that the disease is a metaphor for race and racism. As Joan Gordon suggests, "confronting" an Other, made nonhuman, "literalizes the dehumanization of racism" (208). Those with the disease do present a significant danger to themselves, since they in effect commit suicide unless restrained, and they are of some danger to society because they can be violent in the process of killing themselves. The story also reveals that some state facilities where victims of the disease are placed are essentially no more than warehouses and that particularly violent DGD victims are occasionally allowed to kill themselves while in quarantine. These expectations are clearly failures of the story's medical and political establishment, especially because a new method of treating patients is much more effective; however, as in our world today, few patients have access to proper health insurance and powerful lawyers.

While the surface meaning of this story is about a genetic disorder, the deeper meaning concerns the sociocultural illness of racism as it affects the lives of the characters. Quoting Susan Sontag, Delany states, "Diseases should not become social metaphors," yet they do so because diseases bring an exclusionary impulse to bear on parts of society ("Tale" 184). Healthy people, symbolically white, project this racism, and those who suffer from this projection are figuratively black. Butler is looking at the consequences of this (probably universal) human impulse to Otherize parts of society to create an identity. Her general process is Otherization, and race, disease, and gender are her selected methodology for defining an Other in this story. Lynn struggles to escape from this form of oppression, from the knowledge that one day this monstrous Other will be unleashed, clawing its way out from its flesh prison. Her difficulty symbolizes her hardship in leading a "good" life as an afflicted person confronting a racist society. In this framework, if all DGDs are raced, the broader cultural message is that racial constructions are destructive, embedded as they are in the social consciousness, because they function like pathogens by killing potential friendships, harmony, and goodwill among people.

Butler's unwillingness to disclose the race of her female characters is a very deliberate critique of the feminist movement. Many readers assume that *woman* is tantamount to *white woman*, a manifestation of racism by the feminist movement. Butler does not deny "the existence of nonwhite women in America," which is why Lynn should be perceived as an everywoman, particularly one of color (hooks 8). "There is no more powerful position than that of being 'just' human," according to Richard Dyer, who also suggests that "raced people can't do that—they can only speak for their race" (2). Lynn does precisely that as she confronts serious issues related to race, health, and feminism. In this respect, Butler's science fiction tells stories about what it is to be human, to be black, to be female, to be a slave, to be betrayed by biology, to be Other. In Butler's stories as in life, these categories, these differences, overlap and transform one another. Richly deserving of all the accolades bestowed on her, Butler yanks her audience outside its comfort zone and continuously "digs" into their thoughts.

Notes

1. For example, sociologist Nicole Rousseau has found that North Carolina's eugenics program "admits that of the 7,686 sterilizations that had been performed in the state by the early 1960s, 'about 5,000 of the sterilized persons had been black'" and that "North Carolina continued to perform sterilizations at the same alarming rate, of 65 percent Black compared to 35 percent White, for the next twenty years" (110).

2. Alan's decision could also be interpreted in light of his awareness that all of his offspring would have DGD. Such a difficult decision may not be uncommon for people who are genetically predisposed to have severely disabled children.

3. Other places of containment or isolation exist in Butler's work. For example, the aliens, Tlic, confine humans to the Preserve in "Bloodchild" (1984).

4. These biscuits are the staple of her DGD diet, designed and proven to inhibit drifting, much as "insulin [has] done for diabetics" (38).

Works Cited

Alsultany, Evelyn. "Los Intersticios: Recasting Moving Selves." *This Bridge We Call Home: Radical Visions for Transformation.* Eds. Gloria E. Anzaldúa and Analouise Keating. New York: Routledge, 2002. 106–10. Print.

Banks, Taunya L. "Funding Race as Biology: The Relevance of 'Race' in Medical Research." *Minnesota Journal of Law, Science, and Technology.* 12.2 (2011): 571–618. Print.

Bonilla-Silva, Eduardo. *Racism without Racists: Color-Blind Racism and the Persistence of Racial Inequality in the United States.* 2nd ed. New York: Rowman and Littlefield, 2006. Print.

Butler, Octavia E. "Bloodchild." *Bloodchild and Other Stories.* New York: Seven Stories, 1996. 1–32. Print.

———. *Clay's Ark.* New York: Warner, 1984. Print.

———. *Dawn.* New York: Warner, 1987. Print.

———. "The Evening and the Morning and the Night." 1987. *Bloodchild and Other Stories.* New York: Seven Stories, 1996. 33–70. Print.

———. *Kindred.* 1979. Boston: Beacon, 1988. Print.

———. *Parable of the Sower.* New York: Warner, 1993. Print.

———. "Speech Sounds." 1983. *Bloodchild and Other Stories.* New York: Seven Stories, 1995. 87–108. Print.

———. *Wild Seed.* New York: Warner, 1980. Print.

Collins, Patricia H. *Black Sexual Politics: African Americans, Gender, and the New Racism.* New York: Routledge, 2005. Print.

DeGraw, Sharon. "'The More Things Change, the More They Remain the Same': Gender and Sexuality in Octavia Butler's Oeuvre." *Femspec* 4.2 (2004): 219–38. Print.

Delany, Samuel R. *The Jewel-Hinged Jaw: Notes on the Language of Science Fiction.* 1978. Rev. ed. Middletown: Wesleyan UP, 2009. Print.

———. "The Tale of Plagues and Carnivals; or, Some Informal Remarks towards the Modular Calculus, Part Five." 1984. *Flight from Nevèrÿon*. 1985. Hanover: Wesleyan UP, 1994. 181–360. Print.

DiChario, Nick. "A Conversation with Octavia Butler." 2004. *Conversations with Octavia Butler.* Ed. Consuela Francis. Jackson: UP of Mississippi, 2010. 206–12. Print.

Du Bois, W. E. B. *The Souls of Black Folk.* 1903. New York: Signet Classic, 2003.

Dyer, Richard. *White.* New York: Routledge, 1997. Print.

Fink, Marty M. "AIDS Vampires: Reimagining Illness in Octavia Butler's *Fledgling.*" *Science Fiction Studies* 37.3 (2010): 416–32. Print.

Foucault, Michel. *The Birth of the Clinic: An Archaeology of Medical Perception.* 1963. Trans. A. M. Sheridan Smith. New York: Vintage, 1994. Print.

Gordon, Joan. "Utopia, Genocide, and the Other." *Edging into the Future: Science Fiction and Contemporary Cultural Transformation.* Eds. Veronica Hollinger and Joan Gordon. Philadelphia: U of Pennsylvania P, 2002. 205–16. Print.

Green, Michelle E. "'There Goes the Neighborhood': Octavia Butler's Demand for Diversity in Utopias." *Utopian and Science Fiction by Women: Worlds of Difference.* Eds. Jane L. Donawerth and Carol A. Kolmerten. Syracuse: Syracuse UP, 1994. 166–89. Print.

Hall, Stuart. "Race, Culture, and Communications: Looking Backward and Forward at Cultural Studies." *What Is Cultural Studies?: A Reader.* Ed. John Storey. New York: Arnold, 1996. 336–43. Print.

Hairston, Andrea. "Octavia Butler—Praise Song to a Prophetic Artist." *Daughters of Earth: Feminist Science Fiction in the Twentieth Century.* Ed. Justine Larbalestier. Middletown: Wesleyan UP, 2006. 287–304. Print.

hooks, bell. *Ain't I a Woman: Black Women and Feminism.* Boston: South End, 1981. Print.

Jackson, H. J. "Sci-Fi Tales from Octavia E. Butler." 1994. *Conversations with Octavia Butler.* Ed. Consuela Francis. Jackson: UP of Mississippi, 2010. 43–47. Print.

Kalbian, Aline H., and Lois Shepherd. "Narrative Portrayals of Genes and Human Flourishing." *American Journal of Bioethics* 3.4 (2003): W1–W21. Print.

Larson, Edward J. *Sex, Race, and Science: Eugenics in the Deep South.* Baltimore: Johns Hopkins UP, 1995. Print.

Le Guin, Ursula K. "Introduction." *The Norton Book of Science Fiction: North American Science Fiction, 1960–1990.* Eds. Brian Attebery and Ursula K. Le Guin. New York: Norton, 1993. 15–42. Print.

Leonard, Elisabeth A. "Race and Ethnicity in Science Fiction." *The Cambridge Companion to Science Fiction.* Eds. Edward James and Farah Mendlesohn. New York: Cambridge UP, 2003. 253–63. Print.

Morrison, Toni. *Playing in the Dark: Whiteness and the Literary Imagination.* New York: Vintage, 1992. Print.

Moynihan, Daniel P. *The Negro Family: The Case for National Action.* U.S. Department of Labor, Mar. 1965. Web. 10 Jan. 2011.

Rousseau, Nicole. *Black Woman's Burden: Commodifying Black Reproduction.* New York: Palgrave Macmillan, 2009. Print.

Schoen, Johanna. *Choice and Coercion: Birth Control, Sterilization, and Abortion in Public Health and Welfare*. Chapel Hill: U of North Carolina P, 2005. Print.

Shinn, Thelma J. "The Wise Witches: Black Women Mentors in the Fiction of Octavia E. Butler." *Conjuring: Black Women, Fiction, and Literary Tradition*. Eds. Marjorie Pryse and Hortense J. Spillers. Bloomington: Indiana UP, 1985. 203–15. Print.

Sontag, Susan. *AIDS and Its Metaphors*. New York: Farrar, Straus, and Giroux, 1988. Print.

Wilson, David. *Inventing Black-on-Black Violence: Discourse, Space, and Representation*. Syracuse: Syracuse UP, 2005. Print.

Winant, Howard. *The New Politics of Race: Globalism, Difference, Justice*. Minneapolis: U of Minnesota P, 2004. Print.

Wolmark, Jenny. *Aliens and Others: Science Fiction, Feminism, and Postmodernism*. Iowa City: U of Iowa P, 1994. Print.

THE LAUGH OF ANANSI

Why Science Fiction Is Pertinent to
Black Children's Literature Pedagogy

• • •

MARLEEN S. BARR

A current Kindle television commercial adroitly addresses my notion that SF is especially pedagogically pertinent to black children. The commercial portrays a black boy who cannot contain his excitement when he tells his grandmother that he wishes to use his new Kindle to read about "wizards," "vampires," and "magic zombies." Although marketing rather than pedagogy is most certainly this commercial's goal, its creators correctly indicate that black children love fantastic genre fiction. The boy, after all, does not tell his grandmother that he cannot wait electronically to peruse texts about slavery and civil rights. He clearly wants to use his e-reader to access Martians, King Arthur, and starships, not Martin Luther King Jr. and slave ships. Because the black American historical reality is, to say the least, athwart with struggle, it is no wonder that black children eschew history and reality in favor of the unreal and the fantastic. Or, as Walter Mosley explains in "Black to the Future" (2003), SF may have a special allure for African Americans:

> Black people have been cut off from their African ancestry by the scythe of slavery and from an American heritage by being excluded from history. For us, science fiction offers an alternative where that which deviates from the norm is the norm. Science fiction allows history to be rewritten or ignored.... This power to imagine is the first step in changing the world. It is a step taken every day by young, and not so young, black readers who crave a vision that will shout down the realism imprisoning us behind a wall of alienating culture.... The power of science fiction is that it can tear down the walls and windows, the artifice and

laws by changing the logic, empowering the disenfranchised or simply by asking, What if? (202–3)

What if educators tore down the elitist walls that separate classrooms from
SF? What if asking "what if" was an integral part of the curricula?

My purpose is to apply Mosley's ideas to the notion that SF is a useful
pedagogical tool and an empowering genre for black children. The chapter
title is derived from my interpretation of statements by some of the participants at the New York University conference, "A Is for Anansi: Literature for
Children of African Descent" (8–9 Oct. 2010). I do not advocate jettisoning
realistic texts. I am merely calling for replacing knee-jerk discrimination
against SF with an open door in relation to the genre's pedagogical benefits,
the willingness to teach children about jumping through fantastic portals.

It is important to note that Anansi, a trickster god who appears in the
form of a spider and who one of the most important characters in West African and Caribbean folklore—is now engendering SF and is being featured in
children's popular culture. China Miéville cast Anansi as a prominent figure
in his first novel, *King Rat* (2000). Neil Gaiman's *American Gods* (2001) features Anansi (called Mr. Nancy), and Gaiman's sequel, *Anansi Boys* (2005),
follows Anansi's sons as they discover their heritage. Two major practitioners
of a genre that was almost devoid of black authors (with the noted exception of Samuel R. Delany and the late Octavia E. Butler and the not-so-noted
exception of Virginia Hamilton) are now featuring the black literary tradition in their work. And, most crucial to my objective, naming the New York
University conference for Anansi directly links black literature for children
to science fictional tropes appearing in popular culture aimed at children. In
"Static in Africa" (8 Feb. 2003), an episode of a WB network series, *Static Shock*
(2000–2004), Static travels to Africa, where he meets a superhero, Anansi the
Spider. The heroic team depicted in the D.C. Comics series *Justice League of
America* faces Anansi (McDuffie). *Spider-Man Fairy Tales*, part of the Marvel
Fairy Tales series, involved Spider-Man becoming Anansi (Cebulski). Spider-
Man and Anansi certainly share a great deal. Anansi is currently delighting
children in a manner that has nothing to do with racial distinctions. By referencing Anansi, the New York University conference's creators were in league
with those who authored the Kindle commercial: they indicate that SF is
appropriately at the center of literature that is productively aimed at black
children. What is helpful for black children? Is it a real bird? Is it a real plane?
No, it is a science fiction protagonist of Anansi's ilk. The fantastic is a "supergenre" for black children (Rabkin 147).

I have devoted my career to explaining why SF is a supergenre for women, but everything I have said also applies to black children. Reality, as we are all aware, has often not been a positive place for women and blacks; realistic literature is replete with negativity vis-à-vis both groups. SF is the location of empowering female images. SF provides a respite from such stalwarts of the realistic American feminist literary canon as Sylvia Plath's *The Bell Jar* (1963) and Kate Chopin's *The Awakening* (1899). Plath killed herself by sticking her head in an oven. Edna Pontellier, the protagonist of *The Awakening*, drowns herself. Ditto for Virginia Woolf. As an undergraduate student, I very consciously turned away from realistic feminist literature because I was seeking something other than death and dying. I exalted in the fact that the women in SF were alive and well and living on feminist planets. Black children who are interested in something other than slavery and civil rights can productively turn to SF, too, and inhabit their own black planets.

Realism: Often the Wrong Stuff for Black Children

Realistic black canonical literature, after all, is as depressing as realistic feminist canonical literature. The subject of Alex Haley's *The Autobiography of Malcolm X* (1965) was assassinated. Being shot to death is as distressing as death by dint of oven asphyxiation. *Black Like Me* (1961)? Contemporary black children are not black like John Howard Griffin's experience in mid-twentieth-century racist America. A fantastic griffin would be less alien to them than Griffin's reality. Young denizens of Obama's America are not native to the world Richard Wright created in *Native Son* (1940). Richard Wright is Mr. Wrong for black children. They are not fated to be the socially invisible, the "ectoplasm" Ralph Ellison describes in *Invisible Man* (1952) (3). They would be more interested in H. G. Wells's *The Invisible Man* (1897), the fun, fantastic invisible person who can magically be discerned only by a hat and sunglasses. Leo G. Carroll playing *Topper* (1953–55)[1] contending with ghosts would be more relevant to twenty-first-century children than Ralph Ellison's invisible man.

Black women authors point the way out of the problematic history reality trap. The ghost at the center of Toni Morrison's *Beloved* (1987) is certainly not appropriate for children. But as I have stated elsewhere, the feminist separatist community Morrison depicts in *Paradise* (1998) is akin to the ones appearing in feminist SF (see Barr). Although the complex relationships between the women and men Alice Walker depicts in *The Temple of My Familiar* (1989) are also not appropriate for children, Lissie, Walker's protagonist who experiences many past lives, also points the way to the fantastic. I mention Morrison and Walker because the presence of the fantastic in their work is a precursor to the young black women SF writers who are presently creating children's literature: Nnedi Okorafor, and Alaya Dawn Johnson, for example. Okorafor's *Zahrah the Windseeker* (2005) and Johnson's *Racing the Dark* (2009) are akin to Mosley's notion that SF enables black children to dream their futures. Okorafor creates black protagonists who fly.[2] As the experience of astronaut/ physician Mae Jemison (the first black woman in space) and the history-making 2011 domestic flight featuring the first all-black female crew show, black children who read about flying people really can fly when they grow up.

Black SF is as empowering for black children as feminist SF is for women. The same marginalization attributed to the fantastic and women is also directed toward the fantastic and blacks. Jeannie was told to go back in her bottle at her "master's" command; feminists would do well not to dream of Jeannie. As for Samantha, the all-powerful magic woman in *Bewitched* (1964–72), well, she spent her energy trying to comply with her husband's desire that she not use her power. In this vein, young adult SF book cover art involving black protagonists is being whitewashed. Brown-skinned Ged, the protagonist of Ursula Le Guin's *Earthsea* trilogy,[3] was originally pictured as blond. The black female protagonist of Justine Larbalestier's *Liar* (2009) was portrayed as white. Liar indeed. There is hope, though. In her blog entry "The Elephant in the Room," Elizabeth Bluemle emphasizes that enlightened members of the publishing and critical community empire are banding together and striking back against book cover whitewashing and other practices of that ilk: "We must open the gates of our publishing houses to a greater variety of voices and cast aside outdated assumptions of what people will or won't want people to edit or publish or sell. So how do we do it? . . . [C]hildren's book people [want] to address these important imbalances and make real change happen. . . . [T]he internet [has] made it possible for like-minded people to respond . . . quickly and vocally to unacceptable practices, like book-cover whitewashing."

The necessity of nullifying the power of the black fantastic was recognized close to a hundred years ago in a blatantly racist passage from a 1914 story written by Elizabeth Gordon, "Watermelon Pete":

> Once there was a little darky boy, and his name was Watermelon Pete. They called him Watermelon Pete because his mouth was just the shape of a *big*, piece of *ripe* watermelon. . . . He said "Oh dear, I wish I had a *big* piece of watermelon to eat!"

> And then a naughty little Blackie, who was sitting on Watermelon Pete's
> bedpost, just *hoping* that he would want to get out of bed and get into mis-
> chief[,] said, "I know where there are some watermelons. Farmer Brown has
> some down in the watermelon patch." ... Then he ate, and he ate, and he *ate* so
> many watermelons! ... But the naughty Blackie couldn't have any. (11, 13, 14, 23)

The "naughty little Blackie" is a fairy depicted as a tiny male version of Tinkerbell. Tinkerbell is of course beautiful. In a move to equate a magical black
creature with vermin, however, this black fairy has insect antenna protruding
from his head. Baby boomers who as children watched the televised production of *Peter Pan* (1960) might deep in their hearts still feel that they must
believe in and hence rescue Tinkerbell. In contrast, this black insectoid fairy
is portrayed negatively to the extent that the logical impetus would be to use
Raid to kill him dead. As if the story's racist illustrations are not sufficiently
damaging, the black fairy is punished: to add insult to injury, he cannot eat
any watermelon. He does not even deserve to be denigrated. "Watermelon
Pete" exemplifies how to do things with words (and pictures) to alienate black
children from the fantastic. This attitude caused Zora Neale Hurston's efforts
to record black folklore initially to be unvalued. I would like to think that
when Alice Walker found Hurston's grave, a little black female fairy was sitting on her headstone in the manner of the little Blackie sitting on Pete's bed-
post. I imagine that because Walker believed in the fairy's worth, this fantastic
character, like Tinkerbell, was rescued and became Tiana, the black Disney
princess from *The Princess and the Frog* (2009). Farfetched? Certainly not. I
describe a positive version of the fact that Hollywood debased women's relationship to the fantastic when it turned Jane Fonda into *Barbarella* (1968),
which portrayed Fonda in an exceedingly sexist fashion and has garnered a
cult following.

Bluemle advocates lessening the attention given to black children's books
about slavery and civil rights and increasing the attention given to normal
subjects. She also emphasizes the particular relevance of the fantastic—what I
describe as the boy's excitement about using his Kindle to read about wizards,
vampires, and magic zombies: "Give books by or about people of color more
than one or two 'slots' per season. That leads to the inevitable predictable del-
uge of books about slavery and civil rights. These are important books, of
course. But, imagine if we only published books about pilgrims for white children, and you'll quickly see that this approach is absurd. Children are hungry
to see themselves in books about regular kids doing regular everyday things.
Or as fantasy heroes. Where is the black *Twilight*?"

Science Fiction: Powerfully Black

While there is no black equivalent to Stephenie Meyer's *Twilight* (2005), an honored black writer specifically wrote SF for children. Virginia Hamilton's forty-one books include folktales, mystery, and SF. Hamilton, who has been overlooked by the SF scholarly community, was concerned with black spiritual legacy, tradition, and memory. Adhering to Mosley's black SF manifesto, Hamilton called her work "liberation literature" (Adoff and Cook 188). A recipient of major children's literature awards and the first African American to win the Newberry Award, Hamilton should be as reverently remembered in the SF critical community as Butler is. Hamilton's work—especially her *Justice Trilogy*, consisting of *Justice and Her Brothers* (1978), *Dustland* (1980), and *The Gathering* (1981)—positions her as the precursor to the black women currently writing SF for children.

These women—notably Okorafor—draw on the tradition of flying black people in black folklore. So too for Hamilton in her *The People Could Fly* (1985). The book's illustrators, Leo Dillon and Diane Dillon, who are known for their SF pictorial art, succinctly point to the importance of Hamilton's work: "Virginia brought magic, fantasy and fairy tales to children who were rarely included in these worlds." In terms of Carol Farley Kessler's feminist utopian literature anthology, *Daring to Dream* (1984), Hamilton enabled black children to dare to dream. Or, in Hamilton's own words, "'The People Could Fly' was first told and retold by those who had only their imaginations to set them free" ("Author's Note"). Hamilton did nothing less than set black children's imaginations free. She acted to negate the "naughty" Blackie fairy's racist implications. Or, As Gregory Hampton and Wanda Brooks put it, "Hamilton's *Justice Trilogy* . . . is an intriguing collection of African American children's literature because it writes black children into a future that does not seem to be concerned with the racial differences of the twentieth century. . . . Justice's ability to observe the present and predict the past enables her to manifest the future. . . . For Hamilton the highest goal for humanity is survival by any means necessary, but mainly by accepting difference and acknowledging the inevitability and omnipotence of change . . . primarily because sameness is not in Hamilton's definition of a better world. As the three books seem to suggest, sameness, or conformity, does not ensure the survival of a species in a hostile environment" (73–74). Mosley would applaud these scholars' insights about Hamilton. Hamilton's SF enables black children to write themselves into the future—that is, to go black to the future. Hampton and Brooks articulate a black-centered version of Hélène Cixous's call for women to use fantastic white ink (derived from mothers' milk) as a means to write themselves back into the past and present. According to Cixous, "Woman must write herself: must write about women and bring women to writing, from which they have been driven away as violently as from their bodies—for the same reasons, by the same law, with the same fatal goal. Woman must put herself into the text—as into the world and into history—by her own movement. . . . The Medusa is laughing" (875). Cixous, like Mosley, addresses the need for marginalized people to write themselves into history; SF is especially suited to enable black people to do so.

Perhaps the project of garnering respect for black children's literature in general and SF aimed at black children in particular can be called the laugh of Anansi. The participants in the Anansi Conference directly called for valuing black children's literature and, according to my interpretation, allude to the importance of SF vis-à-vis black children. Myisha Priest argues that black children are central to American culture. She points out that the connections within black literature written for children as well as for adults provide a whole picture of black literature, and that—most relevant to SF—"children's literature is a site of resistance that alters formations of power." Zetta Elliott deplores the failure of children's literature to address black children's imaginations: "Kids have to dream and incorporate history into their dreams." Fabienne Doucet adds that "you are here because someone is writing about you."

To my mind, Ann Petry best epitomizes the aims of the Anansi Conference and hence is the reason why black SF is pertinent to black children. Petry describes black urban rage from a female viewpoint in *The Street* (1946), the first book written by a black woman to sell more than one million copies. In addition, she has authored children's books. In her *Tituba of Salem Village* (1964), Tituba, who is brought from Barbados to be a slave in seventeenth-century Salem, Massachusetts, is accused of being a witch. This novel juxtaposes the real and the unreal to portray how the fantastic is skewed to disadvantage black people. Tituba is the punished naughty darkie fairy made real in the fictitious world Petry creates. As we are aware, as a consequence of fantastic scenarios made real, women cast as witches were in fact murdered in Salem. In this vein, we can understand the horror of slavery as based on biological SF. There is no such thing as a witch; there is no such thing as biological inferiority. Enslaving people as a result of their biological characteristics is as science fictional as burning women as a consequence of their gender characteristics. All stories about some groups of humans being inferior to other groups of humans are examples of what Roland Barthes (1957) called "mythologies."[4] Racism is based on fantasy narratives in which science fictionesque lies are erroneously presented as master narratives about reality.

When Madeleine L'Engle commented on *Tituba* in the *New York Times,* she addressed the link between black adult realistic literature and black children's fantastic literature that Petry's work exemplifies. SF directed at black children causes a wrinkle in time, a respite from the history of oppression. SF is an opposing force that can counter the biological SF stories that write black people out of the space reserved for human dignity.

Tony Medina, a Howard University professor of creative writing who was raised in a New York City housing project, made remarks at the Anansi Conference that exemplify this point. Seeming to evoke both Hamilton and his contemporary, Okorafor, he read a poem about Barack Obama that ends with images of flying black people. According to Medina a SF work, Daniel Keyes's *Flowers for Algernon* (1966), sparked his interest in writing, a statement that corroborates my thoughts about the positive impact SF can have on black children. Medina said, that *Algernon* "changed my entire world. Daniel Keyes used words to create a world. This made me want to be a writer. Reading humanizes black boys in a system that dehumanizes them. Science fiction shows black boys that they are not alien and belong in the mainstream world." SF shows that black children in general—and Medina in particular—are not the alien Other.

The Anansi Conference also included the most knowledgeable experts on the subject of the positive impact of SF on black children—black children themselves. These children, like members of Medina's generation, can also fruitfully position fantastic literature positively to affect their lives. Four young New York City public school students who participated in the conference—Nadi Tall, Hatim Mohamed, Ibraham Mohamed, and Earl Davis—echoed the enthusiasm for the fantastic communicated by the boy featured in the Kindle commercial. They underscored the idea that children do not like to read about race, struggle, and slavery because it is cruel. Hatim Mohamed said that he liked fantasy books: "They sort of bring you away from real life. You can go off to another world if you have a bad day." Tall says, "I agree. In fantasy, anything can happen. That's better." Davis, too, was very excited by books about vampires, and his favorite books are SF novels. Just after saying that he loved Orson Scott Card's *Ender's Game* (1985), Davis stated that "black people shouldn't be a problem in books. There should be less books about people going through problems. I can't relate to a book about an older man like Richard Wright. It is too sad." Ibraham Mohamed, too short to be seen behind the podium, presciently asked, "What's genre fiction? I just like stuff that's not real but could be real, like fantasy and sci-fi."

These children want to read about a place that is elsewhere in relation to the depressing aspects of black American history. They prefer haunted houses to plantation houses. Eschewing the real past, they desire to look toward an as yet unreal future that could include them. For example, Mary Pope Osborne's

Magic Tree House series (fifty-two volumes published between 1992 and mid-2014) delights young readers because it is about children who travel through time. Children who read the series's *Midnight on the Moon* (1996), about children who go to the moon in 2036 to assist Arthurian sorceress Morgan Le Fey, might really go to the moon in 2036. Granted, they will not encounter Morgan Le Fey there, but accessibility to Morgan Le Fey and the ability to engage with fantasy—dreaming the future—could propel them on that journey. African folk tales about flying people, SF visions, and black people's aspirations that enable them to fly are all connected: real-life astronaut Mae Jemison appeared on *Star Trek: The Next Generation* (1987–94), playing Lieutenant J. G. Palmer in an episode called "Second Chances." And no less an eminence than Martin Luther King Jr. told Nichelle Nichols that she could not resign from the original *Star Trek* series, on which she played Lieutenant Uhura, because she had the first nonstereotypical television role for a black actor (Martin). *Star Trek* (1966–69) is a utopian future fantasy dream; the first televised interracial kiss, which included Nichols as Uhura and William Shatner as Captain Kirk, was very real. *Star Trek* has fueled many other baby boomers' aspirations as well: Whoopi Goldberg, for one, was so intrigued by *Star Trek* and inspired by Nichols that she played the alien Guinan on *Star Trek: The Next Generation*. Further, *The Matrix* (1999) includes both a fictitious black woman who is portrayed as the smartest person in the world and the real Cornel West, who is one of the smartest social critics in the world. Where is the boundary between fiction and reality? What is the limit to black people's achievements? Answer: the sky. Perhaps after watching black actor Avery Brooks play Captain Sisko on *Star Trek: Deep Space Nine* (1993–99), Americans no longer were alienated by the idea of electing a black man as the U.S. president.

SF can act as a catalyst for turning black children into successful adults. SF should not face pedagogical discrimination; realistic texts should not be valorized at the expense of imaginative texts. Toni Morrison, after all, exalts Mark Twain, who "talked about racial ideology in the most powerful, eloquent and instructive way I have ever recalled" (Schappell 74). Twain, the creator of the quintessential literal American literary whitewasher, Tom Sawyer, would most certainly not approve of the practice of "whitewashing" black protagonists on SF novel covers. Twain talks about racial ideology in a manner that includes both fiction and realistic texts. His "A Double-Barreled Detective Story" (1902) posits that a lynch mob pursues and arraigns none other than Sherlock Holmes. Twain describes how Holmes escapes being burned at the stake because a brave sheriff intervenes. In addition, in "The United States of Lyncherdom" (1901), Twain uses a nonfictitious essay to reiterate the fantastic aspects of his detective story: strong personalities who can face "mobs without flinching" are the only means to stop mobs from carrying out lynchings—what Twain called an "epidemic of bloody insanities." Together, Twain's story and his essay form a non–O.K. Corral to contain lynching when this atrocity faces a double-barreled shootout on the insane American planet called Lyncherdom. Twain talks about the impact of fiction on reality—especially American black reality—when he argues (in *Life on the Mississippi* [1883]) that medievalism justified hierarchal society, and he traces medievalism's influence on southern American society to Walter Scott's *Ivanhoe* (1820). According to Twain, *Ivanhoe* was responsible for the Civil War: "A curious exemplification of the power of a single book for good or harm is shown in the effects wrought by *Don Quixote* and those wrought by *Ivanhoe*. The first swept the world's admiration for the medieval chivalry-silliness out of existence; and the other restored it. As far as our South is concerned, the good work done by Cervantes is pretty nearly a dead letter, so effectually has Scott's pernicious work undermined it" (267). Twain teaches us that reality, history, and classic fiction, such as *Ivanhoe*, are not the only textual right stuff for black children. The right stuff is not Scott's *Ivanhoe* and its impact on the antebellum south. The right stuff is Osborne's Morgan Le Fey and her impact on the moon.

Conclusion: The Laugh of Anansi

Black children can imagine climbing to the moon, as Barack Obama's sister, Maya Soetoro-Ng, describes in her children's book, *Ladder to the Moon* (2011). Or they can contemplate eventually being mentioned in a future potential sequel to a best-selling children's book called *Of Thee I Sing: A Letter to My Daughters* (2010). This imagined sequel might be written by either Malia or Sasha Obama, daughters of the man who wrote *Of Thee I Sing*. Barack Obama's book, like the all-inclusive utopian multiracial vision *Star Trek*'s starship crews represent, contains women and men from many races and time periods—Billie Holiday, Jackie Robinson, Abraham Lincoln, George Washington, and Neil Armstrong. While *Of Thee I Sing* is certainly not SF, an Amazon.com reviewer described it as a "fantastic book! Very simple yet deep, inspiring, stirring, and magical" (Acegb). The book, which is indeed "fantastic" and "magical," shows how what was once SF can become real. America really did send Armstrong to the moon. According to Mosley, "Through science fiction you can have a black president, a black world or simply a say in the way things are" (202). America really did send Barack Obama to the White House; President Obama has a say in the way things are. Anyone who now argues that black people do not belong on the moon or in the White House can be chastised by the phrase Jackie Gleason used on *The Honeymooners* (1955–56) to express the ridiculous: "To the moon, Alice!"

Loren Long, the illustrator of *Of Thee I Sing*, implies that racism itself is unreal and that color is not a barrier to becoming president: Obama "brings [the book] home by saying 'and I have told you that [the exemplary people the book describes] are all part of you and you are one with them.' My hope for this book is that every child will get that message to dream about what they can be when they grow up." Obama's notion that, regardless of race, all children are one with and a part of all exemplary individuals reveals that supposed biological racial difference is a SF fantasy. The president's literary place called hope is situated within the textual geography that emerges when SF is placed at the nexus of children's literature pedagogy. SF is the hopeful place where children can best receive Obama's message and dream of what they can be when they grow up. Or, in the words of Hampton and Brooks, *Of Thee I Sing* works in the manner of the SF written by Butler and Hamilton: "Through their reinterpretation of the issues of alienation and marginalization, Octavia Butler and Virginia Hamilton have forged a path in a genre that is prime for African American exploration. 'Otherness' is posited in Butler's and Hamilton's science fiction narratives as functions of difference and likeness that demonstrate both the flaws and strengths in human behavior. The genre of science fiction is the new frontier for African American literature that might lead to a more critical view of the past and a future that dismantles the concepts of alienation and marginalization, while it reinterprets the meaning of 'otherness'" (74). Like Butler's and Hamilton's fiction, Obama's book offers an inclusiveness— an insistence that America is one America in which *all* Americans have an impact on each other—that reinterprets alienation, marginalization, and the meaning of Otherness. John F. Kennedy's New Frontier involved a mandate to place a man on the moon. America answered his mandate by saying "Yes we can." President Obama's new frontier involves, in part, ending whitewashing in literature and in life—erasing the supposed racial genres that act as social barriers. Or, in Mosley's terms, if walls are torn down, they cannot be whitewashed. People can live in an America Mark Twain would exalt. In fact, all Americans—and all people—originated in Africa. Or, from the standpoint of SF's very biologically correct take on the human condition, all humanoids are Earthlings—as *Of Thee I Sing* proclaims this fact. It nullifies color difference in that it includes black people and white people (and all humanoids) and it is read (not in terms of the color red or any other color) all over.

His book's utopian vision ensues on *Star Trek*—and it ensued in historical American reality. On 11 September 2001, during the horrific destroyed space odyssey the terrorists wrought, neither the victims nor the rescuers gave a thought to skin color. The victims and the rescuers wanted to retard red (the color of flames) and turn burning lethal red into positive "read"— that is, reading all people as their fellow Americans who asked not what those who share their skin color can do to save or to be saved by them. This *Star Trek*–inspired utopian SF vision really happened on 9/11. When we evoke the universal human heroism that transpired on that day, we go black/ back to the future.

I like to think that Anansi would approve of *Of Thee I Sing*. After all, first dog Bo Obama, Anansi's fellow nonhumanoid, is featured prominently on the book's cover. Bo exemplifies that the Obama family exalts inclusion to the extent that even their family dog is black and white. Hillary Clinton has famously pointed out that it takes a village to raise a child. Malia and Sasha insisted that it also takes a dog. When Clinton connects a village to child rearing, she cites an African folklore concept. The fantastic elements of African folklore do apply to the problems inherent in raising all children. Toni Morrison has proclaimed that Bill Clinton was the first black president. This statement, too, is true. What Hillary Clinton and Toni Morrison say—their real/ unreal verbal female texts—are echoed in the laugh of the Medusa—and in the laugh of Anansi.

Notes

1. Ann Jeffreys and Robert Sterling played the ghosts that haunt Carroll's Topper on the CBS show.

2. Okorafor acknowledges Virginia Hamilton's influence by dedicating *Zahrah the Windseeker* to her.

3. The *Earthsea* Trilogy consists of *A Wizard of Earthsea* (1968), *The Tombs of Atuan* (1971), and *The Farthest Shore* (1972). *Tehanu: The Last Book of Earthsea* (1990) and *The Other Wind* (2001) are subsequent *Earthsea* novels.

4. Barthes's *Mythologies* explores how contemporary social value systems create modern myths.

Works Cited

"A Is for Anansi: Literature for Children of African Descent." Institute of African American Affairs. New York University. 8–9 Oct. 2010. Conference.

Acegb. Rev. of *Of Thee I Sing: A Letter to My Daughters*, by Barack Obama. 19 Dec. 2010. Web. 27 Aug. 2012. http://www.amazon.com/review/R3IHYKZ6F17MSW.

Adoff, Arnold, and Kacy Cook, eds. *Virginia Hamilton: Speeches, Essays, and Conversations.* New York: Blue Sky, 2010. Print.

Barbarella. Dir. Roger Vadim. Paramount, 1968. Film.

Barr, Marleen S. "'Everything's Coming Up Roses'—or, Mainstream Feminist Science Fiction, the Uncola." *Future Females, the Next Generation: New Voices and Velocities in Feminist Science Fiction Criticism.* New York: Rowman and Littlefield, 2000. 1–9. Print.

Barthes, Roland. *Mythologies.* 1957. Trans. Annette Lavers. New York: Farrar, Straus, and Giroux, 1972. Print.

Bewitched. ABC. 1964–72. Television.

Bluemle, Elizabeth. "The Elephant in the Room." *Shelftalker.* Publisher's Weekly. 10 June 2010. Web. 27 Aug. 2012. http://blogs.publishersweekly.com/blogs/shelftalker/?p=700.

Card, Orson Scott. *Ender's Game.* 1985. New York: Tor, 1991. Print.

Cebulski, C. B. *Spider-Man Fairy Tales: The Spirits of Friendship, Issue #2.* Illus. Niko Henrichon. New York: Marvel, 1 Aug. 2007. Print.

Chopin, Kate. *The Awakening.* New York: Stone, 1899. Print.

Cixous, Hélène. "The Laugh of the Medusa." Trans. Keith Cohen and Paula Cohen. *Signs* 1.4 (1976): 875–93. Print.

Dillon, Diane, and Leo Dillon, illus. *The People Could Fly.* By Virginia Hamilton. New York: Knopf, 1985. Print.

Doucet, Fabienne. "Issues of Identity and Representation." "A Is for Anansi: Literature for Children of African Descent." Institute of African American Affairs. New York University. 9 Oct. 2010. Panel.

Elliott, Zetta. "Issues of Identity and Representation." "A Is for Anansi: Literature for Children of African Descent." Institute of African American Affairs. New York University. 9 Oct. 2010. Panel.

Ellison, Ralph. *Invisible Man.* 1952. New York: Vintage, 1995. Print.

Gaiman, Neil. *American Gods.* New York: Morrow, 2001. Print.

———. *Anansi Boys.* New York: Morrow, 2005. Print.

Gordon, Elizabeth. "Watermelon Pete." *Watermelon Pete and Others.* Illus. Clara Powers Wilson. Chicago: Rand McNally, 1914. 11–23. Print.

Hampton, Gregory J., and Wanda M. Brooks. "Octavia Butler and Virginia Hamilton: Black Women Writers and Science Fiction." *English Journal* 92.6 (2003): 70–74. Print.

Griffin, John H. *Black Like Me.* Boston: Houghton Mifflin, 1961. Print.

Haley, Alex. *The Autobiography of Malcolm X.* New York: Grove, 1965. Print.

Hamilton, Virginia. "Author's Note." *The People Could Fly.* Illus. Leo Dillon and Diane Dillon. New York: Knopf, 1985. Print.

———. *Dustland.* New York: Greenwillow, 1980. Print.

———. *The Gathering.* New York: Greenwillow, 1981. Print.

———. *Justice and Her Brothers.* New York: Greenwillow, 1978. Print.

———. *The People Could Fly.* Illus. Leo Dillon and Diane Dillon. New York: Knopf, 1985. Print.

The Honeymooners. CBS. 1955–56. Television.

I Dream of Jeannie. NBC. 1965–70. Television.

Johnson, Alaya D. *Racing the Dark*. Chicago: Agate, 2009. Print.

Kessler, Carol F., comp., ed., and intro. *Daring to Dream: Utopian Stories by United States Women, 1836–1919*. Boston: Pandora, 1984. Print.

Keyes, Daniel. *Flowers for Algernon*. New York: Harcourt, Brace, and World, 1966. Print.

Larbalestier, Justine. *Liar*. New York: Bloomsbury, 2009. Print.

Le Guin, Ursula K. *The Earthsea Trilogy: A Wizard of Earthsea; The Tombs of Atuan; The Farthest Shore*. New York: Science Fiction Book Club, 2005. Print.

———. *The Other Wind*. New York: Harcourt Brace, 2001. Print.

———. *Tehanu: The Last Book of Earthsea*. New York: Atheneum, 1990. Print.

Long, Loren. "Video Commentary on Barack Obama's *Of Thee I Sing: A Letter to My Daughters*." Amazon.com. 16 Nov. 2010. Web. 27 Aug. 2012.

Martin, Michael. "Star Trek's Uhura Reflects on MLK Encounter." NPR.org. 17 Jan. 2011. Web. 8 Jan. 2014.

The Matrix. Dir. Andy and Larry Wachowski. Warner Bros., 1999. Film.

McDuffie, Dwayne. *Justice League of America: #24—The Second Coming, Chapter Three: The Blood-Dimmed Tide*. Illus. Alan Goldman. New York: DC, 1 Oct. 2008. Print.

Medina, Tony. "Literacy and Education for/of the Black Male." "A Is for Anansi: Literature for Children of African Descent." Institute of African American Affairs. New York University. 9 Oct. 2010. Panel.

Meyer, Stephenie. *Twilight*. Boston: Little, Brown, 2005. Print.

Miéville, China. *King Rat*. 1998. New York: Tor, 2000. Print.

Morrison, Toni. *Beloved*. New York: Plume, 1987. Print.

———. *Paradise*. New York: Knopf, 1998. Print.

Mosley, Walter. "Black to the Future." *Envisioning the Future: Science Fiction and the Next Millennium*. Ed. Marleen S. Barr. Middletown: Wesleyan UP, 2003. 202–4. Print.

Obama, Barack. *Of Thee I Sing: A Letter to My Daughters*. Illus. Loren Long. New York: Knopf, 2010. Print.

Okorafor, Nnedi. *Zahrah the Windseeker*. Boston: Houghton Mifflin, 2005. Print.

Osborne, Mary Pope. *Midnight on the Moon*. Magic Tree House, no. 8. New York: Random House, 1996. Print.

Peter Pan. Dir. Vincent J. Donehue. NBC. 1960. Film.

Petry, Ann. *The Street*. 1946. New York: Mariner, 1998. Print.

———. *Tituba of Salem Village*. 1964. New York: HarperCollins, 1991. Print.

Plath, Sylvia. *The Bell Jar*. 1963. London: Faber and Faber, 1966. Print.

Priest, Myisha. "Issues of Identity and Representation." "A Is for Anansi: Literature for Children of African Descent." Institute of African American Affairs. New York University. 9 Oct. 2010. Panel.

The Princess and the Frog. Dirs. Ron Clements and John Musker. Walt Disney. 2009. Film.

Rabkin, Eric S. *The Fantastic in Literature*. Princeton: Princeton UP, 1976. Print.

Schappell, Elissa. "Toni Morrison: The Art of Fiction." *Toni Morrison: Conversations*. Ed. Carolyn C. Denard. Jackson: UP of Mississippi, 2008. 62–90. Print.

Scott, Walter. *Ivanhoe*. 1820. New York: Oxford UP, 2010. Print.

"Second Chances." *Star Trek: The Next Generation.* Written by René Echevarria and Michael A. Medlock. Dir. LeVar Burton. Paramount. 22 May 1993. DVD.

Soetoro-Ng, Maya. *Ladder to the Moon.* Illus. Yuyi Morales. Sommerville: Candlewick, 2011. Print.

Star Trek. NBC. 1966–69. Television.

Star Trek: Deep Space Nine. CBS. 1993–99. Television.

Star Trek: The Next Generation. CBS. 1987–94. Television.

"Static in Africa." *Static Shock.* WB. 8 Feb. 2003. Television.

Topper. CBS. 1953–55. Television.

Twain, Mark. "A Double-Barreled Detective Story." 1902. Electronic Text Center, University of Virginia Library. Web. 27 Aug. 2012.

———. *Life on the Mississippi.* 1883. Cutchogue: Buccaneer, 1986.

———. "The United States of Lyncherdom." 1901. *Europe and Elsewhere.* Ed. Albert B. Paine, 1923. Web. 27 Aug. 2012. http://people.virginia.edu/~sfr/enam482e/lyncherdom.html.

Walker, Alice. *The Temple of My Familiar.* San Diego: Harcourt, Brace, Jovanovich, 1989. Print.

Wells, H. G. *The Invisible Man: A Grotesque Romance.* 1897. Project Gutenberg. Web. 27 Aug. 2012.

Wright, Richard. *Native Son.* 1940. New York: Harper Perennial, 2005. Print.

PART TWO

. . .

Brown Planets

HAINT STORIES ROOTED IN CONJURE SCIENCE

Indigenous Scientific Literacies in
Andrea Hairston's *Redwood and Wildfire*

• • •

GRACE L. DILLON (ANISHINAABE)

Several years ago Robert Warrior (Osage) spoke at the Native Student and Community Center at Portland State University in Oregon. Almost digressing from his prepared comments on social justice issues, he brought up his advocacy for the decolonization and restoration of Freedman peoples to their Cherokee bands and for recognition of Seminole Black Indians as accepted members of the Seminole Nation. Was he amplifying his own views in "Native Critics in the World: Edward Said and Nationalism" or echoing Taiaiake Alfred's *Peace, Power, Righteousness: An Indigenous Manifesto* (2009)? Both sources call for a new generation of native leaders who will work toward decolonization "in concert with the restoration of an indigenous political culture within our communities . . . not a matter of nostalgia, or any other uncritical attempt to capture the past in the present" (Alfred 143–44). Restoration is, in Warrior's rephrasing of the idea, "a sincere attempt to find ways to use insights, practices, and structures from our Indigenous traditions as the basis for contemporary forms of democratic polities in the Native world" (208).

A good bit of internal conflict and controversy exists in the broad native community on these issues. Advocating for restoration of status to "Black Indians" and decrying recent attempts to legally disenfranchise currently enrolled tribal members who share African and native heritage amounts to openly reprimanding the Cherokees, the Seminoles, and many other nations. As he humbly spoke to us about how one cannot ask another nation to shift its policies generally, he acknowledged moments—civil rights moments—that require speaking out, and he had chosen this moment to bear witness. Witnessing Professor Warrior's reaction to his Portland audience's wholehearted endorsement was therefore amusing. He probably did not realize that a Black Indian who had recently discovered his native heritage had anonymously donated substantial seed money for the center in which he was speaking that afternoon. Nor did he know that Portland State's Indigenous Nations Studies Program is closely affiliated with our Department of Black Studies in the ongoing development of a graduate degree in gender, race, and nation. In fact, our chair of black studies, Kofe Agorash, is an African archeologist famed for his digs in Jamaica, which have established the direct ancestral lineage of the Maroons to the Tainos/Arawaks, as runaway African diasporic slaves joined communities of indigenous peoples who sought safety from colonial enterprises by living in remote parts of the Jamaican mountains. Nor could he have known that this particular audience included members of a literary studies class on indigenous science fiction who had been busy consuming Andrea Hairston's "Griots of the Galaxy" (2004) and *Mindscape* (2006) and would soon be reading her *Redwood and Wildfire* (2011), which I was fortunate enough to have in manuscript form prior to its release the next spring. *Just wait,* I told my students, *until you get to hear the story of Aidan.*

We had the great honor of inviting Andrea Hairston and Pan Morigan to give a reading and performance at the same Native Student and Community Center once *Redwood and Wildfire* was released. Andrea's "readings" are mesmerizing *performances*, and in this case she and Pan were introduced by the ceremonial drumming and singing of Indigenous Nations Studies director Cornel Pewewardy (Comanche), while Pan later accompanied Andrea's spoken words with music and song.

In *Bodies in Dissent: Spectacular Performances of Race and Freedom, 1850–1910* (2006), Daphne A. Brooks chronicles the performance tradition that Andrea Hairston extends into the present generation. Describing the careers of Aida Overton Walker and Pauline Elizabeth Hopkins, Brooks writes, "They shared much in their visions of how black women might utilize performance as a place from which to explore and express the social, political, and sexual politics of black womanhood in America. In the midst of this fruitful era when leading black female activists conjoined the political with the aesthetic in myriad ways and forms, Hopkins and Walker experimented with classic and Pan-Africanist aesthetic practices to imagine how performance culture might serve as a site of revision and self-making for black women and their overdetermined bodies in the cultural imaginary" (286). Hairston casts Aida Overton Walker as a walk-on in the narrative, where she takes in Redwood, Aidan, and Saeed's performance; in turn, a worn-out copy of Hopkins's fantastic SF adventure novel *Of One Blood* (1903) makes its appearance, a marker of influence on Redwood's sister, Iris, on Aidan, and obviously on Hairston herself.

Redwood and Wildfire has been categorized as a "historical novel" but is better recognized as a renewed form of the speculative novel—a renewed form of the speculative novel that emphasizes conjuring as science, science as conjuring explicitly. Conjuring, all too often described as a form of magic, might be argued to be in opposition to scientific thought. However, China Miéville's writings, sometimes categorized as the New Weird, are, as the author himself states, additionally about "magicking science," and his work is steadily studied in the top peer-reviewed journals of the SF field. Less noted but still implicit is his experimentation with indigenous thinking and sciences more directly in his SF/New Weird novels, *The Scar* (2002) and *Embassytown* (2011), the former in a parallel world of Bas-Lag and the latter in a futuristic discovery of a species on a world of truly alien tongue and speech. Even on the back flap of Nnedi Okorafor's *Who Fears Death?* (2010), some reviews identify the novel as a future apocalyptic fantasy, but Okorafor assured audiences and readers in a WisCon Guest of Honor speech of her distinctive use of science in this novel, her fascination from childhood with classification and the science of animals/insects/fauna, and her Nigerian uncle's concept of science as "magic" (198). Nalo Hopkinson accomplishes an Afro-Canadian and Caribbean islander remix of Taino/Arawak stories in the midst of the organically constructed science of a postcyberpunk novel, *Midnight Robber* (2000). However, the *Los Angeles Times* recently termed her and the bulk of her SF thought experiments "cross-fabulist," mingling SF, horror, and fantasy (Farabee). These dynamic shifts in the SF field, recognizing the science of more than Euro-Western ways of thinking, along with numerous other examples such as indigenous science fiction stories (see Dillon), express better the stance of Hairston's forms of conjuration as science and embedded experiences of life itself. Or as Andrea herself might term it, her work shows art as a spectral aesthetic from a polyrhythmic perspective ("Upstaging" 237).

The overall feel of *Redwood and Wildfire* undermines the late nineteenth-/early twentieth-century pulpish but electrifying adventures of American Edisonades without resorting to closely intertextual satire, as is evidenced in Joe R. Lansdale's wickedly funny "The Steam Man of the Prairie and the Dark Rider Get Down: A Dime Novel." Hairston's novel instead emphasizes both the agency and presence of Native and African American sciences intertwined with art via the use of African diasporic, African American, and native indigenous methodologies and epistemologies.

Her main characters in this aesthetic of interminglings are a young black woman, Redwood Phipps, and a half-Irish, half-Seminole man, Aidan Wildfire. Events take place primarily in rural Georgia and Chicago between 1898 and 1913. The main actions of the narrative involve responses to the lynching of Redwood's mother, Miz Garnett, by a white mob. Miz Garnett was a well-regarded conjurer whom the white community viewed as a healer. When she killed the white man who raped her, racial affiliations became clear. Miz Garnett becomes a "Haint" to young, quaking Aidan, who witnessed the lynching and will be forever tormented by his guilt for failing to intercede. But this horrific event ultimately inspires Aidan to recover his own native identity and to preserve memories of his Seminole's father's stories and the languages of the Seminoles, Cherokees, and Muskogee Creeks as well as his Irish mother's Gaelic and family stories. Miz Garnett had taught young Aidan to write down these stories in a red leather-bound journal, which she characterized as "the good medicine" that will keep his mind and heart open. Gullah Sea Islanders, such as Miz Garnett and Miz Subie, who becomes Redwood's mentor for conjuring, as well as Cherokees, Seminoles, and Creeks emphasize the power of literacy, since all their cultures have faced sequestration, lynching, and erasure if found reading or understanding words in print.

A decade after the lynching, Redwood has grown into a woman as capable of conjuring, as her mother had been. While Aidan's guilt has wasted his gifts and led him to alcoholism and failed marriages, his friendship with Redwood greatly increases her powers, as is demonstrated by a signature event that reappears throughout the novel: Redwood's ability to capture a thunderstorm in her fist. Aidan and Redwood are soul mates, kept apart by the illegality of interracial marriage in the South.

Yet another tragic event carries forward the narrative. Redwood is raped by Jerome, the son of a former plantation owner, represents white desire to reclaim Cherokee and Choctaw lands and the properties of the colored folk of Peach Grove, including the Phippses' acreage. After Redwood accidently kills Jerome by conjuring with her thunderstorm fist, she knows that she risks the same fate as her mother by staying in Georgia, so she begins a trek to Chicago. Underscoring the element of performance discussed previously, she becomes a singer in a traveling show, finding her place in the theater and film businesses that were hallmarks of Chicago's cultural identity at that time. Aidan follows later, bringing along Redwood's younger sister, Iris. Together, they work on stage and in films. Redwood sings in choruses and picks up "African savage" parts; Aidan is cast in multiple roles as the "noble Indian savage." These compromises keep them working and ultimately give them access to a wealthy middle- and upper-class black community in Chicago, along with the more mixed communities that were springing up quickly at the time. Redwood's conjuring, which she gifts freely, gives her stature as a healer in this community, where she and Aidan realize her dream of making a film by and for diasporic and indigenous peoples, a dashing Sea Islander adventure and romance of an interracial marriage called simply *The Pirate and the Schoolteacher*. The film is based in Hog Hollow, a Sea Island town off the coast of Georgia.

The novel does not present a series of oppositions: science versus magic, minority cultures versus dominating culture. Rather, the reader soon senses what Arnold Krupat (Cherokee) terms a "double-sidedness of reality." Unlike the rhetorical figure dealing in contraries, a Western discursive practice, this "double-sidedness of reality" has different things "*appear to belong together, both* subversive and normative." Native philosophy[1] suggests not an antagonistic relationship of supremacy between them but an emphasis of balance and complementarity, a "dynamic and relational perspective" much like Hairston's polyrhythmic perspective (Krupat 10–13). Aidan and Redwood's relations to each other and to all others explore the science of conjuring and imagination. Redwood is simultaneously spread out and rooted, a healer, a dancer, a singer, an actress, a root digger, and a transformer; she can, in fact, embody animals, feel animals *be*. For example, she mediates Scar the bear scrounging for food at a Peach Grove picnic and a lioness who is beaten and finally slaughtered in spite of Redwood's heroic efforts to save her life. She can also transform others during dances, songs, and moments of receptiveness of celebration and joy. Aidan complements her conjuring skills with an open heart, open mind; he is a musician, composer of songs, and singer, an eager farmer practicing indigenous scientific literacies, a medicine bag keeper, and a serious writer journaling his life experiences.

In his memoir, *Brother West: Living and Loving Out Loud* (2009), Cornel West details conjuring of this kind of breadth. As a young Baptist and born-again Christian, he experienced life-threatening asthma. Madame Marie, the "voodoo lady" who had remedies for him, lived in a one-room home with roots, peppers, and beads hanging from her ceiling like Miz Subie's in *Redwood and Wildfire*, which is strung with herbs and medicines that Redwood and Aidan have gathered for her. West credits Madame Marie with a conjuring cure: she used incomprehensible language (most likely Gullah like that used by Miz Subie) and blessings that shift him in a "more ecumenical direction [where he] began to understand that answers to problems—physical, emotional, spiritual—often require enquiries that go beyond the confines of narrow dogma" (33–35). This kind of double-edged reality has room for African Baptists as well as Cherokee, Creek, Seminole, and Sioux Christians while opening up avenues for Africana and indigenous ways of thinking and ceremony, *aadizookaaanan* (sacred knowledge). Clarissa, Redwood's sister-in-law, is a composed, urbane, upper-middle-class African American who holds to the "uplift" model of Booker T. Washington. When she first meets Redwood,

Clarissa holds rigid views against on conjuring or hoodooing of any kind transformations so strongly that Aidan is startled to see "hoodoo talk coming out Clarissa's good Christian mouth" as she declares "if the good Lord sees fit to let us help one another this way, then who am I to argue?" (427)

Raymond Fogelson (Cherokee) notes that among Eastern Cherokees, "all of today's conjurers consider themselves to be good Christians and feel their work is completely consistent with Christian doctrine" (219–20). Moreover, according to Krupat, "the close rapport between Christianity and conjuring does not seem to be a recent event": he notes that much of the "best material" in James Mooney's *Myths of the Cherokee* (1900) "came from persons who combined the profession of native doctor with Sunday school preacher" (Krupat 219–20). Mooney's ideas were repeated by Robert Conley (United Keetoowah Band of Cherokee) in his explanation of *duyulta*, a moral code translated as "the right way" or "the path of being in balance." The medicine people maintain that being in balance means "the traditional Cherokee way of living: placing importance on the good of the whole more than the individual; having freedom but taking responsibility for yourself; staying close to the earth and all our relations. And how does one do this? By taking time to dream; by understanding our nature and our needs and taking care of them; by doing ceremonies that keep us in balance like going to water and using the sweat lodge; by listening and praying; by recognizing our dark and light sides; by having the support of family, extended family, clan, and tribe. The medicine people say it requires understanding ourselves and our place in the world around us" (qtd. in Teuton 199).

When Redwood dream-travels before conjuring and shares the ceremonial midsummer First Fruits and green corn ceremony and sweat lodge with Aidan as an extended "family" member of his Seminole clan, there is no contradiction in the sense felt by her Peach Grove Baptist minister and by the African Methodists, who shoo her away with shovels and guns while Sequoia (Redwood's stage name) travels north with Milton and Eddie as part of the act. Redwood/Sequoia's "Master of Breath" is also God; "God had mercy on her. God might even forgive her too, 'cause once she was beloved by the spirit on everything" (*Redwood* 151). This belief rings true consistently with many native bands, including Creeks. Craig Womack (Muskogee Creek) aligns the areas of Creek Baptist Church and conjurer woods grounds with an actual creek/river flowing as running water over stones, the "place where we touch medicine" (308). In the traditional circles, the balancing of Ofunka (Creator) and the Christian (here, Baptist) God, Hessaketemmessee, remains no riddle (314–15). The opening scene of *Redwood and Wildfire* and intertwined histories of red and black are established almost immediately by the first story of the Peach Grove colored folk eighty-five years earlier. The House of the Lord, built by slaves in the starlight after sweating and groaning all day, reappears in story form in 1898: "Half these devout slaves, filled with the spirit of the Holy Ghost, took their freedom into the swamps and onto Florida to live and die with the Seminoles." The story continues, "Paddy rollers chasing behind them got struck down by lightning, and their hound dogs got fried too. Overseer aimed to torch the church but set fire to his own self—man ran 'round for hours, burning everyone he touch, and nobody could put him out. Even if this was a tall tale, the angry God of the Baptists made Aidan nervous" (6–7). A 1929 film, *Hearts in Dixie*, features an all-black cast and portrays conjuring but plays it safe for a white Hollywood audience by deconstructing the abilities of the conjure woman.[2] In contrast, the film in Hairston's novel—directed by Redwood, written by Iris, and reinscribed by Aidan in his red leather journal—depicts effective conjuring with Seminole and Gullah medicines.

Abbaseh, Saeed's Persian sister-in-law, inquires about a red pouch in the film and its symbolic significance. More ambiguously, this pouch, faithfully worn at either Redwood's or Aidan's side most of the time, reveals this type of crossroads and soft translations going on all the time in the novel as a whole. Milton describes the pouch as a West African and Gullah conjuring *"mojo,* a prayer in a bag," whereas Rose, a Seminole of the Hutalglagi Wind Clan and a distant cousin of Aidan's, refers to it as an indigenous "medicine bag, holding you to a promise" (*Redwood* 435). This complexity, then, is not a monolithic blur but a cascade of a "polyrhythmic perspective," with readers expected to note even these small details of variety.

As a native science, conjuring may have multiple layers, including not merely its symbiogenesis and coevolution, in quantum mechanics and organic physics terms (spelled out explicitly in Hairston's SF novel *Mindscape*), but also forms of conjuration such as reading, writing, and literacy in general. As Aidan reminds his friend, Walter Jumping Bear, "Writing myself down, it's—a hoodoo tonic spell" (404). Further, *Redwood and Wildfire* conjures aspects of indigenous scientific literacies and the inversion of environmental hegemony, now acknowledged as environmental justice with an awareness of economic inequalities and racial groups whose homes bear the brunt of environmental degradation. Finally, conjuring is changing the weather, as Redwood does with her storm fist, time travel, dance and songs of celebration, and the love of *anogetchka*, a Creek rendering of a participatory act, calling things into being and enacting relationships (Womack 308). These conjurings are fully attributed to Isti Seminoli (free people), whether the freed people of long ago gone off to join the Seminoles; the freed of Cherokee, Choctaw, Chickasaw, and Muskogee Creek peoples; black and brown liberated together; or the main characters of this novel, colored folk, Indians, Persians, Dahomeans, Abyssians, and/or mixed peoples, such as the elderly guide, "colored and Indian too," who fills Aidan in on the Buffalo Bill Wild West show at the 1893 Chicago World's Fair.

Aidan writes and records samples of this kind of mixing: stories of his and Redwood's voyage ten years back in time to the fair; stories about his great-great Muskóki Creek ancestor, Okefenokee (Trembling Earth), born on a floating island, "A Time before Time" (47); stories from his Seminole father, Big Thunder, such as "Walking the Stars" (57–60); "stories and songs medicine too" (101); tales from his Irish mother, Aislinn O'Casey, a "story spell" (157); stories of his own "medicine work" for Miz Garnett of the "Cherokee *nunnehi*, invisible spirit people, liv[ing] inside the mountain and also the tiny *Yunwi Tsunsdi*. Perhaps the fairies of Ireland too" (231–33) He also records stories of his youth in the enchanted land of the Cherokees, Blood Mountain, and the Blue Ridge Mountains, where the 1883 *Pace v. Alabama*, legal restrictions on interracial marriage were disregarded, where his parents married in the traditional Seminole way in 1876 and slipped away to these communities; where Aidan received his mother's white seashell on Cherokee-sacred Mount Enotah, "*isti seminoli*, free folks, coloured and Indian" (345–46); where "all sorts of free folks were mixing 'round up there in them mountains" (435); where one celebrates first fruits, lights new fires, and forgives what can be forgiven.

While the European privileging of an alphabetic writing system interrupted the oral, graphic, and critical impulses of indigenous peoples in the Americas, memory as well as recordings were famously enunciated by Sequoyah, whose English name was George Guess. Sequoyah was the nineteenth-century "American Cadmus" often described as "inventing from scratch a written language" through "idea diffusion"; his "talking leaves" culminated in eighty-five signs of the Cherokee syllabary and took twenty years to create. More recent native scholarship suggests that this so-called invention came from a much older language used by the ancient priesthood, the Ani-Kutani (Teuton 3). At the same time, scholars recognize that a "continuing legal force of a long established, deeply embedded and widely dispersed language of racism directed at Indians" represents an ongoing attempt to eradicate the knowledge of indigenous recorded and written systems of language (Teuton 218–19). Both Lisa Brooks and Stephen Greenblatt write convincingly of how imperial forces strategically destroyed extant indigenous orthographies as a strategy of colonial dominance. As far back as 1828, Elias Boudinot, the first editor of the *Cherokee Phoenix* (still published today), pointed out that the Cherokees and other native peoples had been misrepresented by whites as static primitives locked in time when they, like whites, had in reality changed over time. Cherokees had hesitated to reincorporate "talking leaves" with the corruption of the former priesthood and the decimation of the remaining strands of administration (war chiefs, peace chiefs, and medicine peoples), but soon after the Civil War, the Cherokees founded the country's (and perhaps the world's) first free, compulsory public school system. Education quickly became the largest single item in the Cherokee Nation's budget, and by 1907, the Cherokee Nation had produced more college students than the states of Arkansas and Texas combined. All Cherokee youth learned from literary sources as well as grandparents and elders in both English and Cherokee (Teuton 3–22, 190–96).

Aidan's ability to read and write so easily may well have been linked to this kind of outreach in Cherokee education, since he lived on tribal lands until he was eleven or twelve. Conjurers' roles as healers led them to become the keepers of public ceremonies and old stories, graphically and orally. This role included singing to animals and copying their steps and manners to better communicate with them, a function Aidan often performs with his mule, Princess; the bear, Scar; and other animals. Miz Garnett's first advice to Aidan is to write all of life in story form in his red leather journal. Miz Subie's Gullah friend reminisces about Miz Subie's willingness to die before Civil War by learning to read. And Iris possesses a fierce love of books and writing, is determined to be a journalist someday, and writes the script for the movie/play.

Reading and writing become powerful conjuring and healing spells when one's people have been denied their history of writing or when they have been banned from learning to read or write. Such actions represent the essence of racialized relations embedded in the formation of imperialism and conquest and slavery, as Michael Omi and Howard Winant have established. *Mindscape*'s Lawanda Kitt speaks of this "spiritual assault" on enslaved and conquered Africana and indigenous peoples for more than five hundred years.

Redwood and Wildfire also takes on the misuse of native lands in light of the post–Civil War rise of mechanized industry, which had negative effects on former slaves and indigenous communities. There are ample instances in literature that show slaves finding themselves transformed into crossbreeds (people of mixed ancestry) (see Chesnutt, "Goophered"; Chesnutt, "Po' Sandy"). Consistently in this tradition, "conjure women," like Hairston's Redwood, help to mitigate or to exacerbate the effects. Charles W. Chesnutt praised W. E. B. Du Bois's efforts to highlight increasing debt peonage, refused to "pass" although friends urged him to do so, and chose to write controversially on the environmental catastrophes of his day (Crouch and Benjamin 143–44). In Chesnutt's "Po' Sandy," a conjure woman turns her husband into a tree so that he can remain on the plantation. Ironically, however, he is cut down, and

the bound and screaming conjure woman is forced to watch the dismember-
ment of both her husband and the forest "in a metonymic whirr of ecosublime
terror and shock" (Rozell 24–28). Such stories suggest the ecological context
of the period between 1860 and 1900, when poverty-stricken southerners
drained swamplands on a massive scale, cut virgin timber, and attempted to
farm on a landscape depleted of the nutrients required to sustain crops. These
stories thus explore relationships between exploited African Americans and
natural environments plagued with misuse in the developing South (Rozell 24;
Outka 103–7). Glimpses of this sort of exploitation occur throughout *Redwood
and Wildfire*: the trees at Mount Enotah have been devastated between Aiden's
childhood and Redwood, Milton, and Eddie's visit there (156); Chicago in general and especially the stockyards are plagued by pollution, dirt, and noise;
even the film site outside Chicago is sullied by "greasy rain off the lake—half-
water, half-factory spew," as Lake Michigan has become badly polluted only
a few decades after the Chicago World's Fair highlighted the lake's sparkling
waters and the ultraclean "White City" (*Redwood* 391; Sotiropoulos 12–41).
Each individual has the power to harm the common pot: for example, "George
came out to hunt the snowy egrets and purple swamp hens. A company in
England was paying thirty-two dollars an ounce and didn't care 'bout the color
of the man doing the selling. Long as they got purple jewel feathers and snowy
white plumes for high-fashion hats. All over Europe, fancy rich ladies were
styling Georgia birds" (33). Redwood makes a conscious effort to tread lightly
on the earth, reminding George, that it is bad for his insides "to go killing what
you don't need" (34); similarly, celebrating her birthday with a new lighting of
First Fruits on the shore of Lake Michigan, "she silently promised the lake to
do no harm and asked the *crossroads* spirits to open the way" (382–83).

Redwood and Wildfire follows this conjuring tradition of environmental responsibility, or better put, mutual reciprocity, by bestowing indigenous
scientific literacies, a forward-thinking way of characterizing indigenous
knowledge in opposition to Euro-Western characterizations of "native superstition" and magic, with the traditional figure of the conjure woman. Hairston
incorporates several key characteristics of indigenous scientific literacies. For
example, she emphasizes a place-located knowledge of medicines, roots, and
other elements of the landscape, showing an awareness of the importance of
careful use of all parts of the plants at all times. Scenes in the film, feature the
Seminole dish of *sofkee*, made with corn hominy and meat; Seminole agriculture; eating smoked fish in canoes; and using a single arrow to kill a bear
(395). A life-threatening spider bite and extensive blood poisoning are almost
immediately counteracted when Redwood dashes into the woods to grab a
root, while the precise administration of an herbal tea allows Clarissa to avoid

a life-threatening pregnancy (142, 236). Controlled burnings and fires started with ceremonial torches ignited by lightning, a significant indigenous science for tens of thousands of years, appear along with natural forest fires. The dangerous Boneyard fire haints of ashes of the Chicago Fire wipe out the World's Fair and later the Phipps Dry Cleaning business., the latter first started by envious Irish roughs and the exquisite balance of Miz Garnett Phipps, a fire haint that tells Aidan to "do right," that dances in on train tracks as Iris and Aidan join the city crowd, and a person-fire haint that exchanges stolen heart beats to save her children, George, Iris, and Redwood along with other lives (70–72, 409–21).

The distinctions among of various indigenous methods and embedded, mentored Africana knowledge are distilled. Aidan uses "Indian medicine," as Redwood calls it, knowing that greenbrier can be quite dangerous if not used properly: "Roots be poison, if you take too much, but just enough clean you out real good" (51). In the swamp, Aidan covers himself with bear grease to protect himself against chiggers, ticks, and mosquitoes, while Redwood employs a different technique with Miz Subie's cure-all bag of roots around her neck to ward off "no-see'ems and stinging demons" (47, 53). Further, Redwood engages in a little provocation with Aidan: "Miz Subie say I could work out my own understanding" with the insects, and "then I wouldn't need funky bear grease or nasty herbs" (53). This recognition in my Anishinaabowin tongue is called *gikendaasowin* and suggests being attuned to tribal knowledge, information, and the synthesis of personal teachings (see Genius).

Native activist scholars are publishing more explicit information regarding other forms of *gikendaasowin* in an effort to foster environmental sustainability (see, for example, Cajete; Nelson; Silko). The novel also suggests this kind of transformation among communities, along with a recognition of the significance of theater, entertainment, dance, and the arts. Clarissa's group of thoughtful progressive African American female thinkers projects her own increased awareness, especially after she realizes the significance of Redwood's conjuring as actual scientific practices after they are gathered, known in the heart, and learned through practice accompanied by ceremonial vigor.

Respect for indigenous scientific traditions is consciously cast in opposition to colonialism, slavery, debt peonage, lynchings, and segregation. Tradition not only encompasses timelessness but also marks out indigenous knowledge as ever-changing and dynamic, forms of native science that include dance, music, ceremony, and all art forms. Gregory Cajete (Acoma Pueblo) and Leslie Marmon Silko (Laguna Pueblo) contend that this kind of traditionalism gets away from the stark polar distinction between the scientific and indigenous ways of thinking. Chris Teuton (Cherokee) qualifies this outlook by reminding readers that science and literature, oral and graphic impulses are kept dynamic by the critical impulse of balancing one another experientially. In this sense, Redwood displays a critical impulse when she suggests that her conjuring skills may someday "overgoe" Aidan's acquired scientific literacies.

This novel, then, recenters the conversation and critical impulses within Africana, indigenous, and mixed communities about these environmental sustainabilities and provides a sharp contrast with the general mainstream thinking of the time—a reckless haste to obtain more and more. Iris knows more than even her teachers about Darwin's evolutionary ideas, while some citizens of Peach Grove are depicted as well-meaning and civilized: Doc Johnson, for example, lends books to both Redwood and Aidan .

Iris's mastery of Darwin is particularly noteworthy. According to Patrick B. Sharp, Darwin's *Descent of Man, and Selection in Relation to Sex* (1871) generated a much more positive initial Euro-American response than did Darwin's earlier *The Origin of Species* because the later volume offered a compelling "adventure of the English evolving, clambering up from the apes, struggling to conquer savagery, multiplying and dispersing around the globe" (32). In fact, *Descent* reestablished the polygenist perspectives and omitted the argument about separate species, since, as Darwin argued, all humans can cross-fertilize and thus must be all of one species. But *Descent of Man* also supported regressive ideas with his references to the industrial-age notion of progress and of humans as toolmakers, and he surmised that various races such as Africans and islanders (including all natives he had not yet met) were best-termed "subspecies." He allowed the term *race* to remain in use "from long habit" (Sharp 37).

Darwin's thinking had enormous impact at the time. His narrative of human progress asserted that Europeans were superior tool users and the most evolved branch of the human species. Darwin's vision of racial progress provided a "worldview not only for future scientists but also for historians and fiction writers trying to account for the importance of race and technology in the modern world" (Sharp 32). Lois A. Cuddy and Claire M. Roche further this argument by examining the growth and migration of the U.S. population during the late nineteenth century: in 1860, sixteen cities had populations of greater than fifty thousand, but by 1910, that number had grown to more than eighty, partly as a consequence of immigration and the rise of eugenics. Evolution's requirement for reproduction of the best human species and obsession with pathology after outbreaks of various diseases creates a climate in which homosexuals, the poor, and even the working classes encounter revulsion as "unfit" members of society. While also obsessing about science, authors writing as realists carefully aligned their thinking with the sciences of the day, and even naturalists, modernists, and socialists were "seduced consciously or unconsciously by the evolutionary and eugenic ideologies that placed these eminent authors themselves as the highest level of human development," committed to the idea of "scientific objectivity" (Cuddy and Roche 17). In *Descent*, Darwin argues specifically that natives and Africans cannot think abstractly (18) and that they are "the lowest savages" connected directly with "the most highly organised ape" (85). He quotes a Spanish maxim, "Never, never trust an Indian" to illustrate the savagery and ethical defects of the uncivilized Indian (142).

In this historical context, *Redwood and Wildfire* can be seen as a tale of nineteenth- and twentieth-century social revolution on two fronts. The novel is a revolutionary text as a conjured love story that is not just about the legal banning of interracial marriage during this neoslavery period. It is also a reaction to Darwin's stated "scientific" thinking that actual human qualities evolve over millions of years. Thus, the revolutionary idea of *Redwood and Wildfire* as a love story between an African American female and an indigenous male also functions radically at an immersive scientific/philosophical level: All human qualities evolved over millions of years—compassion, loyalty, love of beauty, sense of community, and so on—are "undermined by the animal natures that take over when poverty and hunger impel people to act" (*Redwood* 29).

In *Redwood and Wildfire*, conjuring is science, a recognizable application of indigenous scientific literacy, and in the indigenous sense of *gikedaasowin*, it includes all the kineticism of our lives, the performance of our lives, and the revolutionary tactics of sharing via stage performance. Redwood, Aidan, and Saeed engage in these revolutionary tactics when they shift from "cooning" to white/immigrant audiences to "redfacing" in Wild West shows to coming out as themselves before a breathless audience. Creating abstractions, conjuring with storm fists, or flying on stage are not only true, not only science, but are also revolutionary and resistant to the Euro-American mind-set illustrated by Darwin's "scientific" thinking. Conjured science and conjured art as science fiction cause people to brighten "at entertainment gracing their path" (*Redwood* 434). The transformations of a bright-destiny spell in *Redwood and Wildfire* are glimpsed in the delight of dusty travelers stepping off the train: for a delicious instant, the station crowd turned into swooping osprey, elegant buzzards, and playful otters. Hardly nobody really believed what was happening to them. And after Aidan and Redwood passed, folk just settled back down to coming and going. Yet every once in a while, in the days to come, these good people would hop and soar and feel as if they could just get up and do anything (434).

Notes

1. Justice's theorizing of Cherokee nationhood—an upper world of order and a lower world of chaos supports Hairston's native philosophy.

2. For more on *Hearts in Dixie*, see Friedman.

Works Cited

Alfred, Taiaiake. *Peace, Power, Righteousness: An Indigenous Manifesto.* Ontario: Oxford UP, 2009. Print.

Brooks, Daphne A. *Bodies in Dissent: Spectacular Performances of Race and Freedom, 1850–1910.* Durham: Duke UP, 2006. Print.

Brooks, Lisa. *The Common Pot: The Recovery of Native Space in the Northeast.* Minneapolis: U of Minnesota P, 2008. Print.

Cajete, Gregory. *Native Science: Natural Laws of Interdependence.* Santa Fe: Clear Light, 2000. Print.

Chesnutt, Charles W. "The Goophered Grape Vine." 1887. *The Conjure Woman and Other Conjure Tales.* Durham: Duke UP, 1996. 31–43. Print.

———. "Po' Sandy." 1888. *The Conjure Woman and Other Conjure Tales.* Durham: Duke UP, 1996. 44–54. Print.

Conley, Robert J. *The Cherokee Nation: A History.* Albuquerque: U of New Mexico P, 2005. Print.

Crouch, Stanley, and Playthell Benjamin. *Reconsidering the Souls of Black Folk.* Philadelphia: Running, 2002. Print.

Cuddy, Lois A., and Claire M. Roche, eds. *Evolution and Eugenics in American Literature and Culture, 1880–1940: Essays on Ideological Conflict and Complicity.* Lewisburg: Bucknell UP, 2003. Print.

Darwin, Charles. *Descent of Man, and Selection in Relation to Sex.* 1871. New York: Penguin Classics, 2004. Print.

———. *The Origin of Species by Means of Natural Selection, or, The Preservation of Favoured Races in the Struggle for Life.* 1859. New York: Penguin, 1986. Print.

Dillon, Grace L., ed. *Walking the Clouds: An Anthology of Indigenous Science Fiction.* Tucson: U of Arizona P, 2012. Print.

Farabee, Mindy. "Nalo Hopkinson's Science Fiction and Real-Life Family." latimes.com. 21 March 2013. Web. 9 Jan. 2014.

Fogelson, Raymond D. "Change, Persistence, and Accommodation in Cherokee Medico-Magical Beliefs." *Symposium on Cherokee and Iroquois Culture.* Eds. William N. Fenton and John Gulick. Washington, DC: Bureau of American Ethnology, 1961. 213–25. Print.

Friedman, Ryan J. *Hollywood's African American Films: The Transition to Sound.* New Brunswick: Rutgers UP, 2011. Print.

Genius, Wendy Makoons. *Our Knowledge Is Not Primitive: Decolonizing Botanical Anishinaabe Teachings.* Syracuse: Syracuse UP, 2009. Print.

Greenblatt, Stephen. *Marvelous Possessions: The Wonder of the New World.* Chicago: U of Chicago P, 1992. Print.

Hairston, Andrea. "Griots of the Galaxy." *So Long Been Dreaming: Postcolonial Science Fiction and Fantasy.* Eds. Nalo Hopkinson and Uppinder Mehan. Vancouver: Arsenal, 2004. 23–45. Print.

———. "I Wanna Be Great!: How to Rescue the Spirit in the Wasteland of Fame." *Upstaging Big Daddy: Directing Theater as If Gender and Race Matter.* Eds. Ellen Donkin and Susan Clement. Ann Arbor: U of Michigan P, 1993. 235–52. Print.

———. *Mindscape.* Seattle: Aqueduct, 2006. Print.

———. *Redwood and Wildfire.* Seattle: Aqueduct, 2011. Print.

Hearts in Dixie. Dir. Paul Sloane. Fox, 1929.

Hopkins, Pauline E. *Of One Blood: or, The Hidden Self.* 1903. New York: Washington Square, 2004. Print.

Hopkinson, Nalo. *Midnight Robber.* New York: Warner/Aspect, 2000. Print.

Justice, Daniel H. *Our Fire Survives the Storm: A Cherokee Literary History.* Minneapolis: U of Minnesota P, 2006. Print.

Krupat, Arnold. *All That Remains: Varieties of Indigenous Expression.* Lincoln: U of Nebraska P, 2009. Print.

Lansdale, Joe R. "The Steam Man of the Prairie and the Dark Rider Get Down: A Dime Novel." 2000. *The Long Ones.* Sanford: Necro, 2000. Print.

Miéville, China. *Embassytown.* New York: Macmillan, 2011. Print.

———. *The Scar.* New York: Macmillan, 2002. Print.

Mooney, James. *Myths of the Cherokee.* Nineteenth Annual Report of the Bureau of American Ethnology, 1897–98, Part I. 1900.

Nelson, Melissa K., ed. *Original Instructions: Indigenous Teachings for a Sustainable Future.* Rochester: Bear, 2008. Print.

Okorafor, Nnedi. *Who Fears Death?* New York: Daw, 2010. Print.

———. "WisCon 34 Guest of Honor Speech." *The WisCon Chronicles: Writing and Racial Identity.* Vol. 5. Ed. Nisi Shawl. Seattle: Aqueduct, 2011. 196–201. Print.

Omi, Michael, and Howard Winant. *Racial Formation in the United States: From the 1960s to the 1990s.* 2nd ed. New York: Routledge, 1994. Print.

Outka, Paul. *Race and Nature from Transcendentalism to the Harlem Renaissance.* New York: Palgrave Macmillan, 2008. Print.

Rozelle, Lee. *Ecosublime: Environmental Awe and Terror from New World to Oddworld.* Tuscaloosa: U of Alabama P, 2006. Print.

Sharp, Patrick B. *Savage Perils: Racial Frontiers and Nuclear Apocalypse in American Culture.* Norman: Oklahoma UP, 2007. Print.

Silko, Leslie Marmon. *The Turquoise Ledge: A Memoir.* New York: Viking, 2010. Print.

Sotiropoulos, Karen. *Staging Race: Black Performers in Turn of the Century America.* Cambridge: Harvard UP, 2006. Print.

Teuton, Christopher B. *Deep Waters: The Textual Continuum in American Indian Literature.* Lincoln: U of Nebraska P, 2010. Print.

Warrior, Robert. "Native Critics in the World: Edward Said and Nationalism." *American Indian Literary Nationalism.* Eds. Jace Weaver, Robert Warrior, and Craig Womack. Albuquerque: U of New Mexico P, 2005. 179–224. Print.

West, Cornel, with David Ritz. *Brother West: Living and Loving Out Loud: A Memoir.* Carlsbad: Smiley, 2009. Print.

Womack, Craig. *Art as Performance, Story as Reflection in Native Literary Aesthetics.* Norman: U of Oklahoma P, 2009. Print.

QUESTING FOR AN INDIGENOUS FUTURE

Leslie Marmon Silko's *Ceremony* as Indigenous Science Fiction

• • •

PATRICK B. SHARP

Recent studies have highlighted how science fiction functions within a *system* of genres: discussions of whether a text is "science fictional" enough to be included in the genre have been left behind, along with the taxonomic definitions of genre that supported them. A text that includes science fictional elements is now understood to be engaged with—and a part of—the genre, whether or not science fiction is the "primary" or "dominant" genre of the text. In this new approach to science fiction, it becomes possible to reexamine a host of texts that were previously excluded from critical consideration for their engagement with and contributions to the genre of SF. Leslie Marmon Silko's now-canonical novel, *Ceremony* (1977), can therefore be understood as a text that provides a science fiction vision of an indigenous future that leaves behind the dominant assumptions and narrative preoccupations of post–World War II apocalyptic SF. In particular, Silko shows how the narrative logics of Cold War nuclear apocalypse stories propel authors down a path toward inevitable destruction. Silko's novel rejects the stories of the "destroyers," linking them to the colonial imagination that produced both modern science and the "grammar of race" that codes all nonwhites as incapable of contributing to the futures promised by SF. Apocalyptic SF is evoked in the novel as a symptom of illness and witchery and as a white narrative that is trying to complete the colonial destruction of all peoples, including whites. In place of this narrative of destruction, Silko presents a heroic quest narrative about healing the identities and the lands of indigenous characters by having them live an updated version of their traditional lives.

Genre and Science Fiction

Within science fiction studies, this paradigm shift in thinking about genre has encouraged new ideas that have changed our understanding of what SF is and how it emerged. In the 1960s and 1970s, such influential scholars as Darko Suvin and Samuel R. Delany produced definitions of SF that were based on formalist assumptions about genre. Their definitions provided the basis for measuring texts according to narrow, static criteria and excluding texts that did not measure up (Luckhurst 6–7). Their goals were taxonomic: they were trying to come up with definitions of a literary genre that could be used to sort texts into categories and in the process to identify the essence of the genre. One major flaw with such formalist approaches to genre is that they try to pin down an essence that is constantly changing. Over the past few decades, scholars in the humanities and social sciences have developed accounts of genre that attempt to balance the analysis of formal textual properties with an understanding of generic evolution.

One way recent genre studies have avoided lapsing back into an unproductive taxonomic mode of analysis is by emphasizing the "social and historical aspects" of any given text (Miller 24). A genre, as defined by Tzvetan Todorov, is "the historically attested codification of discursive properties" (19). Genres comprise a system that is constantly shaping and is shaped by the ideology and institutions of a particular culture (18–19). Several recent theories of genre—in fields such as sociology, anthropology, linguistics, rhetoric, cultural studies, and film and television studies—have demonstrated that genres arise to solve recurring communicative or representational issues faced by members of a community (Bazerman 324–27; Bourdieu 129; Luckmann 228). However, genres do not spring fully formed from the minds of authors. As Todorov describes, genres come "from other genres. A new genre is always the transformation of an earlier one, or of several: by inversion, by displacement, by combination" (15). As a genre develops, certain formal elements are repeated and become codified because of their familiarity and success in handling communicative or representational issues.

Scholarship on the origins of SF has long emphasized this aspect of genre: SF was cobbled together from existing genres such as the gothic romance, the extraordinary voyage, the tale of the future, and the tale of science (otherwise known as the gadget story) (James 13–26; Kincaid 417). More recent scholarship in this vein has also emphasized *why* SF emerged when it did, the social needs and historical conditions the genre addressed, and the entire system of genres from which early SF authors drew from when writing their stories. In his influential cultural history of the genre, Roger Luckhurst cites such developments as mass education in science and literature, the impact of industrialism on everyday life, and changes in the publishing industry as key "conditions of emergence" for SF (16–29). John Rieder has argued that science fiction's "precursor" genres—and SF itself—"represent ideological ways of grasping the social consequences of colonialism" (20). As Rieder shows and as I demonstrate in *Savage Perils* (2007), SF was heavily influenced by such closely related colonial genres as the scientific race treatise, the travelogue, the "lost race" story, and new narratives of human evolution.

Scholars must address many thorny issues when engaging in genre analysis and discussing the emergence and development of a genre such as SF. One such issue is the degree to which the repeated structures of a genre become unconscious and how specific ideologies become encoded within these structures. In "The Whites of Their Eyes" (1995), Stuart Hall describes how a colonial "grammar of race" became encoded in modern narratives in such a way that the structures of some texts "have racist premises and propositions inscribed in them as a set of *unquestioned assumptions*" (20–21). As I argue in *Savage Perils*, SF authors of the early twentieth century such as Jack London and Edgar Rice Burroughs were quite conscious and explicit about their use of evolutionary discourse, racial "science," and frontier adventure tropes in writing their stories. Over time, people working in many different media began to mimic and repeat the structures of London and Burroughs without being fully conscious of the ideological baggage these structures carried with them. For example, many overtly liberal, antinuclear, antiracist stories written in the 1950s carried with them implicitly racist assumptions and plot structures against which the narratives seem to be arguing in other ways. This is an important issue when addressing the problem of SF's colonial origins and analyzing individual texts that draw on the genre.

Discussing the genre of a novel such as Silko's *Ceremony* requires understanding the historical moment that Silko addressed. *Ceremony* was published in 1977, but it is set in the years following World War II, during the beginning of the "uranium boom" in the Southwest. Beginning in 1946, the newly formed Atomic Energy Commission (AEC) used its mandate to explore, procure, and control uranium mines in the United States. The extensive deposits of uranium in the Southwest quickly led to new incursions onto American Indian lands by the AEC and its corporate uranium suppliers. By the early 1950s, the Laguna and Navajo reservations had numerous uranium mines that employed large numbers of indigenous people. The mines transformed the economies and the cultures of the reservations over the next thirty years. During that time, substandard safety conditions at the mines and uranium ore processing plants led to widespread radioactive contamination of the

reservations as well as to countless illnesses among the miners and reservation inhabitants (Eichstaedt 33–45; Jacobs 42–50). The largest of these mines
was the Jackpile Mine near Paguate, New Mexico, which dominated the landscape of the Laguna reservation.

Silko wrote *Ceremony* during the last decade of the uranium boom on
the Laguna reservation, when the illness and death caused by the uranium
mines was just beginning to be understood. In *Yellow Woman and a Beauty
of the Spirit* (1997), Silko comments, "By its very ugliness and by the violence
it does to the land, the Jackpile Mine insures that, from now on, it, too, will
be included in the vast body of narratives that makes up the history of the
Laguna people and the Pueblo landscape" (44). This comment comes in the
middle of a discussion of the agrarian lifestyle and economy of the pueblo,
which was literally been displaced by mining, thus clarifying the connections
Silko made in *Ceremony*. By centering the witchery in *Ceremony* on the first
uranium mine discovered near Laguna, Silko traces the problems of the 1970s
to their roots in the early years of the uranium boom. Through her protagonist's rediscovery of Laguna traditions as well as through his return to an
agrarian lifestyle, Silko rejects the "progress" that the nuclear age brought to
the Laguna and champions moving on to an updated version of the old ways.

Silko's critique of the nuclear age incorporates elements from a number
of different genres. Her use of traditional Laguna stories, songs, and narrative patterns has been a source of a great deal of discussion and controversy.
However, little attention has been paid to Silko's use of generic elements common to science fiction. In the introduction to the groundbreaking *Walking
the Clouds: An Anthology of Indigenous Science Fiction* (2012), Grace L. Dillon
notes that many indigenous authors write stories that "enclose 'reservation
realisms' in a fiction that sometimes fuses Indigenous sciences with the lat-
est scientific theories available in public discourse, and sometimes undercuts
the western limitations of science altogether. In this process of estrangement
they raise the question, what exactly *is* science fiction?" (2). Like Philip Wylie's
Tomorrow! (1954) and Pat Frank's *Alas, Babylon* (1959), Silko's *Ceremony* creates an imagined world that points out the dangers posed by Euro-American
scientific culture. However, where Wylie and Frank posited a future nuclear
catastrophe, Silko anchors her novel in the past. This mooring is perhaps one
reason why Silko's text is not normally identified with SF. By situating Tayo's
story in a recognizable historical setting instead of the future, Silko provides
a powerful critique of the common SF assumption that a nuclear catastrophe has not yet happened in the United States. Wylie and Frank drew on the
imagery of the frontier and the colonial grammar of race that romanticizes
the struggle of white heroes in a "savage" landscape (Sharp 195–218). Silko's

Ceremony, conversely, offers a way to imagine a return to a simpler life without repeating the implicitly racist assumptions of colonial frontier discourse. Silko does this by disarticulating her vision of the future from the colonial projects of Euro-American culture (and of much twentieth-century SF). Her indigenous future is based on an indigenous vision of progress that does not depend on the concepts of linear time and taxonomized individuals central to Euro-American science.

Colonialism and the Chronotopes of *Ceremony*

Helen Jaskoski observes that the central conflict of *Ceremony* is the conflict between the traditional Laguna worldview and the individualistic, scientific worldview of Euro-American culture (162–63). More specifically, Silko's text dramatizes a struggle between Laguna traditions and the future apocalyptic scenarios imagined by SF authors such as Wylie and Frank. These two worldviews conceptualize the relationship between time and space in dramatically different ways, and the confusion they create in Tayo becomes manifested in the form of the text itself. In essence, the conflict stems from the different "chronotopes" within these worldviews and their attendant narratives. In M. M. Bakhtin's articulation of the term, "chronotopes" are characterized by "the intrinsic connectedness of temporal and spatial relationships" in a text that serve as "the organizing centers for the fundamental narrative events" (84, 250). The temporal sequencing and spatial orientations of events and images in a particular narrative provide the primary means for readers to orient themselves to the world of the text. One of the challenges for readers of *Ceremony* comes with the vertiginous juxtaposition of scenes and events that begins the novel. Silko uses this beginning to orient readers to the protagonist Tayo's confusion and illness in much the same way that William Faulkner used Benji's memories to orient readers to the world of *The Sound and the Fury* (1929): the confused and cryptic temporal and spatial markers included in the beginnings of the novels do not make sense until more information is given much further into the texts.

Silko establishes Tayo's chronotopic confusion in the very opening: Tayo is in a World War II veterans hospital and is afflicted with what seems to be a confused sense of time and space. Tayo is unable to distinguish between cause and effect, past and present, and the geographically local and the geographically distant. While he languishes on the battlefield, in the veterans' hospital, and in his bedroom back home, Tayo's visions are characterized as sick by characters associated with the Euro-American scientific chronotope.

Rocky, the white psychologists, and Tayo's fellow war veterans back on the
reservation dismiss his visions as symptoms of physical and psychological
illness. However, as the text progresses, Silko leads her readers to understand
that there is nothing inherently wrong with Tayo's visions. Tayo's experiences
with the Navajo medicine man, Betonie, and the mysterious Ts'eh—along
with his numerous flashbacks to traditional stories and ceremonies from
his childhood—develop his understanding (and the understanding of the
readers) that his visions are related to the traditional Laguna chronotope. In
the traditional Laguna worldview, all creatures are connected in a way that
makes Tayo's "being" both "within and outside him" (Allen 120). That is to say,
Tayo begins to realize that his visions make sense only within the traditional
Laguna worldview, in which all things are connected, not individuated and
alienated from one another as in the Euro-American scientific worldview.

Silko shows Tayo's "illness" as originating from the act of killing: Tayo
is fighting in the Pacific during World War II, and he is ordered to execute
some captured Japanese soldiers. When Tayo looks at the Japanese soldiers,
he sees his uncle, Josiah, and cannot pull the trigger. Rocky, Tayo's cousin and
fellow soldier, explains the event to Tayo in terms of Euro-American scientific
rationality:

> They called it battle fatigue, and they said hallucinations were common with
> malarial fever.
>   Rocky had reasoned it out with him; it was impossible for the dead man to
> be Josiah, because Josiah was an old Laguna man, thousands of miles from the
> Philippine jungles and Japanese armies. (8)

Rocky's explanation adheres to the scientific conception of time and space: a
man cannot be in two places at the same time. Since Josiah is in New Mexico,
he cannot be in the Philippines. Therefore, Tayo must have seen a hallucina-
tion. However, Tayo continues to insist that he saw Josiah in the jungle. Here,
Silko associates Rocky with assimilation into white society: throughout the
novel, Rocky repeatedly shows embarrassment about Laguna traditions and
refers to school science books as the only reliable source of knowledge.

In one scene from years earlier, Rocky criticizes Josiah for dismissing
books about cattle raising written by white people: "Those books were written by scientists. They know everything there is to know about beef cattle"
(76). While Rocky glorifies the perspectives of Euro-American science (as
embodied in science textbooks), Tayo rejects the Euro-American scientific
worldview. Thinking about his years in school, Tayo remembers the conflict
he felt between traditional Laguna narratives and Euro-American science:

Tayo "knew what white people thought about the stories. In school the science teacher had explained what superstition was, and then held the science textbook up for the class to see the true source of explanations. He had studied those books, and he had no reasons to believe the stories any more.... But old Grandma always used to say, 'Back in time immemorial, things were different, the animals could talk to human beings and many magical things still happened.' He never lost the feeling he had in his chest when she spoke those words" (94–95). Here Silko encapsulates how Tayo is torn between his feelings of pride in traditional Laguna stories and the Euro-American ideology that he read in school. Silko associates Euro-American science with colonization and the destruction of indigenous belief systems. This conflict created in Tayo by colonial education fractures his identity. To heal himself, Tayo embarks on a quest to create a new narrative that embraces and updates the traditional beliefs of his community.

Dillon notes that one common practice of indigenous SF is to "juxtapose western science with what can be thought of as 'Indigenous scientific literacies'... to argue that Native/Indigenous/Aboriginal sustainable practices constitute a science despite their lack of resemblance to taxonomic western systems of thought. In contrast to the accelerating effect of techno-driven western scientific method, Indigenous scientific literacies represent practices used by Indigenous peoples over thousands of years to reenergize the natural environment while improving the interconnected relationships among all persons (animal, human spirit, and even machine)" (7). Silko's text exemplifies this tendency of indigenous SF when Tayo rejects Euro-American scientific ideology and embraces his Laguna traditions at the end of the tale. This acceptance finally allows him to make sense of his jungle "hallucinations" through a story that follows the traditional Laguna sense of time and space: "From the jungles of his dreaming he recognized why the Japanese voices had merged with Laguna voices, with Josiah's voice and Rocky's voice; the lines of cultures and worlds were drawn in flat dark lines on fine light sand, converging in the middle of witchery's final ceremonial sand painting" (246). While in the Philippine jungles, Tayo sees the connection between all living things, not their separation as unique biological entities. What connects Josiah and the Japanese soldier in Tayo's vision is witchery and the global illness of nuclear weapons that the witches bring. The story of the ceremony—and of Tayo's life—is the story of this illness as well as its remedy. By immersing himself in traditional Laguna cultural life, including the cultivation of plants and animals, Tayo makes sense out of his experience: he completes the story that heals himself, his people, and the Earth itself. Tayo finally embraces the perspectives of traditional Laguna culture and rejects the Euro-American worldview that would have led to his violent death or institutionalization. In this way, Silko charts a path to rediscovering indigenous "scientific literacies" that can create a healthy future for the indigenous peoples of the southwestern United States.

Overcoming the Chronotope of the Nuclear Wasteland

Since 1914, when H. G. Wells wrote *The World Set Free*, SF authors have written countless stories about apocalyptic nuclear wars. As I argue in *Savage Perils*, the nuclear war narratives produced by most writers in the post–World War II United States were contained within a white, middle-class, suburban imagination. In the aftermath of a nuclear attack, the landscape is described through a mixture of wasteland and frontier imagery, with the survivors reduced to a Darwinist existence struggling to survive against some form of savagery (170–218). Most nuclear apocalypse narratives in SF are warnings about nuclear technologies; however, they have a tendency to represent the coming nuclear war as inevitable. Before the 1960s, they often represented life after a nuclear attack as even better than before. In Wylie's *Tomorrow!* and Frank's *Alas, Babylon*, for example, the white characters who survive on the nuclear frontier are revitalized by their Darwinist struggle with savagery. In terms of landscape and plot, *Ceremony* clearly qualifies as this type of SF. However, by situating Tayo's story in a recognizable historical setting instead of the future, Silko provides a powerful critique of the usual SF assumption that a nuclear catastrophe has not happened in the United States. With the radioactive contamination, blasted landscape, and cultural devastation at Laguna Pueblo, Silko did not need a future setting to imagine a nuclear wasteland. At the same time, her use of traditional Laguna concepts of cyclical time challenges the scientific Euro-American mania with apocalyptic endings.

Like John Hersey's *Hiroshima* (1946) and its future-war-story descendants, *Ceremony* is filled with modernist wasteland imagery of life, death, and rebirth. However, this wasteland imagery is contextualized within traditional Laguna stories rather than in the ancient European myth of the Fisher King. In this sense, Silko's text marks a clear departure from the T. S. Eliot tradition evoked by Hersey and SF authors such as Wylie and Frank (see Sharp 139–69). While the Laguna reservation suffers from a prolonged drought, Tayo resists viewing the desiccated landscape as a wasteland. Rather, the characters who are associated with assimilation and the Euro-American chronotope view the reservation in this fashion. Early in the text, for example, Tayo thinks about the way that his fellow war veteran, Emo, complains about the landscape of the reservation: "Emo liked to point to the restless dusty wind and the cloudless skies, to the bony horses chewing on fence posts beside the highway; Emo liked to say, 'Look what is here for us. Look. Here's the Indians' mother earth! Old dried-up thing!' Tayo's anger made his hands shake. Emo was wrong. All wrong" (25). Emo explicitly rejects his Laguna traditions, instead seeing the landscape in terms of a wasteland. While rejecting "mother earth," Emo desires to return to the white cities that he experienced during the war. Like most of the other veterans, Emo ardently believes in his ability to assimilate and glorifies a scientific Euro-American ideology. The veterans' regular drinking binges, which resonate with the wasteland stories of authors such as Ernest Hemingway, provide a repeated ceremony that eases the veterans' pain and alienation at being rejected by the white world after the war. However, Silko represents this ceremony as a false healing that only deepens the illness that has afflicted Emo, Tayo, and the other veterans.

One of Emo's stories about the war is narrated through free indirect discourse, which is the same manner in which many traditional Laguna stories are narrated. In this sense, Silko uses Emo and the other veterans' stories about the white world as a counter to Laguna traditions: rather than celebrating the landscape of the reservation, the veterans' stories denigrate this landscape as a wasteland and long for the white world of machines and killing. This killing is explicitly related to the atomic bomb, as in one story where Emo begins his regular practice of vilifying his wartime Japanese enemy. With some teeth he had "knocked out" of a dead Japanese soldier, Emo begins a ceremony associated with death:

> The night progressed according to that ritual: from cursing the barren dry land the white man had left them, to talking about San Diego and the cities where the white women were still waiting for them to come back to give them another taste of what white women never got enough of. But in the end, they always came around to it.
> "We were the best. U.S. Army. We butchered every Jap we found. No Jap bastard was fit to take prisoner....
> "We blew them all to hell. We should've dropped bombs on all the rest and blown them off the face of the earth." (60–61)

Emo's hatred of the Japanese and his desire to use atomic bombs to commit genocide against them echoes the sentiments of many Americans after World War II (Sharp 125–29). In this respect, Emo is demonstrating his loyalty to a racist Euro-American ideology. However, this ritual also brings together all of the elements of witchery that Emo and his companions represent: denigration of the reservation as a wasteland, celebration of white cities, and murder using the atomic bomb. Tayo struggles against this ritual through much of the text, and Silko identifies it as a source of illness afflicting the reservations of the southwestern United States.

As the text progresses, Silko increasingly associates wasteland imagery not with the landscape of the reservation but rather with the lives of the veterans and those who try to assimilate into Euro-American culture. Like characters from T. S. Eliot's *The Waste Land* (1922), the veterans wander aimlessly through their lives tortured by the alienation and separation they feel from the modern (white) world. As they wander through the landscape that they view as a wasteland, they use alcohol as a means to escape their problems (lines 139–73).[1] In the imagery of *The Waste Land*, dust represents land without water and land that is infertile because of drought. When water is present in the poem, it becomes not a source of life and rebirth but rather a source of death. This imagery expresses the sense that something is out of balance with nature and that the traditional cycles of life, death, and rebirth are somehow broken. For Silko's characters, dust represents alienation from the traditional life of the Laguna. As they trek toward a bar across the reservation, Tayo and Harley must fight the dust caused by the drought. Alcohol is the medicine that the veterans use to fight the wasteland they see around them: "Liquor was medicine for the anger that made them hurt, for the pain of the loss, medicine for tight bellies and choked-up throats" (40). However, alcohol is not medicine that heals. In the course of the text, Silko shows how alcohol always brings out violent urges and eventually leads to the death of many of the veterans. Only Tayo sees that this aimless bar hopping is destructive and that it leads them away from their only hope for healing. Tayo's ability to see this problem makes him the questing hero of the story: he alone can provide the story for how to escape the wasteland brought about by Euro-American colonization and its most terrible weapon.

The possibility for healing in *Ceremony* does not involve a simple return to Laguna traditions. Like Eliot, Silko believes that the traditions of her culture are no longer adequate for the illnesses and destruction endemic to the modern world. Unlike Eliot, Silko does not despairingly offer up cultural "fragments" of her traditions to shore up the "ruins" of her world (Eliot line 431). Nor does she offer up the romantic visions of frontier life put forward by Wylie and Frank. The drought that plagues the Laguna reservation and the alienation that tortures the veterans is a result of the incursion of Euro-American culture in the form of alcohol, war, and the uranium mine. Through the repetition of the text itself, Silko offers a story that accounts for whites within the framework of Laguna traditions. Tayo is introduced to this "modified" story by the medicine man, Betonie, who believes that "after the white people came, elements in this world began to shift; and it became necessary to create new ceremonies" (126). Betonie's hogan is positioned on a cliff that overlooks the Ceremonial Grounds and dump of Gallup, the town near the reservation where indigenous people from all over the area are marketed to white tourists and become lost in alcohol. Looking down over this part of the town, Tayo notices "the glare of the sun on tin cans and broken glass, blinding reflections off the mirrors and chrome of the wrecked cars in the dump below" (117). This view of Gallup positions Betonie as the keeper of a wasteland, living where he can "keep track of the people" who become lost there (117). By following Betonie's sand painting and completing the story, Tayo finds his way out of the wasteland that traps him and his fellow war veterans. Through Tayo's quest, Silko attempts to provide a way out of the trap created by Euro-American conceptions of progress and the seemingly inevitable drive toward apocalypse.

The End of Apocalypse

Silko's understanding of apocalypse is best described by Dillon, who notes that "one possible Native conception of Apocalypse" is the representation of a "state of imbalance, often perpetuated by 'terminal creeds.' . . . Imbalance further implies a state of extremes, but within those extremes lies a middle ground and the seeds of *bimaadiziwin*, the state of balance, one of difference and provisionality, a condition of resistance and survival. Native apocalyptic storytelling . . . shows the ruptures, the scars, and the trauma in its effort ultimately to provide healing and a return to bimaadiziwin" (9). In Silko's novel, Tayo's struggle to return healing and balance to his people revolves around two spaces that do not become clear until near the conclusion of the text. The first space that serves as a chronotopic center in the text is the kiva, the sacred center and location for traditional Laguna rituals and ceremonies. The *sipapu* (the hole in the ground near the center of the kiva floor) represents the place of emergence for all life, including human life. In this sense, the *sipapu* is a birth canal, like a vagina, and is the center of the earth mother in traditional Laguna culture (Jaskoski 166). Tayo returns to this center of life at the conclusion of the text to complete his ceremony of healing, telling the story of his journey to the elders gathered there. In this way, his story—and the story of the novel as a whole—provides a narrative pathway out of both the colonial mind-set and the drive toward apocalypse.

The second chronotopic center Silko creates in the text is the uranium mine, which represents the scientific Euro-American ideology and its

accompanying alienation, death, and destruction. The story of the witches'
contest, which appears in the middle of the text, explicitly associates the
witchery and death brought about by the "destroyers" with the uranium mine
and colonization by Euro-Americans. The contest occurs "way up in the lava
rock hills / north of Cañoncito," where the U.S. government established a uranium mine in 1942 (133). In the story, the witch who wins the contest tells a
story of "white skin people" who "will destroy each other" after conquering
the world and wiping out several tribes (135, 137). The witch goes on to say that

> Up here
> in these hills
> they will find the rocks,
> rocks with veins of green and yellow and black.
> They will lay the final pattern with these rocks
> they will lay it across the world
> and explode everything. (135)

Silko uses this story to connect whites with the uranium mine and establishes
the mine as the center of witchery in the text. The hole of the mine can therefore be seen as a "deadly counter-symbol" to the hole of the *sipapu*: where the
sipapu brings forth all life, the uranium mine brings forth the destruction of
all life (Jaskoski 166). The scientific Euro-American chronotope leads the text
toward apocalyptic death and destruction—that is, toward the usual SF story
of nuclear apocalypse—and Tayo's challenge in completing the ceremony
comes from Emo, Harley, Pinkie, and Leroy, the veterans associated with this
chronotope. When Tayo resists the violence and destruction the veterans put
on display at the uranium mine, he prepares himself to complete the ceremony of healing. By appreciating the interconnectedness of life and resisting
the temptation to destroy, Tayo continues the ceremony and the story that
enables the survival of indigenous peoples in the Nuclear Age.

   The postapocalyptic community imagined by Silko acknowledges the
threat that the witchery of nuclear weapons poses to all humans. At the same
time, the figures that become indistinguishable for Tayo represent communities that have experienced the horrors of nuclear war firsthand: Josiah,
Tayo's Laguna uncle, serves as an image of the Lagunas destroyed by witchery,
whereas the dead Japanese soldier that Tayo sees early in the text is associated
with the victims of Hiroshima and Nagasaki. Recognizing the relationship
between these two characters provides Tayo with the key for understanding his own story. Through its use of chronotopes, the text guides readers
to a similar understanding of the Nuclear Age. With the uranium mine as a

chronotopic center, *Ceremony* establishes the production and development of nuclear weapons as a major aspect of contemporary identity, particularly for Lagunas. This mine also reveals the hierarchies of radioactive colonialism, with indigenous people bearing the brunt of the negative effects of the nuclear weapons production cycle during the Cold War.

Any discussion of *Ceremony* that does not acknowledge the immediate historical context of its production will fail to understand its central organizing conflict. The uranium mine is more than simply a center for witchery; it was a blight on the landscape that lies at the core of traditional Laguna identity. The Jackpile Mine radically changed the conditions and modes of life on the Laguna reservation and was the center of colonial expansion for corporations, the U.S. government, and Euro-American culture. The primary narrative that Silko associates with this colonial history is SF. Silko seeks not only to heal the illnesses of past colonial incursions but also to provide a story that helps the Lagunas of the 1970s imagine a healthy future. Tayo's quest provides a narrative alternative to nuclear apocalypse that exposes the colonial nature of science fiction as a genre. Through her use of indigenous sciences, Silko contributed a landmark of indigenous science fiction that can serve as a model for how future writers can attempt to overcome the colonial origins of the genre.

Note

1. In this passage, nameless characters discuss the details of their unhappy lives in a bar while the barkeeper continues pressing them to leave. Significantly, one of the topics of conversation is soldiers being discharged from the military.

Works Cited

Allen, Paula Gunn. *The Sacred Hoop.* Boston: Beacon, 1986. Print.

Bakhtin, M. M. *The Dialogic Imagination.* Trans. Caryl Emerson and Michael Holquist. Ed. Michael Holquist. Austin: U of Texas P, 1981. Print.

Bazerman, Charles. "Social Forms as Habitats for Action." *Journal of the Interdisciplinary Crossroads* 1.2 (2004): 317–34. Print.

Bourdieu, Pierre. *Language and Symbolic Power.* Trans. Gino Raymond and Matthew Adamson. Ed. John B. Thompson. 1991. Cambridge: Harvard UP, 1994. Print.

Burroughs, Edgar R. *A Princess of Mars.* 1917. New York: Modern Library, 2003.

Delany, Samuel R. *The Jewel-Hinged Jaw: Notes of the Language of Science Fiction.* New York: Berkley Windhover, 1977. Print.

Dillon, Grace, ed. and intro. *Walking the Clouds: An Anthology of Indigenous Science Fiction.* Tucson: U of Arizona P, 2012. Print.

Eichstaedt, Peter H. *If You Poison Us: Uranium and the Native Americans*. Santa Fe: Red Crane, 1994.

Eliot, T. S. *The Waste Land*. 1922. Ed. Michael North. New York: Norton, 2001. Print.

Faulkner, William. *The Sound and the Fury*. 1929. New York: Vintage, 1991. Print.

Frank, Pat. *Alas, Babylon*. Philadelphia: Lippincott, 1959. Print.

Hall, Stuart. "The Whites of Their Eyes: Racist Ideologies and the Media." *Gender, Race, and Class in Media: A Text-Reader*. Eds. Gail Dines and Jean M. Humez. Thousand Oaks: Sage, 1995. 18–22. Print.

Hemingway, Ernest. *The Sun Also Rises*. 1926. New York: Scribner, 2006. Print.

Hersey, John. *Hiroshima*. New York: Knopf, 1946. Print.

Jacobs, Connie A. "A Toxic Legacy: Stories of Jackpile Mine." *American Indian Culture and Research Journal* 28.1 (2004): 41–52. Electronic. *Wilson Web*. 11 July 2011.

James, Edward. *Science Fiction in the Twentieth Century*. New York: Oxford UP, 1994. Print.

Jaskoski, Helen. "Thinking Woman's Children and the Bomb." *The Nightmare Considered: Critical Essays on Nuclear War Literature*. Ed. Nancy Anisfield. Bowling Green: Bowling Green U Popular P, 1991. 159–76. Print.

Kincaid, Paul. "On the Origins of Genre." *Extrapolation* 44.4 (2003): 409–19. Print.

London, Jack. "The Unparalleled Invasion." 1910. *The Strength of the Strong*. 1914. Web. 21 Sept. 2012.

Luckhurst, Roger. *Science Fiction*. Malden: Polity, 2005. Print.

Luckmann, Thomas. "On the Communicative Adjustment of Perspectives, Dialogue, and Communicative Genres." *The Dialogue Alternative*. Ed. Astri Heen Wold. Oslo: Scandinavian UP, 1992. 219–34. Print.

Miller, Carolyn R. "Genre as Social Action." *Genre and the New Rhetoric*. Eds. Aviva Freedman and Peter Medway. Bristol: Taylor and Francis, 1994. 23–42. Print.

Rieder, John. *Colonialism and the Emergence of Science Fiction*. Middletown: Wesleyan UP, 2008. Print.

Sharp, Patrick B. *Savage Perils: Racial Frontiers and Nuclear Apocalypse in American Culture*. Norman: U of Oklahoma P, 2007. Print.

Silko, Leslie Marmon. *Ceremony*. 1977. New York: Penguin, 1986. Print.

———. *Yellow Woman and a Beauty of the Spirit*. New York: Touchstone, 1997. Print.

Suvin, Darko. *Metamorphoses of Science Fiction: On the Poetics and History of a Literary Genre*. New Haven: Yale UP, 1979. Print.

Todorov, Tzvetan. *Genres in Discourse*. Trans. Catherine Porter. New York: Cambridge UP, 1990. Print.

Wells, H. G. *The World Set Free*. London: Macmillan, 1914. Electronic. *Project Gutenberg*. 11 Feb. 2006.

Wylie, Philip. *Tomorrow!* New York: Holt, 1954. Print.

MONTEIRO LOBATO'S *O PRESIDENTE NEGRO* (THE BLACK PRESIDENT)
Eugenics and the Corporate State in Brazil

• • •

M. ELIZABETH GINWAY

Monteiro Lobato's *O presidente negro; ou, O choque das raças* (The Black President; or, The Clash of the Races) (1926) figures prominently among the Brazilian utopias to emerge in the early twentieth century, a time of incipient industrialization.[1] Although Brazilian utopias written during this period do not form part of the established literary canon, they nonetheless speculate about a future in which Brazil might become a new technological power, raising the standard of living and health of its citizens. Published during a time when the country was outgrowing the political structures of the First Republic (1889–1929) and the leadership of the plantation class, Brazil's utopian fiction, like many of the projected futures of this period, has disturbing implications for modern readers.[2] Unlike the Brazilian canonical works that appeared between 1909 and 1929, such as Lima Barreto's *Triste fim de Policarpo Quaresma* [The Patriot] (1913) and Mário de Andrade's *Macunaíma: O herói sem nenhum caráter* [Macunaíma: The Hero with No Character] (1928), which question national identity,[3] Brazilian utopias resonate with a political nationalism rooted in pseudoscientific theories and racial mythologies held over from the nineteenth century. This nationalism stands in stark opposition to the more questioning and multicultural views of nationhood found in Brazilian high literature.

Before embarking on the analysis of race in utopian works, however, examining how this fictional genre reflects trends that began in nineteenth-century Brazilian society is useful. In addition to Arthur de Gobineau, author of *The Inequality of Human Races* (1853–55), who resided in Brazil as a French emissary between 1868 and 1872, the foremost contributor to formation of attitudes toward race and eugenics was Francis Galton. In 1883, he proposed the idea of the genetic inheritance of physical, mental, and moral characteristics, reasoning that measures should be undertaken to select traits that would ensure the improvement of human stock, a science he called "eugenics" for its connotation of being "wellborn" (Adams 3). By the early part of the twentieth century, Brazil's medical elite gravitated toward a loosely defined scientific practice they, too, called eugenics, believing that it would allow for the physical and moral "regeneration" of Brazil to remedy the ills described by scientific racism (Schwarcz 215). Eugenics in Brazil is a complex combination of tropical medicine, hygiene, and two schools of eugenics, the Lamarckian and the Mendelian, an agenda pursued in the name of national progress and pride.

Brazil's literary utopias from the period 1910–30 are based on the idea of eugenic "regeneration" and a type of nationalism that contrasts greatly with that of Brazil's modernist literary works, with their celebration of ethnic diversity and focus on sociological and ethnographic aspects of Brazilian culture. In general, Brazil's intellectual and literary histories overlook utopian fiction, not only for its uneven literary quality[4] but also because it bears the mark of the type of conservative thought modernist writers sought to overcome. Lobato generally rejected modernist experimentation because of its European influence,[5] shifting his creative energies from literary regionalism to the translation of fantasy and science fiction and children's literature. Of Brazil's utopian writers, he has written the best if also the most controversial of such works, *O presidente negro*,[6] which deserves serious consideration within the context of his time. While Brazil's utopian texts generally offer programmatic measures based on mainly neo-Lamarckian eugenics—emphasizing issues affecting children and public health—Lobato's novel marks a break with this focus, revealing deep-seated fears of racial degeneration that he believed condemned Brazil to inferior economic and political status.

In general, Brazil's utopian works take their cue from early twentieth-century advances in the areas of public health, tropical medicine, and disease control. By 1918, Brazil became one of the first Latin American countries to found a eugenic society, adapting to its own reality the predominantly French school of neo-Lamarckian eugenics, predicated on the idea of the inheritance of acquired characteristics, hygiene, and sanitation (Nancy L. Stepan, "Eugenics" 115–21). Since scientific racism considered Brazil's mixed-race society inferior, the elite adopted the ideology of racial whitening. In *Black into White* (1977), Thomas Skidmore shows how this ideology was based on two fundamental assumptions. First, miscegenation was bound to produce a whiter population because of the tendency to choose lighter partners; second, the higher black mortality rate was diminishing their numbers (64–65). Given the belief that whitening was solving the "race problem," paving the way for future advancement, government and medical authorities stressed that "eugenic" measures should be undertaken to improve social relations and health conditions.[7] As Nancy L. Stepan has shown, this discourse was largely directed toward Brazil's urban poor, consisting of blacks, mulattoes, and recent Italian immigrants, whose housing and sanitation conditions were often deplorable. The neo-Lamarckians in Brazil, such as the Brazilian physician Renato Kehl, focused on issues such as working conditions, tuberculosis, venereal diseases, and alcoholism, all of which have significant effects on the health of both parent and offspring.[8]

Brazil followed the French tradition of neo-Lamarckian eugenics, an unsurprising development given Brazil's cultural and scientific affinity for France. However, by the mid-1920s, this school began to lose credibility, giving way to the genetically based Mendelian eugenics and biometrics. Based on Mendel's laws of inheritance, this school distinguishes between traits considered "eugenic," or desirable, and "dysgenic," or undesirable. It sought to increase the proportion of "fit" individuals by encouraging a higher rate of reproduction among these people while simultaneously discouraging the reproduction of the "unfit" (see Davis). In Brazil, the shift from one school of eugenics to the other is reflected in Brazilian utopian literature published between 1909 and 1929, which begins with a focus on neo-Lamarckian eugenics such as hygiene, "puericulture" (the raising of healthy children), and maternal health before they become overshadowed by issues of race and selective breeding, topics more related to Mendelian eugenics.[9] *O presidente negro*, which dates from the mid-1920s, is caught between these two currents of eugenics, which were often treated as "compatible variations of the same science of heredity" (Nancy L. Stepan, "Eugenics" 120).

Lobato was among the first writers to join the Eugenic Society of São Paulo as part of his concern for Brazil's future. In the 1910s, as an ardent nationalist, Lobato was struck by the precarious state of health and the political apathy of Brazil's rural population, representing it in a character that became widely known as "Jeca Tatu" (Azevedo, Camargos, and Sacchetta 114–15), a type of country bumpkin. He later gathered thirty-five articles about rural life and published them as a book, *Ideias de Jeca Tatu* [The Ideas of Jeca Tatu] (1919). Under the influence of the success of public health campaigns and the eugenics movement, Lobato learned that Jeca's situation was more a result of health problems and sanitary conditions than of racial degeneration. He thus recanted his earlier deterministic views in another series of articles that appeared later under the title *O problema vital* [Vital Issues] (1919) (*Mr.*

Slang). By looking at *O presidente negro* as a portrayal of Brazil's social body, we can begin to understand how Lobato struggled with the idea of race, equating physical health with political health. This change in his attitudes demonstrates his gravitation toward American economic and public health models, which he equated with progress and national improvement.

In Brazil, the neo-Lamarckians were mainly concerned with social welfare and the improvement of sanitary conditions, while the issue of race remained on the sidelines. As Stepan points out, the movement was promoted not by scientists but by doctors "eager to promote their role as experts in shaping social life and naively optimistic about their power to do good. It was a group little given to revolutionary analyses of the economic and racial roots of Brazil's social miseries" ("Eugenics" 113). Since racial whitening was seen as part of "regeneration," the issue of race was swept under the rug. Nonetheless, Stepan notes, this use of the word *raça* is ambiguous, meaning both "people" and "race" ("Eugenics" 126), further clouding the issue.

By the mid-1920s, Mendelian genetics began to gain a foothold in Brazil. Stepan notes that the passage of a "eugenically" inspired U.S. immigration law in 1924 sparked considerable debate in Latin American eugenic conferences, replacing nonracist rhetoric with a more overt discussion of race and heredity that addressed whether racial mixture led to "degeneration" or "regeneration" ("Eugenics" 134–37). The ideology of whitening began to come under fire, with several eugenicists contending that mulattoes constituted an unstable element of society. Even though Brazilian Mendelists such as Octavio Domingues attempted to defend miscegenation, explaining the principles of genetic recombination, the idea of racial "blending" became equated with "degeneration." From this perspective, Brazil could not "purify" its racial heritage and was therefore condemned to inferior status.

Given this situation, Lobato began to think about the United States, where, he believed, blacks and whites had remained culturally, legally, and sexually separate. Extrapolating from this firm belief in American racial fear and prejudice, he took the Mendelian scenario to what he believed to be its inevitable conclusion, the elimination of the black race in the United States, in a narrative illustrating principles of social Darwinism and the survival of the fittest. Telling a tale of American racism must have been either a consolation or a fantasy for Lobato, judging by the great enthusiasm he demonstrated in a July 1926 letter: "Sabe o que estou gestando? Uma ideia mãe! Um romance americano, isto é, editável nos Estados Unidos. Já comecei e caminha depressa. Meio à Wells, com visão do futuro. O *clou* será o choque da raça negra com a branca" (Do you want to know what I am developing in my mind? It's a doozy. An American novel, that is, publishable in the United States. I have started, and it's coming along fast. It's sort of Wellsian, with a vision of the future. The key element will be the clash of the black race with the white) (*Barca* 293). Lobato's novel actually illustrates the clash between the two schools of eugenic theory in Brazil, which, according to Stepan, persisted in Brazil well into the 1940s ("Eugenics" 144).

O presidente negro tells the story of a future contest among three U.S. presidential candidates in a didactic tale that has implications for Brazilian politics and society. Although he purports to admire racial and political "struggles" and separatism in the United States, Lobato paints a picture of conflict, deceit, and social discord. He misrepresents the American political system, satirizes feminism, and distorts racial politics. Underlying his vision is the idea of corporatism, according to which members of society should work together as a healthy body under the leadership of a knowledgeable elite.[10] The message seems to be that it would behoove Brazilians to avoid the American approach, which might hinder eugenic improvement and the advancement of Brazilian society.

Lobato belonged to a group of intellectuals born in the 1880s who were caught between the desire for national progress and a fear of popular politics and radical change. For these reasons, he portrays the female and black characters in *O presidente negro* as divisive members of society who threaten its organic or natural operation. The presidential vote is divided almost equally among a white female candidate, black male candidate, and white male candidate. Lobato paints this political campaign in pseudoracial terms, with each candidate representing his or her own self-interests. For example, the white feminists follow a doctrine known as "Elvinism" according to which women descended from a passive species, the "*sabines*," who fell under the domination of the male *homo sapiens*. Thus, the feminist candidate, Evelyn Astor, defends her "race" against the white male oppressor, the current president, Kerlog, who seeks reelection. She seeks an alliance with Jim Roy, the black presidential candidate, counting on the votes of his followers to ensure her victory. Yet Roy secretly plans to run on his own. While blacks in this future America have remained racially and culturally segregated, they do have voting rights and full citizenship and have, strangely enough, chosen to whiten their skin.[11] Because of advances in eugenics, they have also increased their numbers, constituting a full third of the American population. These advances lead to the novel's main conflict, an election in which Astor and Kerlog divide the white vote, resulting in Roy's victory. Learning of this outcome, Astor faints; when she awakens, she realizes that she feels more loyalty to the white race than to women, so she immediately joins forces with Kerlog. Lobato claimed to be portraying American society, yet his scenario reflects the conflicts and concerns of eugenics and modernization in Brazil rather than the ostensible political struggles of the United States.

Lobato's view of society reflects Brazil's political "corporatism," a tradition based on Aristotelian concepts of state, Roman law, and modern Catholic social thought.[12] According to corporatist doctrine, strong national and collective identity takes precedence over individual rights, and citizens should act in a cooperative manner to achieve a great social good. In Brazil, certain advocates of eugenics were suspicious of what they perceived as a misguided faith in democracy, since they believed in the need for a strong centralized government to impose eugenic reforms (Nancy L. Stepan, "Eugenics" 129). In Lobato's novel, Jim Roy at times appears to fulfill the role of a corporatist leader, as he is charismatic and described as a genius who knows what is best for his people. He is also paternalistic, compared to a shepherd leading his flock, like Moses (93, 182). Blacks obey his every command, as if they had no will of their own. On other occasions, Roy is associated with images of primitivism and violence, undermining his legitimate claim to the presidency. For example, the black population is stereotyped as a wild animal—a black panther—that only he can control: "A pantera negra distendia os músculos entorpecidos, com os olhos a se rajarem de sangue. . . . Jim tremeu. Sabia conter os nervos da fera, dominar-lhe todos os ímpetos instintivos" (The black panther stretched its sluggish muscles, with eyes streaked with blood. . . . Jim trembled. He knew he could contain the beast's passions and dominate all its instinctive energies) (140–41). Roy's association with this "wild animal" and the implied repressed violence it represents reflect atavistic racial fears. In this way, Lobato creates a corporatist leader, not a eugenicized, civilized, legitimate leader fit to govern but one who awakens the primeval fears of the white population, justifying its desire to overthrow him.

To contest Roy's victory, Kerlog and Astor convene a "White Convention" that combines political and business leaders who are also dissatisfied with the presidential outcome. They come up with a secret solution to the problem by marketing "Omega rays," a new hair-straightening treatment for black citizens.[13] Since all blacks have whitened their skin, it is logical that they would flock to straighten their hair as well. But unbeknownst to them, a side effect of the process is sterilization. Kerlog later admits this plot to Roy, justifying this immoral act by saying, "Não há moral entre raças, como não há moral entre povos. Há vitória ou derrota. Tua raça morreu, Jim" (There are no morals among races, any more than there are among different countries. There is either victory or defeat. Your race has died, Jim) (186). Thus, whites use their "superior" technology to save their "race," a development that so demoralizes Jim Roy that he dies within a few days. When Roy's death is announced, the black population becomes an "imenso corpo sem cabeça" (an immense body without a head) (189), reinforcing the corporatist image. In the end, the protocol for presidential succession is conveniently overlooked as new elections are held and victory goes to Kerlog, in a type of coup d'état. He is portrayed as a "natural" leader, and Astor falls in love with him and accepts his proposal of marriage. Here, Lobato shows that democratic ideals are less important than genetic perfection and that leadership by a worthy elite is preferable to having the wrong man elected by popular vote. Thus, the story ends with a corporatist solution, not a democratic one.

As Nancy L. Stepan points out, Latin American eugenicists believed that their nations lacked "biological coherence" (*Hour* 105)—that is, the synthesis required for true nationhood. Lobato's novel explores this assumption in several ways. In *O presidente negro*, the United States remains the last oasis for the white race: "Só se salvará da absorção o branco da América" (Only the whites in America will be saved from being absorbed) (52). Lobato also brings up the possibility of relocating American blacks to the Amazon as a way of avoiding racial conflict, but blacks refuse to be deported, asserting their rights as citizens to remain in the United States and proposing instead to divide the continental United States between a white North and black South.[14] These topics are brought up as part of the eugenic education of the Brazilian protagonist, Ayrton, who learns about the future from Miss Jane, the daughter of an American scientist and inventor of a machine that sees into the future. Miss Jane informs her pupil that in the future America, whites cannot agree with the division of the United States, since the Constitution forbids it, leading to heightened racial tensions. Yet just such a division becomes viable in Lobato's future Brazil, as Miss Jane explains that its southernmost states (which received intense waves of European immigrants) secede from Brazil to form a new bloc with the Spanish-speaking nations of the southern cone, leaving behind the darker, Portuguese-speaking North and Northeast, a variation on this separatist theme (89). In this way, Brazil divides peacefully, achieving a type of racial "solution" that eluded the United States.

Lobato chose to set his novel in the United States because he saw it as the only nation that had maintained the separation of the races and remained a powerful country. This belief is reinforced by the frame story, since Ayrton and Jane passively observe America's future elections in her father's machine, never setting foot in the United States. Roberto de Sousa Causo notes, "Essa é a ficção científica brasileira do final do século XIX e início do século XX: suas máquinas do tempo não permitem que se viaje através delas—e, consequentemente, limitam a ação, a aventura de se interferir no processo histórico—mas apenas observação distanciada dos eventos" (This is Brazilian science fiction of the late nineteenth and early twentieth centuries: their time machines do not allow people to travel in them, so they limit any attempt to take action or change historical events, allowing only observation at a distance) (12). In Lobato's novel, this passive time machine serves the purpose of eugenic education. Miss Jane dutifully points out to Ayrton the danger that arose when Europeans mixed with Asians, with only American whites remaining racially pure. While Daphne Patai attributes Lobato's Yellow Peril[15] racism to the influence of Jack London, whose work Lobato had translated, Brazil also had a large influx of Japanese immigrants from 1908 to the mid-1930s, especially in São Paulo. The influence of eugenicists subsequently led to changes in immigration policy that significantly reduced the number of Asian immigrants.[16]

In general, however, Lobato's novel reflects a crisis within eugenic thought in Brazil caused by the change from neo-Lamarckian to Mendelian eugenics. This is confirmed when Miss Jane says "A nossa solução foi medíocre. Estragou as duas raças, fundindo-as" (Our solution was mediocre. We ruined both races by mixing them) (81). Here, Lobato seems to imply that racial "whitening," an ancillary theory of neo-Lamarckian eugenics, could not fully resolve the issue of race because it did not resolve the problem on the genetic level. Lobato's solution was the complete elimination of blacks from society.[17]

While Lobato's adoption of the Mendelian strain of eugenics is clear in his treatment of race, neo-Lamarckian eugenics more readily explains his ideology regarding the role of women. Many neo-Lamarckian eugenicists believed that women have more eugenic and moral influence in society than men and consequently assigned women the purview of the home and family (Kehl 298). In Brazil, the traditional family was represented as the basis for building a "eugenically" strong society. As Susan Besse notes, eugenicists and others conceived of the home as a miniature state on which the larger state operated (62). Thus, in Lobato's novel, after Evelyn Astor is "cured" of feminism, she dedicates herself to her future husband. While ostensibly giving space to feminism and debates on the rights for women, Lobato ultimately characterizes women as manipulative, volatile, and in need of the rational control that eugenics can provide. In many ways it comes as no surprise that the name *Evelyn* contains the name Eve, because in a sense, the female candidate is responsible for the fall that brings on the clash of the races. Lobato uses the associations with Eve to suggest that women should not partake of the forbidden fruit of political rights lest there be a fall from grace. Women must be loyal to the head of the household or, in the case of Astor, to the head of the state. Here, the novel projects a microcosm of domesticity onto the macrocosm of Brazilian corporatist politics.

Lobato does not focus on the ideas of dress reform, maternal health, and reproduction, the main issues of neo-Lamarckianism and other works of utopian literature published in Brazil at the time. For Lobato, the implementation of eugenic reforms and the establishment of legitimate ruling majorities are more important than carrying out neo-Lamarckian health reforms. He focuses on traditional roles for women and the elimination of blacks from the gene pool, ending with a coup d'état by a strong white male leader.

If we consider the text as an allegory, Astor could represent the body of society, won over by the charismatic Kerlog, the head of the nation. This allegorical marriage is repeated in the frame story of *O presidente negro*. Miss Jane initially says that she has no interest in finding a spouse, planning instead to dedicate herself to her father's scientific work. Yet by the end of the novel, she falls in love with and plans to marry the Brazilian Ayrton. Thus, the frame story set in Brazil and the presidential story set in the future United States reinforce the closure of marriage, in which a couple becomes a model of genetic and political legitimacy. Historically, this fictional moment is not so far from what actually happened in Brazil. The populist Vargas staged a successful coup d'état in 1930, consolidating his power for some fifteen years, winning over the working class, and enacting several eugenic "reforms" that modernized some of the traditional institutions of Brazilian society without changing the fundamental corporatist principles inherited from the First Republic (Nancy L. Stepan, "Eugenics" 138–44).

In *O presidente negro*, a white majority essentially rules and makes decisions for the black population that represents a third of the country. Brazil found itself in a somewhat similar situation at the beginning of the twentieth century, with a white elite controlling a large mixed-race population. Stepan explains that whitening "represented the wishful thinking of an elite in control of a multiracial society in an age dominated by racism—a yearning for a real sentiment of Brazilianness in a country divided by race and class" (*Hour* 156). As an ardent nationalist, Lobato felt the need to assert this Brazilianness, yet he is ambivalent about the myth of whitening and the prospects for a multiracial society and democratic rule. He hoped that Brazil could find its own solutions yet apparently could not envision an authentically Brazilian future that included race and gender equality.

In the frame story of *O presidente negro*, Lobato initiates the debate about authenticity when Ayrton attempts to write a novel based on what Miss Jane has shown him of the 2228 U.S. elections. She tells him to write in a more "authentic" style, explaining, "Estilo é como o rosto: cada qual possui o que Deus lhe deu. Procurar ter um certo estilo vale tanto como procurar ter uma certa cara. Sai máscara fatalmente—essa horrível coisa que é a máscara" (Style is like one's face: we have the one God gave us. Trying to have a certain style is like trying to have a certain face. It comes out inevitably as a mask—what a horrible thing, a mask) (196). Lobato seems to be saying that Brazil must stop trying to be what it is not and tear away the mask of whitening. If, in fact, Lobato was struck by the whitening ideal's lack of viability and authenticity, he had no valid replacement for it within the context of the racist discourse of his time. In general, we can see that while neo-Lamarckian eugenics tried to improve the plight of the poor, its racial position was ambiguous. As Stepan points out, "Since the neo-Lamarckian style of eugenics kept open the possibility of regeneration and a place for moral action, it was an approach that fitted in well with Catholic doctrine and allowed for the fusion of moral and scientific language" ("Eugenics" 121); indeed, we find biblical references overlaid on eugenic ideas in Lobato's novel. Evelyn Astor is compared with Eve, and Jim Roy is likened to Moses, a leader in search of a land for his people, associations that familiar archetypes and behaviors. By emphasizing Mendelian genetics and race, Lobato takes his scenario to its logical "final solution," anticipating the dangers of eugenics and corporatist ideology a full ten years before the Nazi rise to power in 1936. As a chilling fictional experiment in genocide, *O presidente negro* stands alone among works of Brazilian science fiction.

Lobato's novel represents the first attempt of a Brazilian science fiction writer to compare Brazil and the United States, the two largest countries of the African diaspora in the New World. While other utopias written in Brazil at the time focus on neo-Lamarckian issues aimed at specific changes, Lobato offers a comparative perspective, and by imagining a future U.S. society, he offers a complex and contradictory vision of Brazilian society.

Lobato wrote *O presidente negro* before taking up residence in the United States, where he served for five years as a commercial attaché beginning in 1927.[18] As he later wrote, "A América que lá pintei está absolutamente de acordo com a América (Estados Unidos) que fui encontrar'" (The America that I portrayed is exactly like the America [United States] that I found there) (qtd. in Azevedo, Camargos, and Sacchetta 222). His novel, based on the notion of a battle between the races (and to a lesser extent, between the sexes), is not a flattering look at the future of the United States. Lobato thought the novel would sell in the United States in translation, writing to his correspondent of some forty years, Godofredo Rangel, "Já tenho um bom tradutor . . . e em New York um agente que se entusiasmou com o plano e tem boa porcentagem no negócio. Imagine se me sai um best seller . . . Um milhão de exemplares" (I already have a good translator . . . and in New York, an agent who is enthusiastic about the plan and will get a good percentage. Imagine if I have a bestseller . . . a million copies) (*Barca* 294). However, Lobato miscalculated the popularity of his views in the United States and later found out that reviewers found the book offensive to American sensibilities.[19] In many ways the novel, a parody of American society, necessarily exaggerates racial and gender tensions by oversimplifying them. Lobato portrays an American society and Anglo-Saxon culture in which politicized women and blacks represent disruptive forces within the social body. By setting his utopia in the United States, Lobato documents a change in the orientation of the eugenics movement in Brazil, taking it to its dire extremes elsewhere. Ultimately, the work is a strange hybrid, predicating its plot on the dilemmas of race and gender in the United States but actually addressing concerns of national regeneration in Brazil. Lobato was both confused and disappointed by the American reaction: "Acham-no ofensivo à dignidade americana, visto admitir que depois de tantos séculos de progresso moral possa este povo, coletivamente, cometer a sangue frio o belo crime que sugeri. Errei vindo cá tão tarde. Devia ter vindo no tempo em que eles linchavam os negros. Os originais estão com o Issac Goldeburg para ver se há arranjo" (They find it offensive to American dignity, given that, after so many centuries of moral progress, how could they possibly commit the lovely crime I suggested in cold blood. I made a mistake in coming here so late. I should have come when they lynched blacks. The originals are with Issac Goldeburg to see if arrangements can be made for it) (*Barca* 304). Lobato apparently believed that Americans would be receptive to his work since he had read of racial prejudice and violence in the United States and fully expected an eager audience for his novel.

Although Lobato accurately perceived tensions in American society, such as the women's movement and the tense state of race relations, his novel was never published in English, although several Brazilian editions appeared during the 1940s and 1950s, first as part of the series "O Círculo do Livro" (a type of book club subscription) and then in editions of his *Obras completas* (Complete Works). The most recent version appeared in 2008, in time to capitalize on the U.S. elections of that year. To his credit, Lobato's fictional characters anticipated the tensions caused when Hillary Clinton, Barack Obama, and John McCain vied for the highest office in the land.

When we take utopias into account as part of Brazilian intellectual life during the first part of the twentieth century, we see a much more conservative view than that of the more multicultural Brazilian modernist movement. These utopias conceive of the state as a harmonious or disease-free body, a concept that also lies at the heart of authoritarian corporatism. However, after World War II, the "marriage" between the female body of the nation and its male leader breaks down. Brazil's authoritarian populist leader Getúlio Vargas laid the groundwork for the modern Brazilian state but was eventually forced to leave office, revealing the illegitimacy of biological metaphors of nationhood and eugenics.

Lobato remained active in causes such as promoting Brazil's fledgling oil industry, eventually going to prison for contesting Vargas's regime during the 1930s (Azevedo, Camargos, and Sacchetta 293–310). Although he took on many political and literary roles during his life, he is best known for writing the country's most beloved works of children's literature (see Albuquerque), which weathered a recent attempt to be banned from school curricula.[20] His reputation and greatest contributions undoubtedly lie in that area. In *O presidente negro*, Lobato's only adult fiction, he found himself unable to envision the long-term social transformation of Brazilian society and the social changes that would eventually be brought about by Brazil's intense process of modernization. Although he did participate in Brazil's larger political life in support of land reform and liberal causes, he remained a product of his time, and like the eugenics movement in Brazil, his life's work remains an odd combination of both progressive and regressive elements.

Notes

1. All translations are mine.

2. The racist views of American utopias are found mostly in utopias from the turn of the twentieth century. Alexander Craig's *Ionia* (1898) has Jews committing crimes, Arthur Vinton's *Looking Further Backwards* (1890) has the Chinese attacking the United States, while Frona Colburn's *Yermah the Dorado* (1897) features an Aryan hero and the White Knights. Other utopian works from this period, such as Benjamin Rush Davenport's *Anglo-Saxons Onward!: A Romance of the Future* (1898) and Stanley Waterloo's *Armageddon: A Tale of Love, War, and Invention* (1898), predict the victory of white armies in global wars resulting in the annihilation of other races. However, none of these works specifically targeted American blacks. In fact, several authors, among them Horace Kallen and Charles Eastman, embraced racial and cultural pluralism, while African American author Sutton E. Griggs (*Imperium in Imperio* [1899]) and Jewish author David Lubin (*Let There Be Light* [1900]) wrote utopias celebrating their racial and religious identities. See Mizruchi.

3. On these authors and their works, see Haberly.

4. See, for example, Martins, which has a section on the Brazilian intelligentsia called "O imenso hospital" [The Immense Hospital], a name given to Brazil by scientist and physician Miguel Pereira. This name became part of the public health debate sparked by Lobato and his portrait of Brazil's rural population. Utopian literature seems to be more of a historical curiosity, as seen in Fiorentino.

5. In general, Lobato belonged to a generation that had a positivist outlook and a desire for an "authentically" Brazilian art. His relationship with the modernists is complex:

although he is known for his criticism of vanguard painter Anita Malfatti in "Paranoia ou mistificação" [Paranoia or Mystification] (1917), he maintained contact with many modernist writers, even publishing their work (Azevedo, Camargos, and Sacchetta 169–84).

6. See the brief section on Lobato's *O presidente negro*, "um livro racista, contra a raça negra" (a racist book, against the black race), in André Carneiro's pioneering 1967 work on the SF genre, *Introdução ao estudo da "science fiction"* (44).

7. Mark B. Adams points out that most books dealing with "eugenics" focus on the United States and Britain. In the early twentieth century, the science of eugenics, whose name derives from the Greek word meaning "wellborn," was developed in more than thirty countries (v). In Latin America, it was principally seen as a way to solve social issues, since it was believed that hygiene could remedy "degeneration" through a series of health practices.

8. As Nancy L. Stepan notes, "We see the French derivation of this neo-Lamarckianism most clearly in Kehl's adoption of Forel's theory of 'blastophthoria' to explain how intoxicants, venereal diseases and tuberculosis could cause hereditary decay" ("Eugenics" 121)

9. For further information, see Haywood Ferreira; Ginway; Smamiotto.

10. In associating corporatism and the presidency, Lobato anticipates Sinclair Lewis's novel, *It Can't Happen Here* (1935).

11. Lobato seems to anticipate George S. Schuyler's *Black No More* (1931), where Dr. Junius Crookman invents a skin-whitening process, causing blacks to leave behind their race and consequently plunge the country into social and political chaos.

12. For further information on this corporatist model, see Alfred Stepan.

13. Madame C. J. Walker was the first black millionaire in the United States, and she made her fortune with black hair and beauty products in the early twentieth century.

14. Lobato's solution is the opposite of Jamaican immigrant Marcus Garvey's Back-to-Africa movement in the United States.

15. For relevant U.S. eugenicist works, see Grant; Stoddard.

16. This sentiment may well reflect Brazil's growing ambivalence toward immigration policies that initially encouraged European immigration after the abolition of slavery in 1888. As Asian immigration to Brazil rose in the early twentieth century, new fears of racial mixture also grew. Renato Kehl and other Brazilian eugenicists influenced the country's immigration policies, convincing Getúlio Vargas to limit Japanese immigration. In *The Vargas Régime: The Critical Years, 1934–1938* (1970), Robert Levine states that the quota for 1934 was 82 percent below the annual level for the previous ten years (26). In this way, Lobato was reflecting racial fears circulating in eugenicist circles that would ultimately influence national policies in Brazil.

17. David H. Keller's "The Menace," which first appeared in *Amazing Stories Quarterly* in 1928, has a similar outcome when a group of mulatto scientists make a wasp poison virus intended to put white people to sleep that instead causes the black population to spontaneously combust.

18. See the chronology in Azevedo, Camargos, and Sacchetta 201.

19. See "Um romance Americano" in Azevedo, Camargos, and Sacchetta.

20. Masson, Maia Junior, and Turrer explore the issue of censoring Lobato's work because of the images of race in his children's stories. Comparing his case to that of Mark Twain, the authors conclude that censorship is the worse of two evils.

Works Cited

Adams, Mark B. Preface. *The Wellborn Science: Eugenics in Germany, France, Brazil, and Russia*. Ed. Mark B. Adams. New York: Oxford UP, 1990. v–viii. Print.

Albuquerque, João Severino. "Monteiro Lobato." *The Dictionary of Brazilian Literature*. Ed. Irwin Stern. New York: Greenwood, 1988. 181–84. Print.

Andrade, Mário de. *Macunaíma*. 1928. São Paulo: Martins, 1981. Print.

Azevedo, Carmen Lucia de, Marcia Camargos, and Vladimir Sacchetta. *Monteiro Lobato: Furacão na Botocúndia*. São Paulo: Senac, 1997. Print.

Barreto, Lima de. *Triste fim de Policarpo Quaresma*. 1913. Rio de Janeiro: Record, 1999. Print.

Besse, Susan K. *Restructuring Patriarchy: The Modernization of Gender Inequality in Brazil, 1914–1940*. Chapel Hill: U of North Carolina P, 1996. Print.

Carneiro, André. *Introdução ao estudo da "science fiction."* São Paulo: Conselho Estadual de Cultura Comissao de Literatura, 1967. Print.

Causo, Roberto de Sousa. "Um resgate da ficção científica brasileira." *Os melhores contos brasileiro da ficção científica*. São Paulo: Devir, 2007. 11–23. Print.

Colburn, Frona. *Yermah the Dorado: The Story of a Lost Race*. 1897. Whitefish: Kessinger, 2010. Print.

Craig, Alexander. *Ionia: Land of Wise Men and Fair Women*. 1898. New York: Arno, 1971. Print.

Davenport, Benjamin R. *Anglo-Saxons, Onward!: A Romance of the Future*. Eureka: Hubbell, 1898. Print.

Davis, N. A. "Eugenics." *Encyclopedia of Gender and Society*. Ed. Jodi A. O'Brien. Thousand Oaks: 2009. 263–65. Print.

Eastman, Charles A. *From the Deep Woods to Civilization: Chapters in the Autobiography of an Indian*. 1916. Lincoln: U of Nebraska P, 1977. Print.

Fiorentino, Teresinha A. *Utopia e realidade: O Brasil no começo do século XX*. São Paulo: Editora Cultrix, 1979. Print.

Ginway, M. Elizabeth. "A mulher e a política da literatura utópica brasileira, 1909–1929." *Cartografias do futuro*. Ed. Alfredo Suppia. Juiz de Fora: Editora UFJF. Forthcoming.

Gobineau, Arthur de. *The Inequality of Human Races*. Trans. Adrian Collins. 1853–55. New York: Putnam, 1915. Print.

Grant, Madison. *The Passing of the Great Race; or, The Racial Basis of European History*. 1916. 4th rev. ed. New York: Scribner's, 1936. Print.

Griggs, Sutton E. *Imperium in Imperio*. 1899. New York: AMS, 1969. Print.

Haberly, David T. *Three Sad Races: Racial Identity and National Consciousness in Brazil*. New York: Cambridge UP, 1983. Print.

Haywood Ferreira, Rachel. *The Emergence of Latin American Science Fiction*. Middletown: Wesleyan UP, 2011. Print.

Kallen, Horace M. "Democracy versus the Melting-Pot." 1915. *Jews and Diaspora Nationalism: Writings on Jewish Peoplehood in Europe and the United States*. Ed. Simon Rabinovich. Waltham: Brandeis UP, 2012. 155–68. Print.

Kehl, Renato Ferraz. *Lições da eugenia*. 1929. Rio de Janeiro: Alves, 1935. Print.

Keller, David H. "The Menace." *Amazing Stories Quarterly* 7.1 (1928): 91–127. Print.

Levine, Robert. *The Vargas Regime: The Critical Years, 1934–1938*. New York: Columbia UP, 1970. Print.

Lewis, Sinclair. *It Can't Happen Here*. 1935. New York: NAL, 2005. Print.

Lobato, Monteiro. *A Barca de Gleyre*. *Obras completes*. Vol. 12. São Paulo: Brasiliense, 1946. Print.

——. *Ideias de Jeca Tatu*. *Obras completas*. Vol. 4. São Paulo: Brasiliense, 1957. Print.

——. *Mr. Slang e o Brasil e problema vital*. *Obras completas*. Vol. 8. São Paulo: Brasiliense, 1957. Print.

——. "Paranoia ou mistificação." 1917. *Ideias de Jeca Tatu*. *Obras completas*. Vol. 4. São Paulo: Brasiliense, 1957. Print.

——. *O presidente negro; ou, O Choque das raças*. 1926. São Paulo: Clube do Livro, 1945. Print.

Lubin, David. *Let There Be Light*. New York: Putnam, 1900. Print.

Martins, Wilson. *História da inteligência brasileira, 1915–1933*. Vol. 6. São Paulo: Editora Cultrix, 1978. Print.

Masson, Celso, Humberto Maia Junior, and Rodrigo Turrer. "Monteiro Lobato merece ser censurado?" *Revista Época*. 11 Nov. 2010. Web. 3 Oct. 2012.

Mizruchi, Susan L. "Realist Utopias." *The Cambridge History of American Literature: Prose Writing 1860–1920*. Vol. 3. Ed. Sacvan Bercovitch and Cyrus R. K. Patell. New York: Cambridge UP. 1994–2005. 727–29. Print.

Patai, Daphne. "Race and Politics in Two Brazilian Utopias." *Luso-Brazilian Review* 19.1 (1982): 67–81. Print.

Schuyler, George S. *Black No More*. 1931. Boston: Northeastern UP, 1989. Print.

Schwarcz, Lilian Moritz. *O espectáculo das raças: Cientistas, instituições, e a questão racial no Brasil, 1870–1930*. São Paulo: Companhia das Letras, 1993.

Skidmore, Thomas. *Black into White: Race and Nationality in Brazilian Thought*. 1977. Durham: Duke UP, 1993. Print.

Smamiotto, Edgar Indalécio. "O futuro eugenizado." *Anuário Brasileiro de Literatura Fantástica 2010: Ficção científica, fantasia, e horror no Brasil*. Ed. Marcello Simão Branco and César Silva. São Paulo: Devir, 2011. 201–21. Print.

Stepan, Alfred. *The State and Society: Peru in Comparative Perspective*. Princeton: Princeton UP, 1978. Print.

Stepan, Nancy L. "Eugenics in Brazil, 1917–1940." *The Wellborn Science: Eugenics in Germany, France, Brazil, and Russia*. Ed. Mark B. Adams. New York: Oxford UP, 1990. 110–51. Print.

——. *The Hour of Eugenics: Race, Gender, and Nation in Latin America*. Ithaca: Cornell UP, 1991. Print.

Stoddard, Lothrop. *The Rising Tide of Color against White World-Supremacy*. New York: Scribner's, 1920. Print.

Vinton, Arthur D. *Looking Further Backwards*. Albany: Albany Books, 1890. Print.

Waterloo, Stanley. *Armageddon: A Tale of Love, War, and Invention*. New York: Rand McNally, 1898. Print.

MESTIZAJE AND HETEROTOPIA IN ERNEST HOGAN'S *HIGH AZTECH*

• • •

LYSA M. RIVERA

I

The narrative strategies of science fiction are germane to political critique, as they enable writers to couch mundane social and political issues in the invigorating rhetoric of speculation.[1] Going where "no man has gone before," SF writers explore not only imaginary and extraterrestrial places but contested sociopolitical spaces as well. As Tom Moylan has argued, the "fictive practice" of imagining alternative worlds, which always already extrapolate from existing ones, "has the formal potential to re-vision the world in ways that generate pleasurable, probing, and potentially subversive responses in its readers" (43). The SF subgenre cyberpunk, the focus of this essay, is clearly no exception to this rule. Frequently set in familiar near-futures and typically concerned with the social, economic, and ecological impacts of transnational capitalism and emergent information technologies, cyberpunk cannot be extracted from its sociohistorical contexts, of which there are plenty. Though cyberpunk might look futuristic, it is deeply concerned with the present and its near future. This political engagement notwithstanding, cyberpunk has been roundly criticized for muting issues of gender and race to focus exclusively on the frustrations and anxieties of the First World white male (see, for example, Csicsery-Ronay). Related critiques spotlight the genre's obsession with disembodiment, its subordination of body to mind, and its diehard fantasies of cybernetic immortality (see, for example, Nixon; Sobchack).

One particular cyberpunk staple that has rankled both feminist and postcolonial critics—and rightly so—is its tendency to set its dystopian stories in criminal and exotic urban spaces that persist in relegating racial and ethnic Others to the very bottom of social hierarchies (see Fitting; Sponsler).

As Andrew Ross has noted, although the majority of fictional cyberpunk cities are "presented as futuristic," their "existing prototype [can] be found in any inner-city environment, populated for the most part by non-whites" (144). Even a cursory glance at the configuration of urban space in classic 1980s cyberpunk provides more than enough evidence to support these critical assessments of the subgenre. William Gibson's enthusiasts, for example, may recall Night City, a sprawling metropolis fueled entirely, as its moniker suggests, by a lawless black market economy of drug and information trafficking (6). Likened to a "deranged experiment in social Darwinism," the dark city stands in stark contrast to the "bright walls" of cyberspace, the novel's privileged zone that is largely only available to its "default white" protagonists (Nakamura 60). In the cyberpunk novel *Metrophage* (1988), Richard Kadrey transformed Los Angeles into a Third World settlement community "home to thousands of local down-and-outers, illegals from Mexico and Jamaica, indentured workers from Thailand and the Ukraine" (72). In this Los Angeles, "whole societies" with "their own customs and languages" populate the streets, where hordes of different ethnic communities survive in makeshift tenements adorned with "tribal banners" and "prayer flags marked with curious symbols resembling Mayan, Nepalese" and other non-Western "schematic diagrams" (72). Kadrey's futuristic Los Angeles mirrors Edward W. Soja's real-life description of the city as a "vast global metro-network of hitherto dispersed loci that increasingly absorbs everyone, everywhere, into commonly shared economic and cultural rhythms" (154). Thus, while functioning as unsupervised playgrounds for the technocultural elite, the cyberpunk cityscape also signifies the changing social and cultural landscape of American cities in the wake of globalization. For some, like Ernest Hogan, these "worlded" cities represent vibrant multicultural heterotopias.[2] For others, like Kadrey perhaps, they are nothing short of cyberpunk's ominous "Blade Runner scenarios," a term Los Angeles business leaders coined in 1988 to describe "the fusion of individual cultures into a demotic polyglottism ominous with unresolved hostilities" (Davis 82).

This essay extends scholarship on cyberpunk SF and in particular the subgenre's treatment of race and ethnicity by bringing into the conversation the work of overlooked Chicano/a practitioners of the subgenre.[3] I focus specifically on the work of Ernest Hogan, a Chicano SF writer whose novel, *High Aztech* (1992), represents one of a small handful of Chicano cyberpunk novels produced during the 1990s.[4] I begin my discussion with a brief but necessary abridgment of postcyberpunk, the second wave of cyberpunk, which departs in very interesting ways from earlier iterations of the subgenre and represents an important aesthetic context for situating Hogan's novel. Here,

I work closely with Neal Stephenson's novel *Snow Crash* (1992), which was published in the same year as *High Aztech* and exemplifies the postcyberpunk aesthetic that best characterizes Hogan's aesthetic. Following this point, I turn to the concept of *mestizaje* (racial mixing), which not only provides the second major context for reading Hogan's novel but also suggests a powerful framework for further inquiry into the theoretical and historical occupations of Chicano/a cyberpunk. Drawing primarily from José Vasconcelos's essay, *The Cosmic Race/La Raza Cósmica* (1925), I establish a firm understanding of how the many valences of *mestizaje* speak well to Hogan's SF, which embeds Chicano/a identity "within systems of asymmetrical power relations, and it suggests *mutability* as mestizo and mestiza bodies enact *new relational subjectivities* arising from a history of racial conflict" (Vasconcelos 7).

II

Critics have argued that while the official cyberpunk movement began to wane in the late 1980s, its critical acumen, energy, and urban-hip sensibilities persisted into the next decade as a type of "second generation" or postcyberpunk. As Claire Sponsler notes, the 1990s witnessed a vast "dispersion of cyberpunk themes and images across the field of recent SF," suggesting that although now passé, variations and appropriations of the cyberpunk "look" continued to inform the direction of this subgenre (252). In "Notes toward a Post-Cyberpunk Manifesto," SF author Lawrence Person announced that SF in general had by the early 1990s "entered the postcyberpunk era," identified in a handful of "hybrid" and "mutant" SF texts that exhibit cyberpunk *tendencies* while taking the genre into new ideological directions. Person cites Stephenson's *Snow Crash* as an exemplary postcyberpunk text that falls outside the cyberpunk "taxonomy" and therefore "must be regarded as [a] mutant or late-arriving 'classic' cyberpunk" text.[5] Person's "Manifesto" presents both an immanent critique of the 1980s subgenre and a desire to distinguish between it and the new "postcyberpunk" novels emerging in its wake.[6] For Person, postcyberpunk writers depart from their bleaker predecessors in two pronounced ways: their futures are not as bleak, and their protagonists are less alienated.[7] Although their worlds are still "impacted by rapid technological change and omnipresent computerized infrastructures," their tone is "suffused with an optimism that ranges from cautious to exuberant" as they "make fundamentally different assumptions about the future." Moreover, postcyberpunk's protagonists, far from being "alienated losers," now function as "integral members of society (i.e. they have jobs)." Cyberpunk's rich inventory of images, motifs, and themes, in other words, now conspires to reinvent new, less dystopian ways of thinking about our now-familiar cyberculture.

In terms of plot, tone, and theme, Stephenson's *Snow Crash* and Hogan's *High Aztech* are remarkably similar and unquestionably postcyberpunk. *Snow Crash* centers on Hiro Protagonist, a mixed-race "freelance hacker" and expert swordfighter who gets involved in selling information to the CIC, the privatized central intelligence corporation that has replaced the CIA after the demise of state power. Hiro's mixed racial identity, which stands in stark contrast to the "default white" protagonists of classic cyberpunk, also mirrors his philosophical views on language and hybridity (Nakamura 53). Early in the novel, Hiro meets a teenage girl, Y.T., a streetwise "skateboard Kourier" whose loyalty and moxie immediately impress Hiro (14). The two eventually team up to stop media tycoon L. Bob Rife from taking over the world through a plot that essentially boils down to mass brainwashing. A powerful entrepreneurial Texan capitalist who glorifies America as a "big old clanking smoking machine that just lumbers across the landscape scooping up and eating everything in sight," Rife is set on spreading a powerful new synthetic virus, Snow Crash, that functions as a mind-altering virus by rewiring the "deep structures" responsible for producing language (110). Distributed by a network of Pentecostal churches, Rife's agenda engages a type of technoideo-logical warfare, relying as it does on hacking away at both computer programs and human brainstems, to "renew America" by homogenizing all linguistic diversity into a type of "unitary language," to borrow from Bakhtin, that only Rife can understand. Conceiving of language as always "ideologically saturated," Bakhtin argues that "a unitary language gives expression to forces working toward concrete verbal and ideological unification and centraliza-tion," a process that is uncannily similar to what Rife intends to do through the dissemination of Snow Crash on a mass scale (271).

Although working well within the conventions of cyberpunk with its soft machines and cosmopolitan urban sprawls, *Snow Crash* immediately dis-tances itself from its 1980s precursors through parody. What in classic cyber-punk is unconscious and normative becomes in *Snow Crash* transparent and self-conscious. As a postcyberpunk parody, *Snow Crash* (like *High Aztech*) is "doubly coded in political terms: it both legitimizes and subverts that which it parodies" (Hutcheon 101). Hiro's introduction, for example, begins with a comical description of the typical cyberpunk protagonist: the techno-savvy hacker who sports mirrored shades and black leather and who "belongs to an elite order, a hallowed subcategory" of the technocultural underground. Yet this cyberpunk hero/Hiro, far from being a console maverick, is actu-ally an underpaid pizza delivery man whom Stephenson mockingly calls the

Deliverator: "The Deliverator used to make software. . . . [N]ow he has this other job. No brightness or creativity involved. . . . Just a single principle: The Deliverator stands tall, your pie in thirty minutes or you can have it free, shoot the driver, take his car, file a class-action suit. The Deliverator has been working this job for six months, a rich and lengthy tenure by his standards, and has never delivered a pizza in more than twenty-one minutes" (3). *Snow Crash* thus opens by appropriating a popular cyberpunk icon that it then proceeds to extol and deflate, all the while referencing the quintessential 1980s cyborg icon: *The Terminator* (1984). Known in the novel as "Hiro Protagonist," our hero's surname signifies the ongoing self-conscious nature of this postcyberpunk novel, which repeatedly calls attention to his literary constructedness. Of course, the phonetic qualities of his first name function in similar fashion: "Hiro" is supposed to be read as the novel's hero.

As a postcyberpunk text, *Snow Crash* also shies away from pure dystopia and offers in its place elements of what Tom Moylan calls the "critical dystopia," a literary cousin of the dystopia that replaces the latter's dread and resignation with alternative scenarios and images of survival and dogged perseverance. Rather than foreclose on the future, *Snow Crash*, like much postcyberpunk, offers its readers "a horizon of hope just beyond the page" (Moylan 81). Moylan situates the emergence of critical dystopia in the "hard times of the 1980s and 1990s," when the "triumph of transnational capital and right-wing ideology" decimated many of the economic and political gains accomplished during and immediately following the civil rights movement of the 1960s (184).[8] Attuned to the difficulties of this time, the critical dystopia articulated nightmare societies beleaguered by oppressive transnational corporate monopolies and harsh economic and environmental conditions, but it also exhibited a "scrappy utopian pessimism" with strong protagonists who endured the nightmare and sought out alternatives to it (Moylan 160, 147). Octavia Butler's *Parable of the Sower* (1993) and *Parable of the Talents* (1998), for example, imagine a postapocalyptic Los Angeles decimated by drought, corporate greed, and the privatization of social services, but they also sow seeds of hope and optimism through the figure of Lauren Olamina, the strong black female protagonist whose dreams of space travel and an alternative social structure ("Earthseed") inform the novel's vision of the future. In other words, the critical dystopia does not entirely abandon the future, even if that future appears bleak beyond imagination.

Despite the bleakness of its projected future, a future ravaged by hyperinflation, xenophobia, and the collapse of social services (state power), *Snow Crash* does not foreclose on the possibility for survival, adaptation, and above all change. In positioning its mixed-race and multicultural protagonist (Hiro) against Rife's homogenizing agenda, the novel implicitly endorses a politics of difference that embraces cultural, racial, and most assuredly linguistic heterogeneity. The urban streets in *Snow Crash* thrive on difference; they do not dread it. Stephenson's blueprint for change manifests most clearly in Hiro's response to Rife. Whereas Rife's plan to rewire linguistic structures toward a unified language (understood and therefore controlled solely by him), Hiro's plan endorses a language of mutation, diversity, and difference. Returning to Bakhtin, one could make the case that whereas Rife promotes a type of "unitary language," Hiro and by extension all hackers promote a type of linguistic "heteroglossia," a type of language that is "consciously opposed" to unitary forms and that is more "centrifugal" than "centripetal" in its tendency to mutate, change, and (therefore) more realistically reflect a culture, like Stephenson's, in flux (Bakhtin 273). Hiro, for example, marvels at the heteroglossic potential of language itself, which the novel endorses early on in its representation of "Taxilingua," the multicultural city-speak on the streets: "a mellifluous babble with a few harsh foreign sounds, like butter spiced with broken glass" (11). An evolving intercultural language, Taxilingua, though at times "harsh," is both "mellifluous babble" and "essential" for social mobility. It represents an organic tendency in language to adapt and transform to meet the demands of a changing (international) community, something that Hiro, a talented hacker who manipulates code, clearly recognizes and values.

After hearing of Rife's plan to cleanse the world of linguistic and cultural diversity, Hiro is the first to suggest that maybe "Babel was the best thing that ever happened to us" (261). The myth of the Tower of Babel, as Hiro reminds us, refers to "an actual past historical event," prior to which "languages tended to converge," and after which "languages have always had an innate tendency to diverge and become mutually incomprehensible" (203). For Hiro, the only thing that keeps people like L. Bob Rife from ruling the world is "the Babel factor," or "the walls of mutual incomprehension that compartmentalize the human race and stop the spread of viruses" (374). Babel thus not only led to "an explosion in the number of languages" (374) but also promoted diverse and concomitantly robust cultures. "Monocultures, like a field of corn, are susceptible to infections, but genetically diverse cultures, like a prairie, are extremely robust," explains Hiro (374). Hiro's goal in the novel is thus to put an end to Rife's linguistic homogenization and to restore "babel" to the masses. Babel preserves difference and hybridity, affording racially ambiguous characters such as Hiro the chance to establish "a precedent of scary randomness" (50). In keeping with his own racial and cultural hybridity, Hiro's mission in the novel is to restore the effects of Babel, the imperative of cultural and linguistic difference, and above all the "human freedom not to be alike" (51).

III

In a *Strange Horizons* interview (2003), Chicano SF writer Ernest Hogan revealed that the inner-city crime stories of Chester Himes had more of a literary influence on him than did "any science fiction novel" (Palmer). Noting that he identifies "more with the experiences of black writers than white authors," Hogan explains that "being Chicano" (like being black) makes him "just another bastard son of Western Civilization, treated like an *alien* by his native land." This personal anecdote is important: it reveals that Hogan's SF is as influenced by his subject position as a writer of color ("being Chicano") as it is by his love for the genre. In other words, this personal anecdote offers insight into understanding his early novel *High Aztech*, which I read as a science fictional allegory for colonial history in Mexico and more specifically theories of *mestizaje* (hybridity) that emerged in the early twentieth century and persist, as evidenced by Hogan's novel itself, today.

High Aztech centers on Xólotl Zapata, a thirty-year-old mestizo from Tenochtitlán (Mexico City) who writes comic books and poetry for the city's "electronic underground" (6). When the novel opens, Xólotl's beloved city, renamed Tenochtitlán to commemorate the city's colonial past, is on the brink of a massive riot. At war are two competing religious ideologies—Aztecan and Christian—that are represented in the novel by the "Neliyacme" (True Aztec Warriors) and the "quixtianome" (non-Aztecans). Xólotl, a writer who documents the "social mutations" of his fair city, represents the expository voice of the novel. In ways remarkably similar to the story line of *Snow Crash*, Xólotl has learned that he and thousands of other city-dwellers have contracted new synthetic viruses that literally rewire deep structures in one's "basal ganglia" to effect new religious beliefs and allegiances (171). As one character puts it, this new "faith virus" rearranges one's "brain cells [and] download[s] the Aztecan religion into a person's mind" (171; see also 198). Xólotl is apprehended first by a North American Christian fundamentalist band of spies who infect him with a Christian virus and subsequently by his mother, who in the name of science infects him with multiple "faith viruses" to test a hypothesis: that one religion will cancel out another until none are left, leaving the host (in this case Xólotl), the ability to "think for him[self]" (171, 234).

Reminiscent of Oscar Zeta Acosta's hallucinatory novel *Autobiography of a Brown Buffalo* (1972) as well as Stephenson's *Snow Crash*, *High Aztech* is pure Chicano cyberpunk. The novel offers readers the look and feel of cyberpunk: a fully "worlded" city where low-tech subcultures mix and collide in a fast-paced urban underground reminiscent of Gibson's Night City, Kadrey's

Los Angeles, and Stephenson's Southern Californian sprawl (Chambers 23). But this cyberpunk cityspace is decidedly indigenous. Its antihero is a dark-skinned "half-breed" mestizo; high-tech *curanderos* dominate the scientific community; neo-Aztecan warriors work day jobs as hackers; and in this "age of affordable beauty" (Gibson 15), one can travel to Mexico to get "Guadalaja-raized," a new trend in body modification that can turn a brown mestizo into a "Twentieth Century movie star" (134).

In ways similar to its 1980s cyberpunk predecessors, moreover, *High Aztech* configures urban space as sprawling and chaotic, difficult to navigate and bursting at the seams with technocultural innovation. Like his predecessor Case from *Neuromancer*, Xólotl must grapple with the new psychic, temporal, and spatial realities of the "global information economy" (3). He, too, finds the strange workings of time/space in the postmodern megalopolis to be simultaneously exhilarating and threatening, delightfully dreadful. But even here, Hogan departs from his predecessors (including Stephenson) by relocating the cyberpunk cityscape to south of the border, specifically Tenochtitlán. In ways strikingly similar to other Chicano/a cyberpunk texts—including Morales's *Rag Doll Plagues*, Gómez-Peña's *Friendly Cannibals*, and Beatrice Pita's and Rosaura Sanchez's *Lunar Braceros, 2125–2148* (2009)—large-scale geopolitical shifts have reversed North-South power relations so that they are no longer as unilaterally in favor of the North as they were prior to the text's imaginary future. *High Aztech* is set after the collapse of the United States and during a time when Mexico is on the brink of ruling the free world. In this near future, "Mexico is now rich while North America is in ruins" and "Tenochtitlán has become the media and cultural capital of the One World" (85). In this novel, "Armageddon" signals the emergence of globalization ("One World"), the fall of white racial dominance, and the rise of indigenous (Aztecan) political power and media control.

High Aztech can be read as a science fictionalization of Vasconcelos's theories of *mestizaje* as the basis for a future (more superior) race, which he elaborated in *La Raza Cósmica*. That is to say, through SF (in particular, cyberpunk), *High Aztech* dramatizes and ponders Vasconcelos's utopian vision of a new race so mixed (so "universal") as to be, in a word, cosmic. Vasconcelos, a Mexican intellectual who was influential in democratizing its modern educational system, wrote the essay during a time of cautious optimism. The 1910 revolution had finally ended, and Mexico found itself electrified by an opportunity to define and rebuild itself as a modern nation-state. Taking advantage of this revolutionary fervor, *La Raza Cósmica* represents Vasconcelos's attempt to influence his country's future direction as it faces the inevitable advent of industrialization and modernization. The essay is

Vasconcelos's call for racial and hemispheric unity; it is a call for transnational alliances throughout Latin America, alliances that transcend nationalisms and unify under the stalwart banner of being brown. *La raza*, which translates literally as "the race," refers to all of the darker-skinned inhabitants of Latin America, the majority of whom identify themselves as indigenous to the land. In fact, Vasconcelos believes that only by uniting under the banner of a transnational "racial" (hemispheric) identity can Mexico and other oppressed, colonized nations in the New World rise to a very bold new occasion: "Precisely in our differences, we find the way. If we simply imitate [Anglo-Europeans], we lose. If we discover and *create*, we shall overcome. The advantage of our tradition is that it has greater facility of sympathy towards strangers. This implies that our civilization, with all defects, may be the chosen one to *assimilate* and to *transform* mankind into a new type; that within our civilization, the warp, the multiple and rich plasma of future humanity is thus being prepared" (17; emphasis added). Here, Vasconcelos lays the groundwork for the emergence of a "fifth race" (25). This "fifth race" is "cosmic" for two reasons: because Vasconcelos believes it to be the race of the future and because this race, like a galaxy, is a constellation in that it consists of all of the other races to have come before it, including "the Black, the Indian, the Mongol and the White" (9). As the product of "all other races fused together," this race will "assimilate" and "transform" into a new race that is not yet here but most certainly is on the horizon (hence the speculative language that permeates his essay).

Assimilation and transformation are central to Vasconcelos's intervention in Western scientific discourse, particularly with regard to theories of evolution and race. In his essay, citing ancient Mesoamerican and African civilizations, Vasconcelos sets out to supplant "the vulgarity of Spencerian Darwinism" with what he calls a "new science" founded not on reason and positivist philosophy but rather "on love" (25). Still holding onto Darwinian notions of survival, adaptation, selection, and evolution, Vasconcelos imagines a future in which the "superior traits of nature and culture will [still] have to triumph," but "that triumph will only be stable if it is based on the voluntary acceptance by conscience and on the free choice of fantasy" (26). His is a notion of evolutionary development "founded on love," a model of hybridity premised on desire, a "mysterious eugenics of aesthetic taste" as the "laws of emotion, beauty, and happiness . . . determine the selection of a mate with infinitely superior results than that of the eugenics grounded on scientific reason" (30).[9]

Vasconcelos turns repeatedly to a fictional city in charting his blueprint for the future. He notes, for example, that the "world of the future will belong to whoever conquers the Amazon region," which will rise from the ashes as a fictional city, "Universopolis" (25). Affording the fertile, resource rich lands of South America a tremendous role in the new world order, Vasconcelos goes on to outline what he believes to be the two most likely scenarios: "If the Amazon becomes English, the world metropolis would not be called Universopolis, but Anglotown, and the armies would come out of there to impose upon the other continents the harsh law of domination by the blond-haired Whites and the extinction of their dark rivals. On the other hand, if the fifth race takes ownership of the axis of the future world, then airplanes and armies will travel all over the planet educating people for their entry into wisdom. Life, founded on love, will come to be expressed in forms of beauty" (25). Embracing difference and a more globalized approach to the future, Universopolis does not endorse a cultural politics of homogeneity and identity. Rather than fearing or dreading the idea of multiracial Latin American future cities, Vasconcelos (like Hogan) finds great value in racial hybridity and cultural syncretism. For Vasconcelos, the development of the new "fifth race" will be entirely "founded on love" (love for the Other or love of difference). All desires for racial purity (Anglotown) are cast aside in Vasconcelos's urban utopia, which he insists is *the* model of the future. Monoculturalism and racial purity are things of the past, argues Vasconcelos, whereas heterogeneous imaginary cities such as Universopolis "belong to tomorrow" (20). What is "going to emerge" in these new future cities "is the definitive race, the synthetical race, the integral race, made up of the genius and the blood of all peoples and, for that reason, more capable of true brotherhood and of a truly *universal* vision" (21; emphasis added).

High Aztech marries the conventions of cyberpunk with many of the core ideas behind Vasconcelos's thesis, itself crafted in decidedly speculative and "cosmic" language and imagery. Xólotl, having contracted multiple "faith viruses," including that of the "Aztec purists" and "Christian fundamentalists," can be read as a colonized subject whose body functions as host to various (self-replicating) cultural and spiritual ideologies. Within the context of colonialism in the Americas, Xólotl's metaphorical significance is fairly obvious: he is the mestizo about whom Vasconcelos writes, the mixed-race Spanish Indian who is the product of colonial American encounters, alien encounters between two races, two cultures, two religions. As Xólotl puts it, "The viruses. They're mixing me up. I'll never be pure anything. I'm a true *mestizatl*—a true Mexican!" (195). Xólotl, who will never "be pure anything" ever again (if he ever was) thus ends up embodying the science fictionalization of Vasconcelos's "new type" of human who, as a member of the "fifth race," is made possible by the fusion of multiple races and cultures (Vasconcelos 16).

Equally telling, however, is how Xólotl's mind ultimately responds to this information overload. Rather than crash and burn like the infected hackers in *Snow Crash*, Xólotl quickly recovers from his initial vertigo and dizziness (which he always experiences after he first contracts a virus) and realizes that the religions are "combining" with each other to form a new religion (191). Xólotl describes how his mind has responded to the multiple infections rewiring his "basal ganglia": "Christianity wasn't replacing my Aztecan faith—it was combining with it! Just like the way my ancestors worshipped the [Aztecan] gods in the guise of Christian saints. The way the Virgin of Guadalupe is really Coátlicue in disguise" (191). Xólotl's postvirus mutation speaks to the history of "transculturation" in the post-Conquest Americas. The term refers to what Cuban anthropologist Fernando Ortiz describes as "a set of ongoing transmutations," a process "full of creativity [that] never ceases" when two or more cultures collide (25). Out of this process, according to Ortiz, "springs a new reality, which is not a patchwork of features, but a new phenomenon, original and independent" (42).

As he experiences the emergence of this strange new identity (or anti-identity), Xólotl is reminded of his earlier exchange with his friend, Izcóatl, a "Surrealist-Voodoo-Aztecan" who married "a woman who ultimately divorce him and become a Catholic nun" (193). When asked by Xólotl why an Aztecan Voodoo artist would marry a Catholic nun, Izcóatl "leered and said, 'Religions fight, but they also fuck!'" (191). Here, Hogan adds the element of desire (presumably for the Other) to the process of transculturation. For, although the colonial contact zone is most certainly a site of hierarchical and unequal power relations, it also has the potential to foster interracial love and cultural hybridity, a point Vasconcelos repeatedly stresses in his own "cosmic" narrative. As Izcóatl points out, hybridity is as much the result of conquest as it is interracial love and desire. Utopian though it may be, Xólotl's final response to the virus—to merge differences rather than cancel them out—resonates clearly with Vasconcelos's utopian project of imagining *mestizaje* as the antidote for outdated notions of racial purity and petty nationalism.

Hogan's version of Universopolis appears in one of the novel's most lyrical chapters, "Tenochtitlan." Totally "high" on the viruses (he is, after all, a "high Aztech"), Xólotl wanders the city streets, constantly seeing visions of complete cultural, racial, and ethnic fusion: "Marilyn Monroe zoomed by like a jet-propelled Earth Mother/Sacred Virgin. Mao Zedong, Karl Marx, Thomas Jefferson and Frankenstein's monster—who looked very much like Boris Karloff—discussed the problem of modernization and introducing advanced technology to feudal and agrarian societies. Mohammed had Salman Rushdie autograph a copy of the first edition of *The Satanic Verses*; the Prophet told the writer that he got all the jokes" (214). Hogan imagines a global city where national and literary icons collide to create a type of urban postnational tableau. Moreover, his vision of the future city not only invokes the average cyberpunk cityscape with its "advanced technology" and urban sprawl but also recalls the work of Morales, whose *Rag Doll Plagues* was published just one year before Hogan's novel. In an essay about that novel, Morales attempts to theorize the fictional setting of "LAMEX," a vast urban industrial sprawl that extends from Los Angeles to Mexico City. As Morales notes. "People are learning to live in heterotopia and they must constantly develop new survival strategies" ("Dynamic" 24). Describing the real (as opposed to a science fictional) Los Angeles as "a profusion of cultural enclaves, a multitude of otherness" and "an unending, unfinished process of continuous movement" and "ceaseless change," Morales, like Xólotl, embraces heterotopia (24). Rather than flee the multicultural zones brought about by globalization and transnational capitalism, Morales and Xólotl not only stay put but survive.

Like the third book in Morales's *Rag Doll Plagues*, Hogan's novel represents cyberpunk filtered through the lens of colonial history in the Americas. *High Aztech* thus functions as a type of postcolonial cyberpunk insofar as it takes the conventions of classic cyberpunk and "from the experience of the colonizee, critique[s] it, pervert[s] it, fuck[s] with it, with irony, with anger, with humour, and also, with love and respect for the genre of science fiction that makes it possible to think about new ways of doing things" (Hopkinson 9). Like so many other postcolonial texts, *High Aztech* is deeply invested in understanding the cultural, racial, and linguistic dimensions of hybridity. Hogan's novel, like Vasconcelos's cosmic essay, resists notions of cultural, racial, and linguistic purity, fascinated as it is with cultural collision and intermixing. Hogan's commitment to this vision appears in the texture of the language itself as he incorporates more than one hundred "Aztecanisms," words from a fictionalized language, Españahuatl, a new creole vernacular made up of Spanish and Nahuatl. Even the language of the text reflects its intellectual message. Bringing to mind Stephenson's Taxilingua (and *Blade Runner*'s cityspeak) insofar as Españahuatl is a vernacular street language in an imaginary near-future city, Hogan's Aztecanisms speak to Hogan's tendency to privilege cultural syncretism over monoculturalism.

IV

Hogan's work falls squarely within the aesthetic and cultural-political parameters of what Catherine Ramirez has called "Chicanafuturism," a vernacular

form of cultural production that includes both Chicana and Chicano practitioners, that questions "the promises of science, technology, and humanism for Chicanas, Chicanos, and other people of color" (31). As a Chicano
futurist, Hogan is well attuned to issues surrounding the effects of technology
on Mexican Americans. In ways akin to Sanchez and Pita in *Lunar Braceros*
and Morales in *Rag Doll Plagues*, *High Aztech* spends a fair amount of time
exploring the ways in which Mexico (and indigenous America more generally) has historically functioned as a dumping ground for the North's technological waste and debris. In *High Aztech*, the Recycling Syndicate most fully
represents the novel's oppositional voice in this regard. Their leader, Blanca, a
mestiza who has been "Guadajaralized" to look white and "refined," describes
the Recycling Syndicate as in direct opposition to entrepreneurial capitalism, which suffers from, as she puts it, "a self-destructive impulse" capable of
destroying all of Mexico and its inhabitants (125). After first entering the Big
Dump, the "headquarters of the Recycling Syndicate," Xólotl recognizes both
garbage and beauty, decay and life: "It took me down a long, twisting path
through the mountains of garbage and the smoking factories, to a strange
green valley, an *island of beauty* in this ocean of ugliness. The greenery
sprouted several fantastic clusters of buildings of an eclectic variety of styles:
Aztecan Modern, Ancient Grecian, Postmodern Orientaloid, Arabian Nightmare, Fairy Tale Gothic, all *haphazardly mixed and matched and synthesized
out of materials that were salvaged from the dump.... I gasped in amazement"
(113). Blanca and the Recycling Syndicate, which turns garbage and refuse into
new, repurposed objects, recalls the Chicano/a concept of *rasquache*, a form
of cultural expression that appropriates "discards, fragments, even recycled
everyday materials such as tires, broken plates, plastic containers," which it
then recombines and elaborately displays to create new, often politically resistant scenarios and images (Mesa-Bains 166). In its broadest sense, *rasquache*
is a "combination of resistant and resilient attitudes devised to allow the Chicano to survive and persevere with a sense of dignity" (166). In other words,
rasquache is the "capacity to hold life together with bits of string, old coffee
cans, and broken mirrors in a dazzling gesture of aesthetic bravado" (168).
At once an aesthetic and a survival mechanism, *rasquache* comes closest to
describing Chicano/a cyberpunk production, which also transforms a found
object (in this case, classic cyberpunk) by repurposing it to speak for a cultural underdog who, like many people of color in American cities, survives by
making do with very little.

    Hogan's *pependores* (garbage people) also survive by repurposing objects
and turning trash into usable items for postmodern living (77). They also
enable Hogan to repurpose a prevalent theme in classic cyberpunk: dealing

with the garbage of consumerism. Yet rather than explore the issue from the vantage point of a white First World subject, *High Aztech* relocates the issue to south of the border, thereby recasting the cyberpunk genre within the context of colonialism in the Americas.[10] In this case, what is being reimagined is the concept of kipple, a term Philip K. Dick introduced in his classic novel, *Do Androids Dream of Electric Sheep?* (1968): "Kipple is useless objects, like junk mail or match folders after you use the last match or gum wrappers or yesterday's homeopape. When nobody's around, kipple reproduces itself. For instance, if you go to bed leaving any kipple around your apartment, when you wake up in the next morning there's twice as much of it. It always gets more and more" (38). If kipple is discarded trash, then the Recycling Syndicate represents a solution to the problem by transforming "useless objects" into fuel for sustainable energy. Here, rather than allow technology and its debris to use the Third World as its dumping ground, Hogan imagines an indigenous, grassroots movement (the Recycling Syndicate) that seeks to counter wasteful capitalism with sustainable practices. As a Chicanafuturist text, then, *High Aztech* not only explores the effects of technology on people of color but also imagines alternatives to those impacts.

The term *Chicanafuturism* recalls, of course, another neologism in American cultural studies, *Afrofuturism*.[11] Briefly, an Afrofuturist critical stance assumes that "inquiry into the *production of futures* becomes fundamental rather than trivial" (Eshun 289). Afrofuturist writers and texts recognize that just as history is a contested discursive terrain, so too is the concept of futurity. No longer <u>as</u> interested in earlier twentieth-century projects of cultural recovery, of excavating lost traditions and cultures buried by imperial oppression, Afrofuturists turn the critical postcolonial gaze toward the future. Thus, while many of their predecessors and contemporaries desire to go back to the past to write African diasporic experiences back into history, Afrofuturists use speculative fiction to bring "black" to the future (Dery). Hogan's text functions as a Chicanafuturist narrative not simply because it is SF written by a Chicano but more specifically because it adopts a critical stance similar to that of an Afrofuturist. Comparable to the ways in which Afrofuturism explores the science fictionality of diaspora—cultural dislocation, marginalization, and alienation—Chicanafuturist texts like Hogan's recast the equally disorienting experiences that attend colonization and migration (the latter a form of diaspora, to be sure) in the speculative scenarios unique to SF.[12] For Hogan and others like him, the motifs and metaphors of SF are best suited to counterdiscourse, not escapist literature. More than other popular genres, SF is most germane to the project of reexamining "colonial and postcolonial histories of *indigenismo, mestizaje*, hegemony, and survival" (Ramirez 187).

Learning to survive in heterotopia requires a new way of being in the world, and what better genre is there than SF to make this happen? Learning to survive in heterotopia requires, that is, a new "mode of thinking that is neither fixed nor stable, but is one that is open to the prospect of continual return to events, to their re-elaboration and revision" (Chambers 3). Hogan and other Chicano SF writers who set their futures in exasperatingly disorienting urban heterotopias not only recognize this fact of our posthuman, postmodern life but practice it by opting to "return to" and revise a genre—science fiction—that has historically silenced their cultural and racial points of view.

Notes

1. My use of the term *mundane* to create juxtaposition between SF texts and non-SF texts follows Samuel R. Delany's use of the word to distinguish between the highly subversive alternative worlds in imaginative SF and the "mundane" real-life worlds in mainstream realist fiction.

2. In *Migrancy, Culture, Identity*, Iain Chambers coins *worlded city* to describe those futuristic and multinational enclaves that foretell the collapse of the local and the global as cities increasingly reflect not just their local color but the "world" as a whole (23).

3. Throughout the essay, I use the terms *Chicano* and/or *Chicana* instead of *Mexican American*. In Chicano/a studies, the term *Chicano/a* connotes a more politicized individual and collective Mexican American identity. Whereas *Mexican American* suffices to distinguish Americans of Mexican descent from other U.S. Latinos, it fails to connote the political history of the Chicano movement and of course the idea that many people now consider us to be post-Chicano.

4. Readers were also treated to Alejandro Morales's *Rag Doll Plagues* (1991) and Guillermo Gómez-Peña's *Friendly Cannibals* (1997), both of which recast the conventions of cyberpunk within distinct Chicano/a cultural contexts.

5. Moreover, in "Hacking the Brainstem: Postmodern Metaphysics and Stephenson's *Snow Crash*" (1996), David Porush echoes Person's reading of the novel when referring to *Snow Crash* as the product of a "second generation" of cyberpunk writing (110).

6. In general, the following writers are routinely cited as making up the core of 1980s cyberpunk: William Gibson, Rudy Rucker, Lewis Shiner, John Shirley, Bruce Sterling, and Pat Cadigan, whose *Synners* (1991) is often heralded for being an exception to my argument(s) against cyberpunk.

7. In a *Wired* magazine interview, Stephenson describes his work as a type of postcyberpunk. When asked how it feels "when people still refer to you as cyberpunk," Stephenson notes, "I think I've been recategorized as post-cyberpunk, so that's over."

8. See also Michael Omi's and Howard Winant's excoriating analysis of the rise of post-1960s neoliberalism and its deep-seated effects on people of color in the 1990s.

9. Vasconcelos's essay has problematic implications elsewhere, not the least of which are his claims about the disappearance of the "Black" and "Indian," who "will be absorbed

by the superior [racial] type" (32). For a very compelling critique of Vasconcelos's essay, see Pérez-Torres.

10. Pita and Sanchez take up this issue of waste (or the wastefulness of capitalism) in *Lunar Braceros, 2125–2148*, a near-future postcyberpunk novel that imagines a future so bleak that it warrants the use of the moon as a large dumping ground for the fallout of imperial capitalism.

11. The term *Afrofuturism* was coined by Dery.

12. For more on speculations on the future of Chicano/a literary studies, see González.

Works Cited

Acosta, Oscar Zeta *Autobiography of a Brown Buffalo*. 1972. New York: Vintage, 1989. Print.

Bakhtin, M. M. *The Dialogic Imagination: Four Essays*. Trans. Caryl Emerson and Michael Holquist. Austin: U of Texas P, 1996. Print.

Blade Runner. Dir. Ridley Scott. Sir-Run Run Shaw/Warner, 1982. DVD.

Butler, Octavia E. *Parable of the Sower*. New York: Warner/Aspect, 1993. Print.

———. *Parable of the Talents*. New York: Warner/Aspect, 1998. Print.

Cadigan, Pat. *Synners*. New York: HarperCollins, 1991. Print.

Chambers, Iain. *Migrancy, Culture, Identity*. London: Routledge, 1994. Print.

Csicsery-Ronay, Istvan, Jr. "Science Fiction and Empire." *Science Fiction Studies* 30.2 (2003): 231–46. Print.

Davis, Mike. *City of Quartz: Excavating the Future in Los Angeles*. New York: Vintage, 1992. Print.

Delany, Samuel R. "Reading Modern American Science Fiction." *American Writing Today*. Ed. Richard Kostelanetz. Troy: Whitston, 1991. 517–28. Print.

Dery, Mark. "Black to the Future: Interviews with Samuel R. Delany, Greg Tate, and Tricia Rose." *South Atlantic Quarterly* 92.4 (1993): 735–78. Print.

Dick, Philip K. *Do Androids Dream of Electric Sheep?* 1968. New York: Del Ray, 1996. Print.

Eshun, Kodwo. "Further Considerations on Afrofuturism." *CR: The New Centennial Review* 3.2 (2003): 287–302. Print.

Fitting, Peter. "The Lessons of Cyberpunk." *Technoculture*. Eds. Constance Penley and Andrew Ross. Minneapolis: U of Minnesota P, 1971. 295–316. Print.

Gibson, William. *Neuromancer*. New York: Ace, 1984. Print.

Gómez-Peña, Guillermo. *Friendly Cannibals*. Illus. Enrique Chagoya. San Francisco: Artspace, 1997. Print.

González, John Moran. "*Aztlán* @ Fifty: Chican@ Literary Studies for the Next Decade." *Aztlán: The Journal of Chicano Studies* 35.2 (2010): 173–76. Print.

Hogan, Ernest. *High Aztech*. New York: Tor, 1992. Print.

Hopkinson, Nalo. Introduction. *So Long Been Dreaming: Postcolonial Science Fiction and Fantasy*. Eds. Nalo Hopkinson and Uppinder Mehan. Vancouver: Arsenal, 2004. 7–9. Print.

Hutcheon, Linda. *A Poetics of Postmodernism: History, Theory, Fiction*. New York: Routledge, 1988. Print.

Kadrey, Richard. *Metrophage*. New York: Ace, 1988. Print.

Mesa-Bains, Amalia. "Domesticana: The Sensibility of Chicana Rasquache." *Aztlán: The Journal of Chicano Studies* 24.2 (1998): 157–76. Print.

Morales, Alejandro. "Dynamic Identities in Heterotopia." *Alejandro Morales: Fiction Past, Present, Future Perfect*. Tempe: Bilingual Review, 1996. Print.

———. *Rag Doll Plagues*. New Mexico: Arte Publico, 1991. Print.

Moylan, Tom. *Scraps of the Untainted Sky: Science Fiction, Utopia, Dystopia*. Boulder: Westview, 2000. Print.

Nakamura, Lisa. *Cybertypes: Race, Ethnicity, and Identity on the Internet*. New York: Routledge, 2002. Print.

Nixon, Nicola. "Cyberpunk: Preparing the Ground for Revolution or Keeping the Boys Satisfied?" *Science Fiction Studies* 19.2 (1992): 219–35. Print.

Omi, Michael, and Howard Winant. *Racial Formation in the United States: From the 1960s to the 1990s*. 2nd ed. New York: Routledge, 1994. Print.

Ortiz, Fernando. *Cuban Counterpoint: Tobacco and Sugar*. Durham: Duke UP, 1995. Print.

Palmer, James M. "Interview: Ernest Hogan." *Strange Horizons*. 10 Feb. 2003. Web. 9 Sept. 2012. http://www.strangehorizons.com/2003/20030210/hogan.shtml.

Pérez-Torres, Rafael. *Mestizáje: Critical Uses of Race in Chicano Culture*. Minneapolis: U of Minnesota P, 2006. Print.

Person, Lawrence. "Notes toward a Postcyberpunk Manifesto." 1998. Slashdot.org. 18 Oct. 1998. Web. 12 Sept. 2012.

Pita, Beatrice, and Rosaura Sanchez. *Lunar Braceros, 2125–2148*. Illus. Mario O. Chacon. San Diego: Calaca, 2009. Print.

Porush, David. "Hacking the Brainstem: Postmodern Metaphysics and Stephenson's *Snow Crash*." *Virtual Realities and Their Discontents*. Ed. Robert Markley. Baltimore: Johns Hopkins UP, 1996. 107–42. Print.

Ramirez, Catherine. "Afrofuturism/Chicanafuturism: Fictive Kin." *Aztlán: A Journal of Chicano Studies* 33.1 (2008): 185–94. Print.

Ross, Andrew. *Strange Weather: Culture, Science, and Technology in the Age of Limits*. New York: Verso, 1991. Print.

Sobchack, Vivian. "Beating the Meat/Surviving the Text; or, How to Get Out of This Century Alive." *Body and Society* 1.3–4 (1995): 205–14. Print.

Soja, Edward W. *Postmetropolis: Critical Studies of Cities and Regions*. Oxford: Blackwell, 2000. Print.

Sponsler, Claire. "Beyond the Ruins: The Geopolitics of Urban Decay and Cybernetic Play." *Science Fiction Studies* 20.2 (1993): 251–65. Print.

Stephenson, Neal. "Neal Stephenson Rewrites History." *Wired*, Sept. 2003. Web. 10 Aug. 2012.

———. *Snow Crash*. New York: Bantam, 1992. Print.

The Terminator. Dir. James Cameron. Pacific Western/Orion, 1984. DVD.

Vasconcelos, José. *The Cosmic Race/La Raza Cosmica*. 1925. Baltimore: Johns Hopkins UP, 1997. Print.

VIRTUAL REALITY AT THE BORDER OF MIGRATION, RACE, AND LABOR

■ ■ ■

MATTHEW GOODWIN

From Frontier to Borderland

Like many emerging technologies, virtual reality calls for metaphor.[1] The "frontier" and "colonization" have proven to be some of the most durable. The frontier metaphor appeared early in cyberpunk fiction with William Gibson's novel, *Neuromancer* (1984), in which the protagonist Case is identified as a "console cowboy" (28). The frontier metaphor also found its way into the writings of virtual reality developers such as Thomas A. Furness III, who stated, "As pioneers, we are obligated to pursue the development of virtual interface technologies in a systematic way and leave a technology base and tools as a legacy for others to build upon" (qtd. in Chesher).[2] A founding member of the Electronic Frontier Foundation, John Perry Barlow, turned to an earlier iconic figure: "Columbus was probably the last person to behold so much usable and unclaimed real estate (or unreal estate) as these cybernauts have discovered." The metaphors of the frontier and colonization are attempts to evoke the ingenuity, individualism, and freedom needed for the long project of virtual reality development. They do so by ignoring the destruction and conquest of European and American colonialism.

As a corrective to this techno-utopianism, a variety of writers in the mid-1990s expanded the metaphors beyond the celebration of computer colonialism. For example, Ziauddin Sardar describes how the military was central to the development of both virtual reality technology and the frontier (737).[3] In fact, the military remains one of the most significant users of virtual reality technology in such things as multiuser combat training programs (Beardsley). Sardar also notes that "colonization would not be complete without the projection of Western man's repressed sexuality and spiritual yearning on to the 'new continent'" (747). This aspect of the metaphor is borne out by the popularity of topics such as virtual sex in films about virtual reality and in cyberculture magazines such as *Mondo 2000* (Rucker, Sirius, and Mu). These expanded metaphors of the frontier and colonization gain a new purpose—they show that virtual reality technology is itself a medium used in the exploitation of labor and racial subjugation of people—in Anibal Quijanjo's terms, the coloniality of virtual reality. The three works discussed in this essay—Guillermo Lavín's short story, "Reaching the Shore" (1994); Guillermo Gómez-Peña's live TV broadcast, "Naftaztec: Pirate Cyber-TV for A.D. 2000" (1994); and Alex Rivera's film, *Sleep Dealer* (2008)—are critical of the coloniality of virtual reality and move toward updating the metaphors. Rather than looking back to a past built on the destruction of other cultures, they turn to the present and show what became of the American frontier once it was settled—the Mexican-U.S. border, the borderlands that developed there, and the migration systems that emerged. They show that virtual reality is a rich palette that can be used to depict migration, race, and labor. They turn to the borderland instead of the frontier as the new geographic center of virtual reality. While the frontier and the borderland are similar terms, both indicating a boundary, the key difference for this essay is that the frontier is expansionist oriented, while the borderland is hybridizing.

The Illusions of Virtual Reality

In his short story "Reaching the Shore," Mexican science fiction writer Guillermo Lavín depicts the production side of virtual reality technology. This quotidian story is set in the border town of Reynosa, where eight-year-old José Paul lives with his family. José Paul's father, Fragoso, works at Simpson Brothers Inc., the Leisure Time Company, a maquiladora (manufacturing operation on the Mexican-U.S. border) that produces virtual reality biochips. When inserted into the head, these chips make one's dreams a reality. Believing in the promise that technology offers for economic development, Fragoso volunteered to be a tester at the factory. Fragoso becomes addicted, however, and instead of buying José Paul the bike he wants for Christmas buys a cheap imported black market biochip. José Paul decides to steal a biochip, enabling him to get his bike, if only in virtual reality. The story ends with José Paul pondering whether he should give the biochip away or continue to use it, like his father.

This story creatively correlates the experience of virtual reality technology with a variety of phenomena that resemble virtual reality. The common logic of these phenomena is that they are colorful and pleasurable, promising something great, yet are fleeting and over time destructive. Virtual reality technology is simply the newest form of this type of experience. The male gaze, for example, is one prominent virtual reality phenomenon. José Paul is accompanying the men leaving work at the end of the day when a woman passes by: "He followed the men's gaze and his eyes glided along the undulating curve of her smooth hips and the dark reflection of legs encased in pants that seemed fused to them. The color of the clothes changed constantly, like a kaleidoscope, and he liked that. A gust of cold wind raised a dust cloud; it crystallized in the men's eyes and compelled them to move on" (226). The reality behind the colorful illusion is signaled by the obscuring of vision by the non-colorful dust: this woman is more than a colorful spectacle; she is someone's family member. This connection becomes clear when the visual description of this woman parallels the description of José Paul's sister, Clementina, arriving home with a young man and wearing "pants tight, cheeks aflame" (230). The commonality of these two descriptions is that color is brought so close to the body that the illusion of the person is total. Illusions can just as easily be attached to nonhuman objects of desire, as when José Paul takes his bike ride: "Thousands of summer butterflies molded their colors onto the bike and the boy's clothes, he felt them like rain, like a new gift from heaven" (234).

That José Paul mimics the male gaze points to the legacy of these virtual reality phenomena. Clearly inspired by his father's decision to volunteer for the company, José Paul volunteered to be the first student in his class to receive a bioport, which he uses for schoolwork. But even though these illusory experiences are learned, they are solitary experiences. The scene in which José Paul watches fireworks gives a lyrical description of the arc of the experience: "It was time for the fireworks. The time when people came out of their houses and hugged each other and contemplated the gift that the municipal government gave the city in the form of fleeting, dazzling signs, simulated stars, ringlets of burning colors.... Alone, with his arms open wide, he bathed in the halos of illusory fire, until reality reimposed itself with a shout and the hiss of steam that escaped from the pot of tamales someone had uncovered" (230). The community holds the belief that these fireworks are a positive contribution, whereas the city is in fact using its limited resources on brief spectacles, not long-term improvements. These illusions isolate those who have them, and they are dangerous. Since the virtual reality biochips transform one's imagination into reality, the experience can be of a wonderful dream come true—or a nightmare come true. The reality of virtual reality is found in the eyes: for example, one evening, after Fragoso uses the biochip, José Paul observes that "tiny red veins had been installed in his father's eyes and that his eyelids formed little dark bags" (230). Later, Fragoso runs "from the bedroom with his eyes popping out of their sockets, bawling like a steer in the slaughterhouse" (232).

This cluster of virtual reality phenomena coalesces at the Mexican-U.S. border, the dangerous point of contact where, as Gloria Anzaldúa writes, "the Third World grates against the first and bleeds" (25). In the story's final scene, after stealing the biochip, José Paul goes on his virtual bike ride: "He could journey far beyond the Rio Bravo, he could leave Reynosa and travel along the riverbanks, along the toll road and the forgotten paths and across bridges. And no sooner had he so decided than he was on his way, racing along a footpath, traveling faster than the greenish current flowing at his side" (234). Virtual reality enables him finally to cross the border, headed for the great spectacle of the United States. Like the dust that crystallizes in the men's eyes as they gaze at the woman, José Paul had earlier seen the reality of the border in the once lively river that separates Mexico and the United States: "The Rio Bravo: a thin thread the color of dirt, as if coffee grounds ran in its great bed" (228). This dystopian detail of the river drying up allegorically points to a deterioration in the relationship between Mexico and the United States. The reality is that these border factories provide little lasting benefit to the community. Instead, they direct the gaze across the border, creating desires for products that the residents of the town cannot afford while providing for the leisure of those living in the United States.

Ethical responsibility for these effects of virtual reality technology is spread evenly in the story. By correlating virtual reality technology with a variety of other virtual reality phenomena, Lavín seems to be pointing to our deeply ingrained desire for dangerous illusions—a universal human problem. But the very specific economic disparity between the United States and Mexico brings the maquiladoras to town. As a microcosm of this problem, Fragoso freely chooses to volunteer for the job of testing chips, but the company does not help him once he is addicted. The title of the story indicates that the responsibility to fix this situation ultimately falls on the individual. "Reaching the Shore" refers to a line in Ray Bradbury's *Fahrenheit 451* (1953) that appears as an epigraph to Lavín's story: "Don't ask for guarantees. And don't look to be saved in any one thing, person, machine, or library. Do your own bit of saving, and if you drown, at least die knowing you were heading for shore" (224). The self-reliance recommended in the quote gains some strength since the institutions (factory, school, government) depicted in the story do not in fact give much help to José Paul and his family. But as the quote makes clear, reaching the shore is not guaranteed. When José Paul's mother calls him out of his bike-riding dream, he repeats, "I really have to think it over. . . . I'll have to think it over" (234). The statement indicates some level of awareness of the problem but remains ambiguous.

The Chicano Virtual Reality Machine

Like José Paul, performance artist Guillermo Gómez-Peña has what he calls a "paradoxical, contradictory relationship with digital technology," attracted to it yet aware of its dangers ("Chicano"). Virtual reality technology in particular becomes his medium for expressing this contradictory relationship. On 22 November 1994 (Thanksgiving Day), Gómez-Peña and Roberto Sifuentes appeared in a live TV broadcast in which they acted as if they had taken over a television station. This performance, "Naftaztec: Pirate Cyber-TV for A.D. 2000," was available to 3.5 million cable viewers, since the two men had convinced more than four hundred program directors to air the show under another listing. Gómez-Peña took on the character of El Naftazteca, while Sifuentes was Cyber-Vato. The performance was a collage of monologues by Naftazteca, video clips from past performances by Gómez-Peña, and live interactions with callers. A centerpiece of the show was a fictional technology, Technopal 2000 (combining the words *technology* and *nopal*, a Mexican cactus), also known as the Chicano virtual reality machine.[4]

Naftazteca lays out the problem: "The U.S. suffers from a severe case of amnesia. In its obsessive quest to construct the future, it tends to forget or erase the past. Fortunately, the so-called disenfranchised groups who don't feel part of this national project have been meticulously documenting their histories." The Technopal 2000 enables such documentation: "With this new system, called Technopal 2000, I can turn my memories into video images, ipso facto, meaning that I can retrieve any episode of my life, any performance I was ever involved in, any persona or hidden self that exists within me, or any historical event involving my family and my raza—the Chicano/Mexicano communities in the U.S. . . . I can edit these memories on the spot and turn them into video footage, like so." The Technopal 2000 enables video documents to be inserted into the mainstream media system, constructing a different future: "Our video memories will soon also be yours," declares Naftazteca. The functioning of the Technopal 2000 is also a metaphor for the process of the performance, since it describes the show itself—that is, the selection, editing, and presentation of video clips from previous performances and family events. The Technopal 2000 is a tool for the creation of political art. The artistic-political vision is expressed by the design of the virtual reality equipment used in the show. Naftazteca does not use actual virtual reality equipment but takes traditional virtual reality equipment and modifies it using a mixture of Mexican and Chicano icons, including ethnic stereotypes and low technology.

There are two principal scenes in which the performers use the Chicano virtual reality machine. The first scene involves the use of the beta version, a virtual reality sombrero that references the type of virtual reality equipment tested by Ivan Sutherland in 1966 that included an enormous head-mounted display (Rheingold 105). Prefacing his use of the sombrero, Naftazteca says, "Immigrants are faced with a hairy predicament. Either we immerse ourselves in a nostalgia for a homeland that no longer exists, or we embrace our present condition as public enemies, as unwanted minorities, as painful as it may be, and become politicized. To choose the road of nostalgia is of course more romantic. But it can also be very, very, very dangerous." As the scene progresses, Naftazteca puts on the virtual reality sombrero, while Cyber-Vato acts as his virtual reality guide. Cyber-Vato performs as a member of the dominant group with control of the media. He numerates various political and cultural problems that worry Naftazteca and then reminds him that he is "not responsible" for these problems. He invites Naftazteca to go back to his first memories in Mexico. As Cyber-Vato begins to count down from ten, Naftazteca reflects, "*La nostalgia, le nostalgie.* It protects me against the gringos, *la migra*, the art world." He begins to remember aspects of his home in Mexico City and increasingly uses Spanish. Cyber-Vato admonishes, "Please, can you remember in English, in English," indicating precisely who this technology is meant to serve.

Cyber-Vato uses a New Age–type voice in his performance, referencing the early proponents of virtual reality, who were more concerned about the mind-altering experiences possible in virtual reality than the political possibilities. This New Age mentality expresses the danger of that arises if immigrant nostalgia ignores the political. Naftazteca affirms that nostalgia is attractive and that it gives a sense of comfort to migrants in a strange world. He engages in some nostalgia after using the virtual reality machine by showing a video clip from his family, praising their influence on his performance art. He does not reject nostalgia but rather moves on from it to more contemporary political issues such as the passage California's Proposition 187, which barred state agencies from assisting undocumented immigrants.

In the second scene involving virtual reality equipment, Naftazteca and Cyber-Vato switch roles, with Naftazteca directing the virtual reality experience. Cyber-Vato puts on the alpha version of the Chicano virtual reality machine, a virtual reality bandana that includes a rope tied in a noose around his neck and a glove, referencing the virtual reality glove created by Thomas

Zimmerman in 1982 (Rheingold 159). Naftazteca guides Cyber-Vato through three programs. In the first two programs, Cyber-Vato initially has a positive impression of the scenario, but it then turns nightmarish. First, Cyber-Vato is sitting in a car with a guy who seems cool; however, it turns out that Cyber-Vato is wearing handcuffs, and the other man is a cop who beats him. When Cyber-Vato wants out, Naftazteca ironically replies, "Man, don't worry. It's just virtual reality." In the second program, "Borderscape 2000," Cyber-Vato is in the Southwest desert, where the beautiful scene causes him to exclaim, "It's gorgeous, man! And I feel happy too, real happy." He sees what appears to be an eagle in the sky but then realizes that it is a border patrol helicopter and that it is chasing his uncle. Naftazteca repeats, "Tranquilo, Carnal, it's just virtual reality." Of course, for a vato (guy or dude), these experiences are not just virtual reality.

These programs exhibit the false promise of the utopian vision of virtual reality—that virtual reality and the Internet were utopian spaces, unblemished by race. Virtual reality proponent Jaron Lanier writes, "Virtual Reality is the ultimate lack of class or race distinctions or any other form of pretense since all form is variable" (Heilbrun 117). Gómez-Peña reports that this idea filtered down into the art world: "The utopian rhetoric surrounding digital technologies, especially the rhetoric coming out of California, reminded Roberto and me of a sanitized version of the pioneer and frontier mentality of the Old West. When we began to dialogue with U.S. artists working with new technologies, we were perplexed by the fact that these artists, when referring to 'cyberspace' or 'the Net,' meant a politically neutral/raceless/genderless and classless territory that gave us all 'equal access' and unlimited possibilities for participation, interaction, and belonging" ("Chicano"). Not only is racism intertwined with who has access to advanced technology, but as Thomas Foster describes, "racialized modes of perception are inevitably imported to cyberspace, and racial fantasies are restaged there" (62). Proponents of virtual reality went further in their estimation of virtual reality, claiming that it had the potential to reduce racism by putting a user in the shoes of someone from another race, thereby causing the user to become more empathetic and compassionate. Ella Shohat and Robert Stam, for example, imagine that virtual reality technology might allow someone to experience what it is like to be an immigrant chased by border patrol or a civil rights demonstrator beaten by police (166). Gómez-Peña satirizes this kind of ethnic training, describing the Chicano virtual reality bandana as allowing Anglo "users to vicariously experience racism" ("Chicano"). For Cyber-Vato, these experiences are too close to home and traumatic, so empathy is not what Cyber-Vato needs to learn. Virtual reality for ethnic training is constructed by multicultural society, not the immigrant or civil rights protester. These two virtual reality programs enabled Anglo viewers to experience the image of what happens when Latinos do not choose the program and have little control over the media that represents them.

In the third program, Naftazteca takes a step in the direction of showing what happens when Latinos control the media that represents them. Naftazteca narrates a scene in which Cyber-Vato is to take on the role of gardener for former California Republican governor Pete Wilson (1991–99), a supporter of Proposition 187 who was later revealed to have hired an undocumented worker as a housekeeper. Cyber-Vato confronts Wilson about murdering the gardener, who was an undocumented immigrant. Instead of seeing how Cyber-Vato reacts, as in the other two programs, the viewers see a clip from the Mexican film *El Hijo de la Calavera* in which El Hijo confronts the man who killed his father and stole the family hacienda. Like the man who stole the hacienda, Wilson is engaged in an unjust act. Unlike the first two programs, Cyber-Vato is not just the victim of an injustice; instead, he can fight back. This moment of empowerment is correlated with the use of a Mexican film, an instance in which Mexicans take control of the media. This scene signals that control of television has shifted. This scene also shows something of Gómez-Peña's perspective on what to do about the unjust use of virtual reality technology. While "Reaching the Shore" indicates that only the individual can improve his or her situation better, Gómez-Peña argues that the individual can change society by working through the Mexican and Chicano communities.

Migration through Virtual Reality

Like "Naftaztec: Pirate Cyber-TV for A.D. 2000," Rivera's *Sleep Dealer* correlates virtual reality with migration, but it does so more directly and in depth. The film's premise is that in the near future, the border has been sealed but the U.S. desire for cheap labor has not vanished. Cybraceros Inc. meets this desire by constructing maquiladoras at the border in which workers in Mexico control robots in the United States via cyberspace. They connect to cyberspace through nodes in their bodies. Contact lenses in their eyes function as screens on which they see whatever their robot counterparts in the United States see. With this technology, they can work in a variety of jobs, among them construction, child care, and agriculture. The plot revolves around Memo, who leaves his home in Oaxaca after his father is killed by the corporate entity controlling the world's water and travels to the border where he works at

Cybraceros Inc. Along the way, Memo meets Luz, a writer who tells his story on the Internet, where it is read by Rudy, the U.S. military pilot who killed Memo's father. Eventually, all of the characters collaborate to find a way out of the system that imprisons them.

Virtual reality complicates the experience of migration and raises the question of whether Memo is a migrant or a nonmigrant. In regard to the common conception of migration as human mobility through geographic space, Memo is an internal migrant, traveling from the country to the city within Mexico, from agricultural labor to factory labor. Once at the border, though, Memo is a nonmigrant laborer. The film correlates Memo with various forms of nonmigratory labor, directly referring to the maquiladoras and to outsourcing in general. For example, when Rudy is traveling into Mexico, the border patrol guard is depicted as a worker in India who interacts with Rudy by camera and phone. Both Memo and the guard are working through cyberspace while remaining in their homelands. Memo's situation as a nonmigrant laborer is elaborated through the correlation between the cybraceros and prisoners. In the film, the closing of the border effectively stops migration from Mexico. This lockdown creates a kind of national prison (the wall is depicted as reminiscent of a prison wall). U.S. citizens can travel south, but Mexican citizens cannot travel north. The film evokes the idea of imprisonment with virtual reality technology. As Lev Manovitch observes, with its goggles and wires, virtual reality technology "imprisons the body to an unprecedented extent" (109). This imprisonment is shared on some level with most technologies, but virtual reality technology raises the paradox to a peak. Virtual reality, which entails visual, auditory, and haptic perception, offers the potential for much greater immersion than does the telephone, for example. The film's virtual reality systems tie the user physically to the machines and are invasive, with nodes in the arms connected to wires and contact lenses in the eyes. The cybraceros are depicted as marionettes and seem to be wearing prison-like uniforms. The technology also enables invasive body surveillance, so that if a worker falls asleep for an instant, the computer wakes her up, registers the lapse, and docks her pay. For Memo, cyberspace is not Gibson's bright geometric electronic "consensual-hallucination" (5) but a construction site.[5]

In addition, the virtual reality equipment gives the workers the appearance of blindness, illustrating the restriction of visual perception to the virtual reality environment and the exclusion of the surrounding world. As in "Reaching the Shore," for those who labor with virtual reality technology, what the eyes see may be virtual, but what the eyes experience is deadly real. In the virtual reality labor depicted in the film, the eyes are the point on the body of intensive usage, and while powerful organs, they are fragile. Cybraceros suffer injuries both progressive and traumatic. Memo reveals to Luz, "The more time I spend connected, the harder it is to see." The potential for progressive eye injury is high, much like the carpal tunnel syndrome suffered by present-day workers in chicken processing plants. And Memo describes one kind of traumatic injury—"You might get hit by a surge, end up blind"—that later affects a worker in the film. Memo meets a group of factory workers who have lost the use of their eyes, been deemed useless by the factory, and thrown out to live in the shadow of the border.

Under the traditional conception of migration, Memo is a nonmigrant. There are important reasons, however, to think of Memo as a migrant. His experience can be read as an allegory of migration. The film contains many references to past and present Mexican migration that support such a reading. The name of the company, for example, is a reference to the Bracero program, during which the United States recruited millions of Mexican agricultural workers from the 1940s through the 1960s. The film also depicts many of the most common migrant experiences. Memo travels from southern Mexico to the border, often the step before migration into the United States. He works hard to help his family, has intense periods of nostalgia, and places value on sending money home. Many of the sociological aspects of migration are present as well. For example, coyotes, the nickname for the guides who help migrants cross the border without documents, are in the film called coyoteks, and they put nodes in the arms of would-be cybraceros, allowing them to enter cyberspace.

The film is not only an allegory of migration but an extrapolation of migration into the future. The idea is that virtual reality technology has created a new form of migration—a migration into cyberspace. This correlation is possible because migration and virtual reality experiences share a common phenomenology an understanding of migration expressed by Vilém Flusser: "Custom and habit are a blanket that covers over reality as it exists" (81). The blanket of habit prevents us from sensing the world and from seeing new things. Both the migrant and the user of virtual reality experience life with the blanket torn away and so enter a new world structure. Though equivalent in this regard, migration into cyberspace is not traditional migration: whereas previously months or weeks would be spent crossing an ocean or desert, migration into cyberspace occurs instantaneously. But even though the travel time has vanished, the experience of an arrival and interaction with a new environment has not. One can travel to and within cyberspace. This connection between virtual reality and migration, like the frontier metaphor, appears in Gibson's *Neuromancer*, where cyberspace is described as the protagonist's "distanceless home, his country, transparent 3D chessboard extending to infinity" (52).

Because of this ability to move within cyberspace, Memo is a migrant not only into cyberspace but also into the United States. He sees the United States, he uses tools in the United States, affects the United States, and at times interacts with people in the United States. He experiences the geography, even if it is a vague notion of exactly where: at one point, he tells his brother that he thinks his job is in California. Memo's experience of migration into the United States is enhanced by the use of telepresent technology, including live video streamed in from the robot, enabling him to have a real presence in the United States. This combination of perceptions, along with the real-time telepresence, gives a sense of reality to the new environment, thus creating an experience of migration. In addition, Memo has the use of an avatar that allows him the ability to manipulate tools and the world connected to those tools. The avatar allows Memo to identify with an abstractly humanoid robot that does in fact take up space in the United States, an important element of migration that would otherwise be missing. While the avatar is not personalized, identification is functionally formed—that is, Memo's movements happen in tandem with the robot, and the robot's gestures mirror Memo's gestures (turning his hand turns the robot's hand). Over time, the identification would deepen.

How, in the end, are we to understand Memo's experience? One possibility is to use the model of the "virtual migrant" as coined by A. Aneesh in a recent study of computer analysts working from India for corporations in the United States. Aneesh describes virtual migrants as workers who "cross national boundaries and directly occupy some employment space in sectors of the American economy" (2). Like these workers, Memo's experience is restricted to the workplace, and he cannot interact with the larger culture (for example, by moving to another state). Only energy and data are traveling through geographic space into the United States. Memo confesses that he feels that his energy or labor power is flowing north, reducing migration to labor. The concept is stated by the manager of the factory: "This is the American dream. We give the United States what they've always wanted. All the work without the workers."[6] Both Cybraceros Inc. and present-day outsourcing keep the physical distance of the worker; however, Cybraceros enables manual labor on U.S. soil. Virtual reality technology, however, makes Memo's experience different from that of a computer analyst. It is stronger and more like an actual migration. The adjective *virtual* should be dropped altogether. To do so may seem at first not to do justice to the idea that Memo is paradoxically both a migrant and a nonmigrant; however, there is a precedent for this idea at the border. We would not call Memo an immigrant, since his experience of migration is not that of immigration, in which a person takes up long-term residence somewhere else. Instead, he is more like a "frontier migrant worker," or someone who has a border crossing card, crosses the border to work in the United States, and then returns to Mexico at night. Memo experiences the dislocation of migration not continuously but daily.

Because of their unique situation, collaborative politics is difficult for these frontier migrant workers. Memo does not connect to other workers in his factory, presumably because the opaque contact lenses prevent him from seeing his coworkers. He cannot communicate easily with the other workers at his job site, since they are present as robots. Instead, he makes a new kind of interclass connection with Rudy and Luz as "node workers" (in Rudy's words). Because of Luz's Internet stories, Rudy travels into Mexico to try to make amends for killing Memo's father. They concoct a plan to have Rudy fly his fighter drone using the virtual reality equipment at Cybraceros Inc. Rudy flies the drone into the dam, freeing the water that was being held back from the people living in Memo's hometown. Their collaboration succeeds; however, it seems to be a one-shot deal. Might there be a way for the factory workers to collaborate? One possibility is that because what appears of the workers in the United States are simulations of their language and gestures, they could at some point find a way to demonstrate their presence through performance-based protest—perhaps a robot march like the 2006 immigration marches across the United States.[7]

New Dystopias in Virtual Reality

On the one hand, the rhetoric surrounding virtual reality and the use of the frontier and colonization metaphors have generally had a strongly utopian element. Cyberpunk fiction, on the other hand, is most often dystopian, depicting a world in which the virtual has overtaken the real. The works discussed in this essay have followed in this tradition of correlating virtual reality with dystopian fiction. These dystopias differ, however, from much of science fiction. In traditional dystopian fiction, such as George Orwell's *Nineteen Eighty-Four* (1949) or Bradbury's *Fahrenheit 451*, the protagonist commonly begins in a privileged position and then falls from that position. The insider citizen becomes an outsider in exile. In mainstream films about virtual reality such as *The Matrix* (1999) or *Avatar* (2009), this same dynamic continues. In the dystopian narratives discussed here, the protagonists do not begin with privilege but are already in the position of maquiladora workers, minorities, and migrant laborers. The dystopian problems depicted in these narratives are not future fantasies but present-day realities, not how things will be but how they are. The beauty of these artworks is that they imagine highly creative protagonists who use virtual reality for their own purposes and find some way to change reality.

Notes

1. Virtual reality technology can be understood on a scale from 3D films to the fictional computer-generated world of *Star Trek*'s holodeck (that is, from very little immersion to full immersion).

2. Chesher was most likely the first to comprehensively draw out the genealogy of these metaphors.

3. Sardar's analysis uses "cyberspace" to refer to both virtual reality and the Internet and shows how they are the newest colonial projects.

4. An edited version of the broadcast is available on DVD through the Video Data Bank. Excerpts from the broadcast are included in Gómez-Peña's *New World Border* (1996).

5. Much of the technology depicted in the film exists in prototype: the contact lens screens are currently being developed and may very well replace the goggles that have been a mainstay of virtual reality according (Choi).

6. Contemporary U.S. immigration policy follows this same logic—periodic mass deportations beginning with the Bracero program and continuing through the Obama presidency. Under Barack Obama, approximately 1.1 million people have been deported. This policy functions as a de facto attempt to give the United States all the work without the workers. The deportation rate will presumably fall in the wake of Obama's 2012 executive order preventing the deportation of young migrants (Preston and Cushman).

7. Rivera mentioned to me at the 2012 Visions of the Future conference at the University of Iowa that he had considered including a scene in the film in which the workers learned to communicate via some kind of robot graffiti.

Works Cited

Aneesh, A. *Virtual Migration: The Programming of Globalization*. Durham: Duke UP, 2006. Print.

Anzaldúa, Gloria. *Borderlands/La Frontera*. San Francisco: Aunt Lute, 1987. Print.

Avatar. Dir. James Cameron. Twentieth Century Fox, 2009. DVD.

Barlow, John Perry. "Being in Nothingness: Virtual Reality and the Pioneers of Cyberspace." 1990. Web. 10 Aug. 2012.

Beardsley, Steven. "Virtual Training Expands as Military Evolves." *Stars and Stripes*. 9 Jan. 2012. Web. 10 Aug. 2012.

Bradbury, Ray. *Fahrenheit 451*. New York: Ballantine, 1953.

Chesher, Chris. "Colonizing Virtual Reality: Construction of the Discourse of Virtual Reality, 1984–1992." *Cultronix* 1.1 (1994). Web. 10 Aug. 2012.

Choi, Charles Q. "Virtual Reality Contact Lenses Could Be Available by 2014." *Scientific American*, 2 Feb. 2012. Web. 10 Aug. 2012.

Flusser, Vilém. *The Freedom of the Migrant: Objections to Nationalism*. Urbana: U of Illinois P, 2003. Print.

Foster, Thomas. "Cyber-Aztecs and Cholo-Punks: Guillermo Gómez-Peña's Five-Worlds Theory." *PMLA* 117.1 (2002): 43–67. Print.

Gibson, William. *Neuromancer*. New York: Ace, 1984. Print.

Gómez-Peña, Guillermo. "Chicano Interneta: The Search for Intelligent Life in Cyberspace." *Hopscotch: A Cultural Review* 2.2 (2000): 80–91. Web. 10 Aug. 2012.

———. *Dangerous Border Crossers: The Artist Talks Back*. New York: Routledge, 2000. Print.

———. "Naftaztec: Pirate Cyber-TV for A.D. 2000." *Border Art Clásicos (1990–2005): An Anthology of Collaborative Video Works by Guillermo Goméz-Peña*. Chicago: Video Data Bank, 2007. DVD.

———. *The New World Border: Prophecies, Poems, and Loqueras for the End of the Century*. San Francisco: City Lights, 1996. Print.

Heilbrun, Adam. "An Interview with Jaron Lanier." *Whole Earth Review*, Fall 1989, 108–19. Web. 10 Aug. 2012.

Lavín, Guillermo. "Reaching the Shore." 1994. *Cosmos Latinos: An Anthology of Science Fiction from Latin America and Spain*. Eds. and Trans. Andrea L. Bell and Yolanda Molina-Gavilán. Middletown: Wesleyan UP, 2003. 223–34. Print.

Manovitch, Lev. *The Language of New Media*. Cambridge: MIT P, 2001. Print.

The Matrix. Dirs. Andy and Larry Wachowski. Warner Bros., 1999. DVD.

Orwell, George. *Nineteen Eighty-Four*. London: Secker and Warburg, 1949.

Preston, Julia, and John H. Cushman Jr. "Obama to Permit Young Migrants to Remain in U.S." *New York Times*, 15 June 2012. Web. 10 Aug. 2012.

Quijano, Anibal. "Colonialidad del Poder, Globalización, y Democracia." *Trayectorias* 4.7–8 (2001–2): 58–90. Print.

Rheingold, Howard. *Virtual Reality*. New York: Summit, 1991. Print.

Rucker, Rudy, R U Sirius, and Queen Mu. *Mondo 2000: A User's Guide to the New Edge*. New York: Harper Perennial, 1992. Print.

Sardar, Ziauddin. "alt.civilizations.faq: Cyberspace as the Darker Side of the West." *The Cybercultures Reader*. Eds. David Bell and Barbara M. Kennedy. London: Routledge, 2000. 732–52. Print.

Shohat, Ella, and Robert Stam. "From the Imperial Family to the Transnational Imaginary: Media Spectatorship in the Age of Globalization." *Global/Local: Cultural Production and the Transnational Imaginary*. Eds. Rob Wilson and Wimal Dissanayake. Durham: Duke UP, 1996. 145–72. Print.

Sleep Dealer. Dir. Alex Rivera. Maya, 2009. DVD.

A DIS-(ORIENT)ATION

Race, Technoscience, and *The Windup Girl*

• • •

MALISA KURTZ

Even if she is New People, there is nothing new under the sun.
—**Paolo Bacigalupi,** *The Windup Girl*

As a part of popular culture, science fiction's imagined futures have always engaged questions of race—either through direct treatment of racial politics or more commonly through the absence of people of color. In fact, if, as John Rieder argues in his influential *Colonialism and the Emergence of Science Fiction* (2008), the ideological basis of colonial practice is central to much of early SF, then it is also inevitable that "some of the racism endemic to colonialist discourse is woven into the texture of science fiction" (97). SF's emergence as a predominantly white, male tradition is reflected in narratives that excluded women, people of color, and the "Third World."[1] Texts that engaged with race often reinforced racist assumptions and fears. For example, figurations of Asia in early SF typically followed in the tradition of Yellow Peril fictions and, as Betsy Huang suggests, reveal "American science fiction's long Orientalist history" and "the West's enduring ambivalence towards Asians as friend or foe in its conceptions of the future" (95). In addition, SF frequently presumed an evolutionary white or color-blind future, marginalizing people of color and depicting race as a matter of little importance. As Mark Bould contends, SF's color-blind futures and visions of one race erase the history of racial struggle and the material conditions that perpetuate racist ideologies (180). Science fiction has recently started to deviate from this tradition, and many SF novels are increasingly concerned with the politics of racial identity, globalization, imperialism, and the Third World.[2] Paolo Bacigalupi's *The Windup Girl* (2009) presents a compelling departure from SF's traditionally white future, portraying a futuristic Bangkok where despite advancements in technoscience, racial tensions and prejudices persist, affecting the daily lives of people of color.

The Windup Girl depicts a dystopian world in which a global energy collapse, known as the Contraction, has led to the rise of biotech companies and their increased control over worldwide food production and distribution. Calories are the new currency, and nations with their own seed banks are rich and not yet tied to the yoke of Western agricultural corporations. Thailand holds its own seed bank and is one of the few remaining countries whose markets are closed off from these multinational corporations. One such American biotech company, AgriGen, attempts to penetrate Thailand's market to integrate the country into the global economy and thus subject Thailand to potentially detrimental economic and social effects as a result of AgriGen's superior technology. Bacigalupi's critique of the imperial practices and environmental consequences of multinational biotech companies permeates his work from *Pump Six and Other Stories* (2008) through *The Windup Girl* and *Ship Breaker* (2010).

The Windup Girl also highlights the complex effects of technoscience on discourses of race. Bacigalupi's use of Thailand as an "exotic" setting in which different ethnicities/races interact depicts a world in which latent ethnocentrism and Orientalism persist, and people of color in the novel struggle for their daily survival in a racist global political economy. Hock Seng, for example, is a "yellow card," a derogatory term for Malaysian refugees of Chinese descent who have fled to Thailand to escape persecution in an increasingly fundamentalist Malaysia. The racial denomination "yellow card" is derived from the literal yellow identification card Chinese-Malays must carry in Thailand. Emiko, the "windup girl," is also a racialized character who as part of a biologically engineered race of "New People" positions discourses of race in relation to developing technoscience. New People—called "windups" for their characteristic "stutter-stop" motions (37)—are created by the Japanese to work as laborers and companions (read: slaves), replacing Japan's dying population. Windups are illegal in Thailand, and only the Japanese are exempt from this regulation in exchange for their technological assistance to the Thai kingdom. *The Windup Girl* positions race and racial politics as a central concern in this imagined future, exploring the historical impact of globalization, migration, and technoscience on the Third World.

This essay examines the complex construction of "Asian" identity in Bacigalupi's novel; specifically, I explore the ways *The Windup Girl* avoids constructing monolithic racial representations, taking into consideration the historical, political, social, and technological structures that influence how race is read and represented. I begin by focusing on the novel's setting and use of ethnically diverse characters, arguing that the novel engages with the historical complexity of race relations in Southeast Asia. The second half of this essay focuses on the intersections of technoscience and the cultural construction of Asian identity in what Peter A. Chow-White calls the "informationalization of race" (1168), or the reduction of racial politics to a matter of informational code and data. Advancements in biotechnology in the novel do not erase but rather perpetuate old racial ideologies, hierarchies, and practices. Orientalism is translated to a form of techno-Orientalism in which prejudices and fears continue with the expansion of global information communication technologies. As such, Bacigalupi's novel does not envision a color-blind future; instead, it portrays race as a matter of life or death, and Emiko's constant fear of being discovered and mulched is but one example of the struggle for daily survival raced characters face. *The Windup Girl* suggests that in an increasingly global political economy, advancements in biotechnology are not utopian possibilities that transcend racism but rather tools that mask racist and imperial ideologies.

Southeast Asia and Variations of Techno-Orientalism

The Windup Girl is set in Thailand, and while it draws on the discourse of Orientalism as outlined by Edward Said, it also reveals the dangers of a different variation David Morley and Kevin Robins define as "techno-Orientalism." Morley and Robins argue that racist assumptions have not disappeared with advancements in technoscience but rather are integrated into the technology itself. Thus, "as the dynamism of technological innovation has appeared to move eastwards, so have these postmodern technologies become structured into the discourse of Orientalism" (169). Though Morley and Robins refer primarily to Japan, their observations may be extended to Thailand, a growing tiger economy in Southeast Asia. In more general terms then, techno-Orientalism may be understood as "the desire to conceptualize the East through a technocratic framework within cultural production [that] leads to a re-articulation and re-emergence of the yellow peril" (Sohn 10). Bacigalupi's novel highlights the discourse of techno-Orientalism while critiquing its assumptions and reorienting its homogenizing framework. The novel does so by critically engaging with its setting and diverse characters to expose the effects of what Istvan Csicsery-Ronay Jr. calls the "technoscientific Empire" (8) that is our current sociopolitical condition.

While setting the novel in a future Thailand may be seen as an instance of Orientalism, by shifting SF's traditionally "Western" focus to a geographic region seldom explored in SF, Bacigalupi's novel opens up the narrative's potential as what Isiah Lavender III calls an "ethnoscape." Lavender contends, "While sf's conventional estrangements populate the fictional environment with, or structure it around, the presence of science, technology, mythology, aliens, androids, humanity, natural and artificial phenomena, politics, culture, language, religion, and so on, the ethnoscape reformulates that construction so as to create an alternative image that enables us to rethink the intersections of technology and race as well as their political, social, and cultural implications" (163). As an ethnoscape, *The Windup Girl* avoids exoticizing Thailand by confronting the relationship between race and developing biotechnologies in a country struggling to keep up with multinational agricultural corporations. By doing so, the novel highlights the racist and colonial practices of the First World and the effects of uneven technological development in an increasingly global economy. Historically, Thailand has never been colonized, but like many Third World countries, it has opened up its borders to the information revolution and foreign investment. Bacigalupi's novel, however, depicts Thailand as sealed off from international markets; thus, attempts to integrate the country into the global economy reflect fears that the country's "irreducible difference will remain aloof from, and impenetrable to, Western reason and universalism" (Morley and Robins 162).

Fear of Thailand's alien culture and its potentially powerful difference is most evident in AgriGen's attempts to penetrate the country's carefully protected seed banks. However, Akkarat, chief of Thailand's Trade Ministry, recognizes AgriGen's offers as an attempt to maintain the company's technological supremacy and economic power. When Anderson argues that opening up Thailand's borders to AgriGen and its science will benefit the kingdom, Akkarat challenges Anderson's claim of "mutual interests," reminding Anderson that the historical record of imperial contact has been one of exploitation and inequality: "This is not a question of perspective. Ever since your first missionaries landed on our shores, you have always sought to destroy us. During the old Expansion your kind tried to take every part of us. Chopping off the arms and legs of our country. . . . With the Contraction, your worshipped global economy left us starving and over-specialized. . . . And then your calorie plagues came" (150). From Akkarat's perspective, technological innovation and Western notions of progress have led only to increased starvation, global plague, and continued dependence on the First World. Akkarat recognizes the social cleavages that have been created by an information/global economy and understands that the consequences of uneven technological development translate to a form of neocolonial rule. As global inequality and suffering increase, *The Windup Girl* challenges the logic of progress and development, revealing the dangers of a global

economy constructed on the basic principles of what Manuel Castells identifies as patriarchalism and productivism.

An analysis of *The Windup Girl* must address the novel's cultural and
social references to Thailand as a place infamous for its sex tourism. Emiko's
status as an illegal windup caught in the sex trade embodies techno-Orientalist attitudes, in which her genetically manipulated body is associated with
assumptions regarding the supposed passivity of Asian women. The novel
suggests Emiko's subservience is a consequence less of her genetic variation
than of her social, political, and economic situation. As Andrew Hageman
states, "Emiko's exploitation in the Thai sex trade demonstrates that she has
been programmed with directives to please, and it is this automation to meet
market demands that in fact makes her an object that humans can treat with
repugnance or with utilitarian apathy" (295). Reduced to the level of technological commodity, Emiko is little better than a slave in every sense of the
word. Because prostitution has been illegal in Thailand since 1960, Emiko's
involvement in that occupation positions her outside legal protection. Furthermore, abandoned by her Japanese master in Bangkok, Emiko is also
an illegal alien with no political status. As an illegal immigrant, sex worker,
and someone considered subhuman, Emiko has no civic rights and is triply
excluded from any position of political autonomy or power. Emiko's narrative, then, reflects the situation encountered by many refugee women from
surrounding countries (including Burma, Laos, and Cambodia) who migrate
to Thailand in search of work, often participating in sex work or manual
labor. Already denied political autonomy as illegal refugees, migrant workers
are further excluded from any position of power as sex workers.[3] Though the
text's fictional representations cannot be seen as representative of prostitution
in Thailand, as an ethnoscape, the novel's setting highlights the economic,
social, and political histories of Thailand, moving readers away from traditionally "Western" focuses.

While a simplistic binary division between the West and the East may
be drawn in Bacigalupi's novel, racial antagonism is not unilateral, and
Thailand harbors many of its own prejudices. This is not a simple reversal
of Orientalism into "Occidentalism" (Robertson 192) but rather a somewhat
accurate reflection of the complex history of racial, ethnic, and religious tensions within Thailand as a whole. For example, in contemporary Thailand and
much of Southeast Asia, white skin is the foremost representative of beauty
and social status. Walter H. Persaud argues that the privileging of whiteness
is an effect of globalization and the history of cultural/political exchange in
Thailand. Furthermore, ethnic tensions in the novel also reflect the historical
record of conflict along the border of Thailand and Malaysia. Hock Seng, a

Buddhist and Chinese-Malay, flees north to Bangkok when "the brown people [turn] on the yellow people in Malaya" (202). "The brown people" to which
Hock Seng refers are "the Green Headbands" of Malaya (67), whose persecution of Chinese-Malays forces Hock Seng to live as a refugee in Thailand.
Hock Seng's escape to Bangkok from Malaysia mirrors the recent migration
of Buddhist citizens in southern Thailand to central or northern Thai provinces to escape the increasing violence between southern separatists (who are
primarily Muslim). Ethnic tensions on the Thai-Malay border can be traced
back to 1902, when Thailand annexed the areas that became its southernmost
provinces, which are populated predominantly by Malay Muslims. Though
violence between separatists and the Thai government has occurred for more
than half a century, it has escalated in the past ten years as a consequence of
poor government relations, lack of representation for local minorities, human
rights abuses by Thailand's military, and poor socioeconomic conditions in
the South.[4]

   The Windup Girl draws on Thailand's complex race relations. For example, the Environment Ministry attempts to impede the negative consequences
of globalization by resorting to a fierce nationalism that encourages antagonism against yellow cards and non-Thais as a way of protecting the "purity"
of Thailand. Consequently, when Hock Seng flees to Bangkok to escape the
Green Headbands, he finds that Thailand is not a haven free from racism. The
flight north enables many yellow cards to escape persecution and death; however, "native" Thais also harbor prejudices against yellow cards. For example,
Jaidee, a captain in the Environment Ministry and a native Thai, expresses his
dislike for Hock Seng and other Chinese-Malays" "Jaidee has a certain respect
for the Chaozhou Chinese. . . . They are utterly unlike the pathetic Chinese
refugees who have flooded in from Malaya, fleeing to his country in hopes of
succour after they alienated the natives of their own. If the Malayan Chinese
had been half as clever as the Chaozhou, they would have converted to Islam
generations ago, and woven themselves fully into the tapestry of that society. . . . The Chaozhou are smart, where the Malayan Chinese are stupid" (117).
Jaidee's extreme sense of nationalism, xenophobia, and fierce loyalty to the
Thai kingdom are reflected in his moniker: the "Tiger of Bangkok" (146). Like
the Environment Ministry, he treats immigrants and non-Thais as invasive
threats to the security of Thai government, economy, and culture, or as Hock
Seng says, "The Environment Ministry sees yellow cards the same way it sees
the other invasive species and plagues it manages" (224). As a result, when the
city breaks into war between the Environment Ministry and the Trade Ministry, yellow cards and foreigners suffer the most physical abuse at the hands
of the Thai military. Thailand's attempts to retaliate against imperialism by

inverting power structures only perpetuates a vicious cycle that feeds into the us-versus-them paradigm on which colonial rule is premised.

Hock Seng's distrust of Thai workers reflects the internalized prejudices and ongoing effects of colonial encounter across Southeast Asia. As manager of Anderson Lake's factory in Bangkok, Hock Seng works primarily with native Thais, though he constantly "curses that he works with Thais. They simply lack the spirit of entrepreneurship that a Chinese would throw into the work" (132). Hock Seng believes that "they are Thai. They are all incompetent" (14). The stereotype of the "lazy native" is a prejudice often rendered against native Thais, and Hock Seng's statement reflects discourses surrounding work/labor in Thailand, where ethnic "natives" are seen as less capable and ambitious than foreigners. Syed H. Alatas's influential critique of imperialism in *The Myth of the Lazy Native* (1977) analyzes the image of Malays, Filipinos, and Javanese as "dependent" (8) and lazy—an effect, Alatas argues, of persistent colonial ideologies and stereotypes in the region. Alatas contends that this myth "has led to certain discriminatory practices [and] a number of employers have avoided Malays because they believe them to be lazy [or] not endowed with the capacity to do business. All these ideas derive their origin from the colonial image of the Malays" (17). Alatas claims the colonial myth of the lazy native permeates even current constructions of Malaysians as dependent and requiring assistance. Though Alatas refers predominantly to the Malay Archipelago, his critique may be extended to Thailand, where the myth of the lazy native is also enacted against native Thais. Hock Seng, then, exhibits this colonial mentality, criticizing Thais for their lack of "the spirit of entrepreneurship" and incompetence (132).

Bacigalupi's novel emphasizes the manner in which ideological constructions of race are reinforced by a history of economic, social, and political relations. Not surprisingly, the list of racial slurs and epithets in the novel is much longer than what has been explored here. For example, as an outsider, Anderson is frequently called a "farang" (white foreigner) (31), "yang guizi" (foreign devil) (29), and "devil cat" (28). Bacigalupi's frequent use of racially loaded language is not, however, in the tradition of ethnocentric colonial fiction. Rather, the emphasis on racial distrust and animosity highlights the growing divisions among peoples forced to survive under the conditions of a brutal capitalist economy. Subject to racial discrimination and under a state of constant uncertainty and competition, Emiko's and Hock Seng's narratives are closely linked in their political exclusion as illegal aliens and their reduction to replaceable labor. This fact is made evident when Raleigh, a nefarious bar owner and pimp, threatens Emiko, "I own every part of you" (159). Emiko's cultural demarcation is not far removed from Hock Seng's status as a yellow card. When Bangkok is locked down after the death of Somdet Chao-praya (protector of Thailand's Child Queen and the most powerful figure in Thai government), "only a few people are allowed in and out, ones who show residence cards. Locals" (224). Because Hock Seng carries "only a yellow card for identification, it took [him] half the evening to traverse the city, avoiding checkpoints" (224). Hock Seng is thus positioned as migrant labor and, like Emiko, a refugee who must live in transit while denied social and political agency. By exploring diverse characters as they are affected by different political, social, and economic positions, *The Windup Girl*'s use of racial representations recognizes the complex history of race relations in Thailand, fracturing an Orientalist construction of Asia as a homogenous region.

Genetic Code and the "Informationalization of Race"

In addition to portraying the continued imperial and racist structures of a future Bangkok, *The Windup Girl* explores the effects of techno-Orientalism on scientific discourses—specifically, on the field of genetics. If "new technologies become subsumed into the discourse of racism" (Morley and Robins 172), Bacigalupi's novel examines the tensions between scientific objectivity and persistent racial prejudice, revealing, as Rieder puts it, that "the crux of racist ideology is not the opposition between civilization and savagery. It is rather the way scientific racism confuses cultural and natural phenomena" (109). This scientific racism is most evident in Gibbons, a genius scientist who has deserted AgriGen and is now harbored by Thailand to help the nation battle the mutating plagues of agricultural corporations and their genetically modified foods. *The Windup Girl* explores the relationships among science, biology, and culture through the development of genetic technologies, revealing that old race models persist in this future world where changes in communication technologies have ushered in a new color-blind age. Race in the novel is positioned through the paradigm of genetics, an equation that reiterates colonial mentalities and represents a disturbing manifestation of techno-Orientalism.

As a "generipper" (357), Gibbons is one of the few people in the novel to embrace New People; however, his scientific interest in New People as products of evolution also reduces the complexity of their lived experience to scientific fact. While New People are "raced" bodies marked by their supposed difference, Gibbons refers to Emiko as a genetic "design" with which he is familiar (357). Gibbons's claims to knowing and understanding Emiko are based on assumptions regarding her genetics, and his treatment of her as a programmed design reflects a shift in what Chow-White calls the "infor-mationalization of race," or the process by which globalization, changes in the global economy, and developments in information and communication technologies (ICTs) have resulted in a new mode of racialization. Chow-White explains that racial knowledge is now constructed in terms of genetic "information," reducing the politics of race to a matter of code (1181). In his words, "Where conventional conceptions of race have been articulated in terms of culture or phenotype, in the digital age, information is the material by which we work on racial meaning. . . . However, race as information does not replace the dependency of racialization on ethnicity or skin color. Rather, as the paradigm of race as culture emerged from the paradigm of race as biology, I would argue that the paradigm of race as information has emerged from both to create a new racial formation—the informationalization of race" (1171). Because genetic technologies that focus on programming DNA are ICTs, such technologies are not merely tools but global systems that act as sites negotiating racial meaning through data that are collected, stored, and analyzed. This results in new racial classification systems that mirror old hier-archal systems with seemingly neutral terms. As Chow-White argues, "Racial classification systems that used terms such as Negroid, Mongoloid and Cau-casian have become African, Asian, and European, which, on the surface, may appear more informational and descriptive than ideological" (1182). In addi-tion, Chow-White argues, the informationalization of race may continue to use the same markers of racialization (physical characteristics, ethnicity, and so forth) but does not always rely on them, as the structures of developing ICTs form new sites of creating and reworking racial meaning. *The Windup Girl* explores the dangers of this suppressed scientific racism through Gib-bons's treatment of Emiko.

Donna Haraway's earlier reflections on technoscience in her landmark essay, "A Cyborg Manifesto" (1985), also examine the implications of develop-ing communication technologies and biotechnology on discourses of race, gender, and class. Haraway outlines the transition from "old hierarchical dominations" to "scary new networks," a development she calls the "infor-matics of domination" (161). Both Haraway and Chow-White consider the development of communication sciences and biology integral in the move from an industrial society to an information system, emphasizing the changes biotechnologies and genetics make to our understanding of DNA as the ulti-mate code of human life (Haraway 162; Chow-White 1168). Gibbons embod-ies this mentality in the technical and often reductive language he uses to describe windups: to Gibbons, New People are subjects who are "easier to build" (243) and whose "mechanics" he "know[s] the secrets of" (358). Though

Gibbons appears to be helping Emiko when he agrees to help reverse her sterility, he in fact reduces her to the status of "genetic material" to be disassembled and reassembled (358). To Gibbons, Emiko's perceived difference is a result of her mechanics or biology. Despite Haraway's appeal for a move away from essentialism and naturalized difference in the face of changing technoscience, Bacigalupi's novel suggests, like Chow-White's study, a renewed (and troublesome) relationship between race and biology as a result of developing ICTs. Chow-White asserts that advancements in human genomics require us to reconsider the ways that technoscience may result in a reification of race, or a return to the "altar of biological determinism" (1185). As new scientific technologies and research develop, the need to examine the effects of technoscience on the discourse and politics of race becomes increasingly evident.

Gibbons's acceptance of New People seems to encourage a move away from identity politics and racist ideology; however, Gibbons's lack of ethical approach in his scientific endeavors reveals that he is motivated primarily by ego and power. His claims of authority over Emiko's genetic design show a paternalism and a desire for domination—a desire made all the more troubling by his wish to be the scientist, or "god," to lead humanity into "the Eden that beckons us" (243). Gibbons fails to see the dangers of a future where he, a white male scientist, continues to rule over racial and ethnic others. Though Gibbons appears only jokingly to call himself a "god" on numerous occasions (244), his sense of superiority permeates all his work. He views genetic manipulation as a technological tool divorced from ideology: "Our every tinkering in nature, our every biological striving. We are what we are, and the world is ours. We are its gods. Your only difficulty is in your unwillingness to unleash your potential fully upon it" (243). This genetic "tinkering," however, has resulted in a growing divide between the wealthy and poor, increased racial tensions, heightened nationalism, and global starvation. Gibbons is clearly not referring to this "potential."

Even as a supposedly objective scientist, Gibbons cannot see how his work is implicated in social and political structures. As a white scientist, protected and maintained by Thailand in exchange for his knowledge, Gibbons is further removed from the streets of Bangkok, where poverty and racism are everyday realities. Kanya realizes that because Gibbons is distanced from the realities of Thailand's struggling people, he sees his work as an intellectual game: "*We are in the hands of a gamesman.* In a flash of insight, Kanya understands the doctor entirely. . . . A man who found his competition too lacking, and so switched sides and joined the Thai Kingdom for the stimulation it might provide. . . . *We rest in the hands of a fickle god. He plays on our behalf only for entertainment, and he will close his eyes and sleep if we fail to engage his intellect....* The man exists only for competition, the chess match of evolution, fought on a global scale" (248). Gibbons's interest in Thailand and genetics is not motivated by compassion or empathy for the condition of others. While Gibbons appears to assist Emiko at the end of the novel, one cannot help but wonder whether he is fulfilling his dream of having "a few more worshippers" (244). Hageman also points out Gibbons's "discourse of deity," asserting that "despite the hospitality he shows to Emiko and the cheshires, Gibbons still frames his vision of the future in terms of 'gods' with dominion from a position atop a hierarchy" (297). Gibbons's supposed scientific rationalism reveals an imperial taste for power and domination. He is not altruistically motivated. As he explains to Kanya, Gibbons worked with AgriGen for so long because "they paid me in the coin I wanted most" (246).

If Gibbons highlights the scientific racism of future technoscience, as a genetically altered human, Emiko highlights the effects of this scientific racism on people of color. New People are engineered and thus considered "unnatural" (302) and "not human" (35). Emiko's genetic structure determines her value and worth, and her "difference" and innate passivity supposedly result from manipulated genetic code. Physically, Emiko's difference is barely visible except in a specific movement marked by its "heechy-keechy" stutter-stop motion (37). However, like Chow-White's assertion that physical traits work alongside the informationalization of race, what marks Emiko's "raced" body is not only her physical difference but her difference as manifested on an *informational* and *genetic* level. Her physical and genetic variation are considered indicative of innate difference, and Emiko often wishes her clients would "look at her, to see her instead of simply evaluating her as a piece of genetic trash" (37). Emiko is treated as "genetic trash" as a result of her race, and New People are considered a group containing immutable and predetermined differences from "natural" people. Because New People are treated as programmed "platform[s]" (357), Emiko is considered inherently subservient and incapable of autonomous thought and feeling, allowing others to continue to abuse her. Bacigalupi's vision of developing technoscience is bleak—this future is not color-blind; rather it is one where biotechnology reduces the complexities of human life to code.

As a windup whose genetic difference renders her subhuman, Emiko provides a narrative that reveals the ways genetic technologies may rearticulate racist and colonial ideologies. Emiko's biology is seen as predetermining her identity as racial Other. Furthermore, her alterity is seen as indicative of psychological and social difference, and Emiko must be trained to control her "animal" urges. Emiko's teacher, Mizumi-sensei, reinforces this idea when teaching New People that "there are two parts to a New Person's nature. The evil half, ruled by the animal hungers of their genes.... And balanced against this, the civilized self, the side that knows the difference between niche and animal urge. That comprehends its place in the hierarchies of their country and people" (154). Mizumi-sensei's instruction that New People must "own their souls" (154) and "civilize" their animal urges is reminiscent of colonial attempts to "civilize" different cultures. Racism has not disappeared, and as Emiko often laments, "Even if she is New People, there is nothing new under the sun" (38). The genetic variation of New People is treated as a condition designating one's inferiority, subservience, and obedience. However, as N. Katherine Hayles argues in her discussion of the posthuman, principles of reflexivity may reveal that "an attribute previously considered to have emerged from a set of pre-existing conditions is in fact used to generate the conditions" (9). In other words, Emiko's supposed inferiority is constructed through the stories, teachings, and prejudices that represent her need to serve as an already naturalized quality. Taught all her life that she is subservient and genetically built to follow orders, Emiko begins to question these narratives: "Does her eagerness to serve come from some portion of canine DNA that makes her always assume that natural people outrank her for pack loyalty? Or is it simply the training that she has spoken of?" (184).[5] Emiko's question reveals the reflexivity and dangers of naturalized difference—she cannot determine whether engineered genes have led to her servitude, or whether, as Hayles suggests, her servitude and submissiveness are attributes that produces precisely the differences they presuppose. Emiko's eventual defiance of her training and her ability to finally break free of her cycle of dependence on Raleigh and Anderson suggest that contrary to her genetic code, Gibbons may be correct in assuring Emiko, "Nothing about you is inevitable" (358).

Emiko's resistance to her training results in a double consciousness in which she is frequently torn by her conflicting feelings to serve or rebel. To draw on W. E. B. Du Bois's discussion of race in his magisterial study *The Souls of Black Folk* (1903), Emiko's internal struggle is a form of self-discipline in which she is constantly subject to a sense of looking at herself "through the eyes of others" (Du Bois 38). Whenever Emiko begins to question her role and hope for an alternative future, "she squashes the thought. It is the other Emiko who thinks this.... Two sides of a coin, two sides of the soul," a Du Boisian double consciousness (Bacigalupi 154).[6] Emiko frequently suppresses her desire to rebel, reminding herself that such desires are not part of her niche. This form of self-discipline divides Emiko's thoughts between what others expect of her and her own desires—"two warring ideals" in one body (Du Bois 38). As a result of this double consciousness, Emiko constantly struggles with her identity. However, as with Haraway's cyborg figure, not until Emiko embraces her partial and contradictory perspective does she begin to question the knowledge of her origins. While Emiko initially believes that her genes dictate her oppression, she complicates this viewpoint when she "wonders if she has it backwards, if the part that struggles to maintain her illusions of self-respect is the part intent upon her destruction. If her body, this collection of cells and manipulated DNA—with its own stronger, more practical needs—is actually the survivor: the one with will" (34). This does not mean that Emiko's body, "with its own stronger . . . needs," defines or preordains her to a predetermined future (even her inability to be fertile is not inevitable). Rather, to think of the body as entrapped by programmed social and genetic code is to deny the possibilities that reside in her multiple contradictions. Her "illusions of self-respect" are social and political structures that have required her to fulfill her role as a passive and subservient New Person, and it is not her supposed genetic difference that reinforces her subjugation. If "bodies are maps of power and identity" (Haraway 180), then Emiko's constant struggle with her identity recognizes that different bodies have been shaped by and participate in different historical, political, and social structures. Not until the latter half of the novel does Emiko begin to understand the effects of institutional regulation and imperial relations between New People and "natural people" as they affect her identity and life (184).

Emiko's politically and socially marginalized status suggests that the "color-blind language in human genomics" masks a return to biological determinism (Chow-White 1182). This color-blind language also hides the formation of new regimes of racial signification and discrimination in everyday practices and institutions. Because Emiko is a windup, she is an illegal alien in Thailand and therefore is denied political and social rights. Put another way, she "is a deeply maligned technoscientific posthuman" (Hageman 294). The Environment Ministry's strict regulations against New People mean that if Emiko is discovered, she will be immediately mulched and killed.[7] Emiko is not only legally marginalized; the physical abuse she must endure at the hands of Kannika, one of Raleigh's "natural" girls, to survive reminds us of the continued effects of institutional racism in her everyday life. Kannika's violence is accompanied by verbal abuse as she calls Emiko a "Japanese plaything," telling her she "will always be nothing, and for once the dirty Japanese get what is coming to them" (38–39). Emiko's association with Japanese high technology, simultaneously revered and despised, subjects her to a form of techno-Orientalism—because she is a female figure and Japanese technological commodity, Emiko's threatening difference reveals techno-Orientalist fears that the West's "loss of its technological hegemony may be associated with its cultural 'emasculation'" (Morley and Robins 167).

As a raced character, Emiko's "heechy-keechy" movements also mark her body as the body of a woman of color—"I am marked. Always, we are marked" (358)—and her continued abuse signifies the domination and exploitation of her body in the global political economy. Judged by her physical movements and genetic difference, Emiko mourns, "All they see are stutter-stop motions. A joke. An alien toy. A windup" (36). Though Judith Butler focuses on the sexed body when she suggests that the body is "shaped by political forces with strategic interests in keeping that body bounded and constituted by the markers of sex" (103), this argument may be extended to race. If the body is shaped by political and cultural forces, race and sex mark Emiko's body as that of commodity, slave, and dangerous Other. Markers such as Emiko's stutter-stop motion are designed to enforce her physical and ultimately social difference. As Gibbons explains to Emiko, "The windup movement is not a required trait. . . . The safeties are there because of lessons learned, but they are not required" (358). In other words, Emiko's body has quite literally been constructed to reinforce her subjugation. While identities cannot be disembodied, they are also always intimately bound by political and social relations.

Emiko eventually realizes that her biology does not predetermine her value or subject her to a life of servitude; rather, the practices and social structures of a world that "trained [her] to the eternal service of a master" do (252). In a world where New People are considered to be under the rule of those who are "natural," Emiko realizes she will always be viewed as simultaneously other than human and as less than human. As a result, Emiko dreams of escaping to the villages of the North, where New People supposedly live away from the laws of the Environment Ministry. During a moment that mirrors Victor Frankenstein's creature and his self-conscious awakening as he gazes into a pool of water, Emiko stares into the *khlong* waters and "sees herself in the canal's reflection with the green glow of the lamps all around. . . . She feels perhaps she could become one with the water. . . . Does she not deserve to float and slowly sink? She stifles the thought. That is the old Emiko. The one who could never teach her to fly" (253).[8] If Emiko once felt torn by a sort of double consciousness, it is at this moment that her "jesses" are cut free (252). A few pages later, Emiko fights against her allegedly ingrained passivity, retaliating against Raleigh, the Somdet Chaoparaya, and the men in Raleigh's bar in a moment of violent rage. Despite recognizing her ability to break free of her supposedly innate dependence and urge to follow orders, Emiko knows that she must eventually reach the northern villages to survive, since Bangkok remains structured on racist principles that privilege "natural" people. As a result, Emiko continues to struggle against her submission until the end, since she is still living in a world that requires her to be submissive despite the urge to rebel she often feels. These boundaries are so ingrained in Emiko and have become so naturalized that even Emiko admits "she has been enslaved to think against New People, even when she herself is one of them" (155). Though Emiko is told she will always serve, when she hears of the villages up north where New People have no masters, "she makes herself stare at the mess and recognize that she is no longer a slave. . . . She is something else" (252). Emiko never reaches these villages, but as Bangkok floods and its inhabitants flee, Emiko receives the space and freedom to begin the process of reversing her cultural training.

Racial Futures

The Windup Girl invokes a number of contemporary racial concerns, and its culturally diverse characters provide a point of departure for examining the importance of race in developing technoscience. Bacigalupi's reference to the social, economic, and political histories of Thailand situates discourses of race in the novel in a local context, avoiding simplistic binaries between East and West. Edward Said argues, "When one uses categories like Oriental and Western as both the starting and the end points of analysis . . . the result is usually to polarize the distinction . . . and limit the human encounter between different cultures, traditions, and societies" (45–46). Bacigalupi's novel avoids replicating the binary division between East and West, instead emphasizing what Haraway calls the "historical systems of domination" that link bodies and power (161). In this future, technological advancement does not result in a color-blind world but instead perpetuates the racist structures of a vampiric global economy. Instead of examining the developments of technoscience and race in an information society from a Western-centered perspective, Bacigalupi's novel attends to the complex history of race relations in Southeast Asia. In so doing, *The Windup Girl* departs from traditions of colonial adventure fiction by refusing to exoticize Thailand and producing an environment that foregrounds the intersections of race, technology, and imperial encounter. Bacigalupi's novel does not suggest a postracial alternative but emphasizes the potential for continuing ethnocentric/racist ideologies and practices in developing technoscience. In this estranged world, familiar patterns continue as bodies are raced by the changing discourses of genomics, information technologies, and globalization.

Notes

1. Despite its outdated and somewhat problematic use, I consider the term *Third World* informative and use it critically, following Ella Shohat and Robert Stam's definition in *Unthinking Eurocentrism: Multiculturalism and the Media*: "The 'Third World' refers to the colonized, neocolonized, or decolonized nations and 'minorities' whose structural disadvantages have been shaped by the colonial process and by the unequal division of international labor" (25; see also 25–27).

2. Some recent science fiction texts concerned with race, globalization, and the Third World include many of Ian McDonald's novels, such as *River of Gods* (2006), *Cyberabad Days* (2009), and *The Dervish House* (2010); Lauren Beukes's *Moxyland* (2008) and *Zoo City* (2010); and Geoff Ryman's *Air: Or Have Not Have* (2004), to name but a few.

3. For an excellent study on the complexities of migration and the sex trade in Thailand, see Jeffrey.

4. For more on the conflict in southern Thailand, see Abuza; McCargo.

5. Though not explored in detail here, Emiko's comparison to animals not only evokes slave comparisons to animals but also emphasizes the anthropocentrism of this future world.

6. Du Bois describes this double consciousness as "a peculiar sensation . . . this sense of always looking at one's self through the eyes of others, of measuring one's soul by the tape of a world that looks on in amused contempt and pity. One ever feels his two-ness,—an American, a Negro; two souls, two thoughts, two unreconciled strivings; two warring ideals in one dark body" (38).

7. Hageman also reflects on this idea, stating that Emiko is "an illegal non-human alien who would be shredded and recycled if discovered" (294).

8. In Mary Shelley's *Frankenstein: or, The Modern Prometheus* (1831), Victor Frankenstein's creature gazes into a pool, comparing himself to the cottage dwellers he so admires: "I had admired the perfect forms of my cottagers—their grace, beauty, and delicate complexions: but how was I terrified when I view myself in a transparent pool! At first I started back, unable to believe that it was indeed I who was reflected in the mirror; and when I became fully convinced that I was in reality the monster that I am, I was filled with the bitterest sensations of despondence and mortification" (116). Like Frankenstein's creature, Emiko is trapped by her marked body and her ambitions of freedom.

Works Cited

Abuza, Zachary. *A Conspiracy of Silence: The Insurgence in Southern Thailand.* Washington, DC: United States Institute of Peace, 2009. Print.

Alatas, Syed H. *The Myth of the Lazy Native: A Study of the Image of the Malays, Filipinos, and Javanese from the Sixteenth to the Twentieth Century and Its Function in the Ideology of Colonial Capitalism.* New York: Routledge, 1977. Print.

Bacigalupi, Paolo. *Pump Six and Other Stories.* San Francisco: Nightshade, 2008. Print.

——. *Ship Breaker*. New York: Little Brown, 2010. Print.

——. *The Windup Girl*. San Francisco: Nightshade, 2009. Print.

Beukes, Lauren. *Moxyland*. Nottingham: Angry Robot, 2008. Print.

——. *Zoo City*. Nottingham: Angry Robot, 2010. Print.

Bould, Mark. "The Ships Landed Long Ago: Afrofuturism and SF." *Science Fiction Studies* 34.2 (2007): 177–86. Print.

Butler, Judith. *The Judith Butler Reader*. Ed. Judith Butler and Sara Salih. Malden: Blackwell, 2004. Print.

Castells, Manuel. *End of Millennium*. Vol. 3 of *The Information Age: Economy, Society, and Culture*. Malden: Blackwell, 1998. Print.

Chow-White, Peter A. "The Informationalization of Race: Communication Technologies and the Human Genome in the Digital Age." *International Journal of Communication* 2 (2008): 1168–94. Online. 15 May 2012.

Csicsery-Ronay, Istvan, Jr. *The Seven Beauties of Science Fiction*. Middletown: Wesleyan UP, 2008. Print.

Du Bois, W. E. B. *The Souls of Black Folk*. 1903. New York: Bantam, 1989. Print.

Hageman, Andrew. "The Challenge of Imagining Ecological Futures: Paolo Bacigalupi's *The Windup Girl*." *Science Fiction Studies* 39.2 (2012): 283–303.

Haraway, Donna. "A Cyborg Manifesto: Science, Technology, and Socialist-Feminism in the Late Twentieth Century" (1985). *Simians, Cyborgs and Women: The Reinvention of Nature*. New York: Routledge, 1991. 149–81. Print.

Hayles, N. Katherine. *How We Became Posthuman: Virtual Bodies in Cybernetics, Literature, and Informatics*. Chicago: U of Chicago P, 1999. Print.

Huang, Betsy. *Contesting Genres in Contemporary Asian American Fiction*. New York: Palgrave Macmillan, 2010. Print.

Jeffrey, Leslie Ann. *Sex and Borders: Gender, National Identity, and Prostitution Policy in Thailand*. Vancouver: U of British Columbia P, 2002. Print.

Lavender, Isiah, III. *Race in American Science Fiction*. Bloomington: Indiana UP, 2011. Print.

McCargo, Duncan. *Tearing Apart the Land: Islam and Legitimacy in Southern Thailand*. Ithaca: Cornell UP, 2008. Print.

McDonald, Ian. *Cyberabad Days*. Amherst: Pyr, 2009. Print.

——. *The Dervish House*. Amherst: Pyr, 2010. Print.

——. *River of Gods*. Amherst: Pyr, 2006. Print.

Morley, David, and Kevin Robins. *Spaces of Identity: Global Media, Electronic Landscapes and Cultural Boundaries*. New York: Routledge, 1995. Print.

Persaud, Walter H. "Gender, Race, and Global Modernity: A Perspective from Thailand." *Globalizations* 2.2 (2005): 210–27. Print.

Rieder, John. *Colonialism and the Emergence of Science Fiction*. Middletown: Wesleyan UP, 2008. Print.

Robertson, Roland. "Japan and the USA: The Interpretation of National Identities and the Debate about Orientalism." *Dominant Ideologies*. Ed. Nicholas Abercrombie, Stephen Hill, and Bryan S. Turner. London: Unwin Hyman. 182–98. Print.

Ryman, Geoff. *Air: Or Have Not Have*. New York: St. Martin's Griffin, 2004. Print.

Said, Edward. *Orientalism*. New York: Pantheon, 1978. Print.

Shelley, Mary. *Frankenstein; or, The Modern Prometheus*. 1831. New York: Airmon, 1963. Print.

Shohat, Ella, and Robert Stam. *Unthinking Eurocentrism: Multiculturalism and the Media*.
     New York: Routledge, 1994. Print.

Sohn, Stephen H. "Introduction: Alien/Asian: Imagining the Racialized Future." *MELUS* 33.4
     (2008): 5–22. Print.

REFLECTIONS ON "YELLOW, BLACK, METAL, AND TENTACLED," TWENTY-FOUR YEARS ON
• • •

EDWARD JAMES

In 1988 or thereabouts, Americanist Philip J. Davies asked me to contribute to a book he was editing, *Science Fiction, Social Conflict, and War* (1990). I offered to write him a piece either on race in American science fiction or on violent revolution. To my consternation, he asked me to write both, which I duly did: I presume they filled what seemed to him to be gaps in the book. The invitation had come at a time when I had begun to do serious work in science fiction (even though my actual job was teaching medieval history). I was editing *Foundation: The International Review of Science Fiction*, on behalf of the Science Fiction Foundation. I had already begun teaching science fiction, under the guise of utopias, within the wonderful slot in the University of York's history syllabus called "Comparative Specials." When I was involved in teaching "Race and Society," which ranged from the Roman Empire to South Africa in the twentieth century, I taught alongside historians of medieval Spain, of the Middle East, of twentieth-century Europe, of the United States, and of Africa. That teaching inspired me to tackle the topic of race in modern science fiction.

In retrospect it was rash of me—a white Englishman, only on the fringes of American studies—to take on the project, and I almost certainly would not have done so had there been anything else that seemed to deal with the topic. I found some useful articles in *Extrapolation* and in *Science Fiction Studies*, but in the absence of the kind of Internet-based research tools that are now available, I was left wondering whether some published work out there made mine quite redundant. I really could not imagine that there had not been a book on the topic. But it seems that there had not. Not until 1997 did Elisabeth A. Leonard publish the first full book on race in the fantastic, a collection of essays called *Into Darkness Peering: Race and Color in the Fantastic*, where she kindly noted, to my surprise, that my article was "probably the best single survey of the issue" (11). The first monographs that concerned themselves with race in fantastic literature took even longer to emerge: they were Sharon DeGraw's *The Subject of Race in American Science Fiction* (2007) and Isiah Lavender III's *Race in American Science Fiction* (2011). Other books had touched on the issue (those by De Witt Douglas Kilgore and Jeffrey Alan Tucker) or had looked at race in the media (Sierra Adare, Daniel Bernardi, Eric Greene, Micheal C. Pounds, and more recently Adilifu Nama). But DeGraw and Lavender were the first to publish monographs on race in SF literature, and both have given us an enormous amount to think about.

The accumulated effect of all this work published since 1997 has been to highlight the defects of my 1990 piece. Of course—that's how scholarship works! Some of these defects resulted from pure ignorance: for example, I had never heard of the science fiction of George S. Schuyler, whose *Black No More* (1931) is the first significant SF work by an African American. I was also almost certainly guilty of making hasty judgments about some of the more significant works by white Americans that allude to or treat race relations. Robert A. Heinlein's *Farnham's Freehold* (1965) is the most obvious of these texts.

My most grievous shortcoming, however, was almost certainly not to think through properly the implications of what Eric S. Rabkin and Robert Scholes argued in *Science Fiction: History, Science, Vision* (1977). Near the beginning of my piece, I summarize, "They suggest that there has for some time been a general assumption among SF writers that in the future the question of black/white relations would wither away. This is often conveyed subtly, by the absence of reference to the problem, that is, by an unstated assumption that it has been solved." This statement of fact is probably accurate, although of course I should have written "a general assumption among white SF writers." If I were writing this piece today, I would have stressed that these white SF writers, few of them right-wing in their politics, had simply failed to think how this problem could have been solved in the future. It is an issue that they almost never address head-on. As a result, an impression is often given that the white person is the default and that "the race problem" has been solved by the disappearance, somehow or other, of minority racial groups. As Richard Pryor put it in *Bicentennial Nigger* (1976), "They had a movie of the future called *Logan's Run*. Ain't no niggers in it. I said, 'Well, white folks ain't planning for us to be here'" (qtd. in Nama 10). The literary erasure of an entire ethnic group (such as was envisaged in Patricia C. Wrede's *The Thirteenth Child*, May 2009 criticism of which unleashed the second phase of the great RaceFail debate)[1] is not something that most people find acceptable today, but I was not alone in being blind about this twenty-four years ago. All I can say in defense of my younger self is that back then at least I thought that "race in American science fiction" was an extremely important topic, and I was right to think so. I was also right to stress, I believe, that the topic should include examination not just of the place of African Americans in the United States, but of Native Americans, Latino Americans, Chinese Americans—there is a very long list. Nevertheless, looking at the books whose authors I have named here shows what great strides science fiction scholarship has taken since 1990.

Note

1. RaceFail was a name given to a heated spring 2009 online science fiction fandom debate tinged by racism, culture clash, and misapprehension between fans and writers regarding the Other being written in science fiction.

Works Cited

Adare, Sierra S. *"Indian" Stereotypes in TV Science Fiction: First Nations' Voices Speak Out.* Austin: U of Texas P, 2005. Print.

Bernardi, Daniel L. *Star Trek and History: Race-ing toward a White Future.* New Brunswick: Rutgers UP, 1998. Print.

Davies, Philip J., ed. *Science Fiction, Social Conflict, and War.* Manchester: Manchester UP, 1990. Print.

DeGraw, Sharon. *The Subject of Race in American Science Fiction.* New York: Routledge, 2007. Print.

Greene, Eric. *Planet of the Apes as American Myth: Race and Politics in the Films and Television Series.* 1996. Jefferson: McFarland, 2006. Print.

Heinlein, Robert A. *Farnham's Freehold.* 1965. New York: Baen, 2011. Print.

James, Edward. "Yellow, Black, Metal, and Tentacled: The Race Question in American Science Fiction." *Science Fiction, Social Conflict, and War.* Ed. Philip J. Davies. Manchester: Manchester UP, 1990. 26–49. Print.

Kilgore, De Witt D. *Astrofuturism: Science, Race, and Visions of Utopia.* Philadelphia: U of Pennsylvania P, 2003. Print.

Lavender, Isiah, III. *Race in American Science Fiction.* Bloomington: Indiana UP, 2011. Print.

Leonard, Elisabeth A., ed. *Into Darkness Peering: Race and Color in the Fantastic.* Westport: Greenwood, 1997. Print.

Nama, Adilifu. *Black Space: Imagining Race in Science Fiction Film.* Austin: U of Texas P, 2008. Print.

Pounds, Micheal C. *Race in Space: The Representation of Ethnicity in Star Trek and Star Trek: The Next Generation.* Lanham: Scarecrow, 1999. Print.

Pryor, Richard. *Bicentennial Nigger.* Warner Bros., 1976. Audiocassette.

Rabkin, Eric S., and Robert Scholes. *Science Fiction: History, Science, Vision.* New York: Oxford UP, 1977. Print.

Schuyler, George S. *Black No More.* 1931. Boston: Northeastern UP, 1989. Print.

Tucker, Jeffrey A. *A Sense of Wonder: Samuel R. Delany, Race, Identity, and Difference.* Hanover: Wesleyan UP, 2004.

Wrede, Patricia C. *The Thirteenth Child.* New York: Scholastic, 2009. Print.

YELLOW, BLACK, METAL, AND TENTACLED
The Race Question in American Science Fiction

• • •

EDWARD JAMES

The "race question," the problem of the relations between different "racial" groups, has been in existence in North America since the earliest contacts between Europeans and Amerindians. With the arrival of other ethnic groups, above all African slaves, and with the rise of nineteenth-century science, which perceived those groups as biologically distinct races and ready to be ranked in terms of ability and potential, the "race question" took a very different form. In some circumstances during the history of the United States it has been the occasion of considerable political and social turmoil; it has always been simmering beneath the surface, with great potential for tension and social conflict. The celebrated English medieval historian E. A. Freeman, who narrated the course of the eleventh-century conquest of the Anglo-Saxon race by the Normans, caused a minor scandal on a lecture tour of the United States in 1881 by pronouncing that this race question would be solved if every Irishman in America could be hanged for the murder of a Negro.[1] It is a useful reminder that historically the "race question" does not just involve American blacks. Nor is the race question in North America, of course, nearly as simple as Freeman envisaged; it involved, and to some extent still does involve, Native Americans, Hispanics, Jews, Poles, Italians, Chinese, Japanese, and others as well as blacks and the Irish. The "science" of race has been written almost entirely by Anglo-Saxons, who used all kinds of measurements—particularly of skulls and of intelligence—to demonstrate the fact (which was obvious to them before they began) that Anglo-Saxons were superior in almost every way.[2] In the late twentieth century, there are very few scientists who subscribe to nineteenth-century racial science, but popular prejudices remain, and those scientific ideas to some extent survive to feed them.

We might expect science fiction writers, as authors of a genre of popular literature, to reflect the racial prejudice in their own society to some extent; we might also expect that as science fiction writers, they may be using their fiction to educate their readers in the current state of scientific opinion— although that, too, of course, is often the product of current political and social realities. It is worth emphasizing at this point that almost all the writers whom we are discussing are themselves white, and most of them WASP; the attitudes of the two best-known black American SF authors, Samuel R. Delany and Octavia Butler, have been discussed by Littlefield, by Bonner, and by Salvaggio.

Eric S. Rabkin and Robert Scholes, in their general book on science fiction, congratulate the science fiction author, collectively, on having moved well in advance of public opinion on race (187–89). They see the xenophobia that created Bug-Eyed Monsters in the early days of SF (as characterized by the Martians of Wells's *The War of the Worlds*) yield to more hospitable notions of the alien in the 1930s, under the influence of writers such as Stanley G. Weinbaum. They suggest that there has for some time been a general assumption among SF writers that in the future, the question of black-white relations would wither away. This is often conveyed subtly, by the absence of reference to the problem—that is, by an unstated assumption that it has been solved; they cite the shock of pleasure felt by the young Samuel R. Delany when he was reading Robert Heinlein's *Starship Troopers* (1959) and "halfway through the book the hero looks into a mirror and a black face looks back at him. In the book, this is not remarkable in any way, and many readers are probably not even aware that the hero is black."[3] Similarly, it would take a very careful reader of Ursula K. Le Guin's *The Left Hand of Darkness* (1969) to notice that the only Earthman in the story is dark-skinned and flat-nosed. William Hjortsberg's *Gray Matters* (1971) is much more direct; the hero chooses to move his consciousness into a black body because of its beauty, but thereafter, in Hjortsberg's book as in Heinlein's and Le Guin's, the reader loses any sense of "race" as being special. Rabkin and Scholes do bemoan the "boys" of Asimov's *I, Robot* stories, which we shall discuss below, and gently chide Bradbury for making his point in "Way in the Middle of the Air" (a story in *The Martian Chronicles*) by means of racial stereotypes (shambling blacks and southern rednecks), but nevertheless they celebrate the fact that SF has moved the racial boundaries: the human race is seen as one and united, and the problem is what attitude to take to the aliens beyond. "Science fiction, in fact, has taken the question so spiritedly raised by the founding fathers of the United States—of whether the rights of man included black slaves as well as white slave-owners—and raised it to a higher power by asking whether the rights of being end at the boundaries of the human race" (Rabkin and Scholes 189).

A cynic might wonder at this point whether the latent xenophobia of so many members of the human race—including SF writers—has not been transferred from the human to the alien. The black soldier of *Starship Troopers* spent his time slaughtering the Bugs; Ender Wiggin, the hero of Orson Scott Card's enormously successful *Ender's Game*, committed successful genocide on the Buggers (although he spent *Speaker for the Dead* feeling guilty about it), while in the 1987 film *Aliens*, another reprise of *Starship Troopers*, Sigourney Weaver's liberated heroine, Ripley, again wipes out insect-like aliens. Bug-Eyed Monsters have perhaps had a revival since Rabkin and Scholes put them to rest in 1977. And, indeed, the role of the race question in science fiction may be rather more complex than Rabkin and Scholes imply. Earthly races do appear in science fiction. But they may also appear in disguise, in what Gary K. Wolfe has seen as two of the most powerful icons in SF, both of which represent the Other in its relationship to humanity: the icon of the robot and the icon of the monster. The problem of the recognition of race in SF will be dealt with at the end, after discussion of the more obvious treatments of the theme.

That science fiction does indeed share the general change in racial attitudes which we have witnessed this century is clear enough, however, and can be appreciated most obviously when looking at the treatment of the "yellow races" in SF.[4] These are much more significant than the blacks in nineteenth-century SF, perhaps because blacks were so disregarded as not to appear a threat. Clareson finds only one story where there is a rebellion of American blacks against the whites: King Wallace's *The Next War* (1892), where the American blacks flee into the southern swamps, there to disappear, after their plot to poison their employers fails (Clareson 54–55). But there are any number of late-nineteenth-century stories of the invasion of the United States by the Chinese, even before the Englishman M. P. Shiel's *The Yellow Danger* (1898) unleashed the Chinese on Europe and created the phrase *the Yellow Peril*.[5] The theme dates back, as Clareson has noted, to the importation of Chinese coolie labor into California, denounced, for instance, in Pierton W. Dooner's *Last Days of the Republic* (1880) as "a race of people whom Nature has marked as inferior, and who are incapable of progress or intellectual development beyond a certain point" (Clareson 69). Robert Woltor in 1882 imagined the Chinese taking over California and Oregon in 1899; Arthur Dudley Vinton's *Looking Further Backward* (1890) had Professor Wun Lung Lai as the successor to Julian West—the main character, of course, of Edward Bellamy's *Looking Backward, 2000 to 1887* (1888)—as professor of modern history at Shawmut College, following the Chinese takeover of 2020. After 1905, and the

Japanese victory over the Russian Empire, the racial epithets once used of the Chinese are transferred to the Japanese, as they attack the States in such books as Marsden Manson's *The Yellow Peril in Action* (1907) or J. U. Giesy's *All for His Country* (1915). Among a welter of racist futures, one eccentric stands out; Clareson reckons him "unique among both American and Western European writers" (76). This is Floyd Gibbons, who published *The Red Napoleon* in 1929. This documents the conquests of Karakhan, the Mongol leader of the Soviet Union, during the 1930s; he takes Poland in 1933 and Boston in 1934. Like most Oriental invaders of the civilized West, Karakhan's hordes rape the white women they find; the idea of miscegenation can be relied upon to horrify (and secretly to fascinate?) readers of the time. Unlike most authors, however, Gibbons almost approves of Karakhan's order to "CONQUER AND BREED" (2), because of his sympathy with Karakhan's aims, which were to end racial prejudice via miscegenation: "The hatred between the colours and the species must be stamped out.... I recognise but one race—the HUMAN RACE" (463).

Most writers are much less broad-minded than Gibbons, and race hatred continues right through the fiction of the 1920s and 1930s. The editor Hugo Gernsback noted in 1930 that both writers and readers of *Air Wonder Stories* seemed to assume that all the magazine wanted to print were stories of air banditry, of men who wanted to control the world, and of aerial warfare between the yellow races and the white.[6] Stories of the Asian conquest of the United States in fact continued to be published for a long time, up to and beyond the greatest of them all, Philip K. Dick's *The Man in the High Castle* (1962), the alternate history novel in which the Japanese and Germans parcel out the world after their victory in the Second World War; a recent example is Frederik Pohl's *Black Star Rising* (1985). The modern manifestation of the fear of the Yellow Peril, I suppose, can be found in those numerous cyberpunk futures of the last decade in which the Japanese are the dominant world power; the classic manifestation is the short story by the "proto-cyberpunk" Norman Spinrad, "A Thing of Beauty." But Dick, Pohl, Spinrad, and the cyberpunks depict the resulting racism in a neutral way and portray the conquerors or dominant people in sympathetic fashion. The last major SF writer to use the theme in an apparently racist way was Robert A. Heinlein, in his very early novel *The Day after Tomorrow*.[7]

In this novel the PanAsians have conquered the United States; the story tells of the founding of the resistance movement and its ultimate success. PanAsians are "monkeys" and "flat-faces" who speak in a "meaningless singsong"; the final battle was "more in the nature of vermin extermination" (157). But alongside the racial invective, Heinlein does offer a more reflective view of the enemy. At the beginning, Ardmore, one of the leaders of the resistance, wonders about this "crazy new world—a world in which the superiority of western culture was not a casually accepted 'Of course'" (15). Soon afterward, another member of the resistance, Thomas, meets Finny, an old anarchist, who makes him realize that he should not view the PanAsians as *bad*. "Since the anarchist believed that all government was wrong and that all men were to him *in fact* brothers, the difference was to him one of degree only. Looking at the PanAsians through Finny's eyes there was nothing to hate; they were simply more misguided souls whose excesses were deplorable" (27). Finny told Thomas, "Don't make the mistake of thinking of the PanAsians as bad— they're not—but they *are* different. Behind their arrogance is a racial inferiority complex, a mass paranoia, that makes it necessary for them to prove to themselves by proving to us that a yellow man is just as good as a white man, and a damned sight better." The PanAsians, "a mixed race, strong, proud, and prolific," are "simply human beings, who have been duped into the old fallacy of the State as a super-entity. '*Ich habe einen Kameraden.* Once you understand the nature of—' He went off into a long dissertation, a mixture of Rousseau, Rocker, Thoreau and others. Thomas found it inspirational, but unconvincing" (27). Thomas is not convinced—but Heinlein very soon puts him in a position which again teaches him that particular characteristics are a result of political conditioning, not racial inheritance. He goes to a hobo hideout and meets his old friend, Frank Roosevelt Mitsui, a Californian farmer, "as American as Will Rogers, and much more American than that English aristocrat, George Washington" (29). Thomas has the common prejudices. He talks of "the swarm of brown kids that were Frank's most important crop," and "the sight of a flat, yellow face in a hobo jungle made Thomas' hackles rise. Well as he knew Frank, Thomas was in no mood to trust an Oriental" (30). But when he learns how much Frank Matsui had suffered (the PanAsians were slaughtering Americanized Orientals), Thomas realizes and conquers his own prejudice: it is a theme which, as we shall see, Heinlein developed in the course of the 1950s.

This novel by Heinlein, published almost on the eve of Pearl Harbor (and the consequent internment of thousands of Americanized Orientals like Matsui), despite its use of racial terminology, seems to be an attempt to get people to think about common prejudices as well as about the nature of religion (the PanAsians are in the end defeated thanks to the creation of a fake religion by the resistance). That no doubt explains how it can have continued to be reprinted in a very different climate. Another fate entirely was in store for a much better known veteran of war against the Yellow Peril: Buck Rogers.

The Buck Rogers opus has been very nicely used by Alan Kalish and others, in the course of an examination of textual variants, as an illustration of the changes in racial attitudes between the heyday of the Yellow Peril and our own more circumspect times. The first versions are the two original stories of 1928 and 1929, by Philip Francis Nowlan; the fix-up novelization called *Armageddon 2419* was produced in 1962; and the most recent revision, by the SF writer Spider Robinson, dates from 1978. The original Buck Rogers stories tell of the invasion of the Chinese, "fierce Mongolians, who, as scientists now [AD 2419] contend, had in their blood a taint not of this earth"; they crush the United States and kill over four-fifths of the "American race." The Mongolians are also referred to as the Hans (the text also, confusingly, refers to the "non-Han Mongolians of Japan"); the possibility that they are in fact not human but alien presumably makes their annihilation somewhat more acceptable. The epic ends as the Han cities "were destroyed and their populations hunted down," and the American example gives a lead to the other subject peoples of the Han, leading to the utter "extermination" of "that monstrosity among the races" (Kalish et al. 305).

Kalish and his coauthors look at a number of different aspects of textual variants in the Buck Rogers opus, reflecting on changes over a fifty-year period in humor, in vocabulary and style, in scientific knowledge, and in attitudes toward gender and sex[8] and toward ethnicity and race. Even the picture of the United States of the future has been subtly altered. Nowlan gave all his future Americans pure Anglo-Saxon names; the later editions made America much more ethnically diverse, with Boss Hart becoming Boss Ciardi, for instance, and Barker becoming Fabre. More importantly, the references to the enemies of America and of Buck Rogers have been softened. "Yellow incubus" becomes "Hans"; "inhuman yellow blight" becomes "inhuman blight"; the fight to the death between the "Yellow and White Races in America" becomes the war between "the Mongolians and our forces." The 1962 edition also removes panegyrics on "the utmost of nobility in this modern, virile, rugged American race," and the 1978 version makes the "simple and spiritual" blacks of Africa "wise and spiritual." The elimination of the racial slurs in the later editions, as Kalish et al. note, makes the final excuses that the Han may in fact be alien in origin rather less hypocritical. But "whether they are 'yellow devils' or just 'Hans,' it is clear that the story's intent is to stir up hatred and attempt to justify massacre. Extraterrestrial or not, the Hans look like humans, talk like humans, breed fertile offspring with humans, and create a recognisably human culture. Ethically considered, they are human beings, and killing one is a homicide. We are asked to rejoice at the end of all three versions at killing all of the Hans, at the utter extermination of a people" (Kalish et al. 315; see also Stephensen-Payne).[9]

Another writer of the early decades of the twentieth century, and far more popular than Nowlan, was Edgar Rice Burroughs. The racism of the Tarzan books, directed against the blacks of Africa, is apparent and open and has often been commented on. The racism of the Martian novels is more apposite here, and if it is equally apparent, it is veiled in what would become typically science fictional guises, as Benjamin S. Lawson has shown (esp. 213–16). Burroughs' Mars is a multiracial and multicolored society—with whites, blacks, reds, greens, blacks, and men "with skins the colour of a ripe lemon" who each play the part of Orientals, Africans, and American Indians rolled into one. This is sometimes revealed by Burroughs with charming simplicity, as when (with perhaps quite unconscious punning) he refers to the magnificent caravan of the green Martians as having "a barbaric splendour . . . which would have turned an East Indian potentate green with envy" (*Princess* 83). But Lawson has convincingly argued that American Indians supply the major analogy;[9] the series starts with John Carter fleeing the Apache in Arizona and being transported to "Barsoom," Mars, with its deserts and exotic natives— one of whom, the red-skinned Dejah Thoris, becomes his own (egg-laying) Pocahontas: it is an Arizona transformed and romanticized to excess. John Carter, with his southern American prejudices, finds this multiracial society difficult, even though the natives act not unlike the lower races back home, with Martians such as the monstrous green Tal Hajus lusting after Carter's red princess. "The thought that the divine Dejah Thoris might fall into the clutches of such an abysmal atavism started the cold sweat" on John Carter; he hoped that she would act like those "brave frontier women of my lost land who took their own lives rather than fall into the hands of the Indian braves" (*Princess* 66). Later Carter imagines her being torn apart by great apes, "her bleeding corpse dragged through the dirt and the dust, until at last a part of it would be rescued to be served as food upon the tables of the black nobles" (*Gods* 162), a centuries-old fear among Europeans, which would have been relished by the celebrated inmate of Charenton. Yet after slaughtering the colored folks of Mars by the thousand, Carter, or Burroughs, comes in the end to imagine the possibility of reconciliation. He learns that the magnificent red men of Mars are in fact the result of the miscegenation between blacks and a yellow-reddish people who flourished in the past. "Ages of close relationship and intermarriage had resulted in the race of red men, of which Dejah Thoris was a fair and beautiful daughter" (*Princess* 63). Carter himself had lived, in disguise, as a red, a white, and a yellow, and his best friend was the jolly green giant Tars Tarkas. *The Warlord of Mars* ends with Carter musing on the possibilities of peace. "The hand of every race and nation was raised in continual strife against the men of every other land and colour. Today, by the might of my sword and the loyalty of the friends my sword has made for me, black man and white, red man and green, rubbed shoulders in peace and good fellowship." All he needed was to cement the "fierce yellow race" to the others and he would rest happy (124).

An appreciation of the un-Americanness of racism became much more apparent to American writers after the rise of Hitler. As early as December 1933, *Astounding* published "Ancestral Voices" by Nat Schachner, which had Attila the Hun being killed in an encounter with a time machine, which caused, in the twentieth century, the immediate disappearance of two of his descendants—a Jew called Max Bernstein and a German called Hans Schilling—all while a dictator called Herr Hellwig is ranting about racial purity. As Carter notes, readers seem to have readily understood the political point but did not comment on this idea that, racially speaking, all Europeans were totally mongrelized (117). It was the same Nat Schachner who in *The Writer* in August 1945 called on authors to avoid the standard ethnic stereotypes, telling them that if they portray members of ethnic minorities as individuals, "we will be doing more to eliminate the vicious Nazi myths . . . than a thousand pulpit sermons and a thousand ponderous editorials" (Carter 138).

After the Second World War, it is clear that the "race question" is above all the question of the place of blacks in American society. Many of the stories we shall be looking at come from the crucial period of the fifties. Let us briefly recall some dates, as a reminder of the political background. In 1950, the NAACP (the National Association for the Advancement of Colored Peoples) agreed to launch a legal assault on racial segregation in schools. In 1954, the Supreme Court created the *Brown* decision, condemning such discrimination as contrary to the Fourteenth Amendment; almost exactly a year later, it ruled that the *Brown* decision be implemented "with all deliberate speed." In December 1955, the young Martin Luther King led the bus boycott in Montgomery, Alabama. In 1957, nine black students were enrolled in the Central High School at Little Rock, Arkansas; thousands of soldiers and National Guard were called in to keep the peace. In February 1960, the restaurant sit-ins began, in Greensboro, North Carolina. In 1963, after a massive protest march on Washington, Kennedy launched a comprehensive civil rights bill; bloody riots swept northern cities as well as states like Mississippi. The bill became law in 1964; Martin Luther King was awarded the Nobel Peace Prize.

Science fiction writers respond to this prolonged process with bitter stories of indignation and with underplayed educational fervor. As an example, we can take four novels—three of them aimed at the young—which Robert Heinlein wrote during a short period in the mid-fifties. Fred Erisman has looked at these recently and sees them, surely correctly, as being a deliberate attempt at education in racial tolerance. Heinlein's interest in the question emerges fairly soon after the war. There is a black among the scientists "who died for the truth that makes men free" in "The Black Pits of Luna" (1948); the Interplanetary Patrol of *Space Cadet* (1948) is multiracial, with race relations emerging as a specific issue when three Patrol cadets have to deal with a clash between a civilian pilot and the natives of Venus. But the four novels of the mid-fifties—*The Star Beast* (1954), *Tunnel in the Sky* (1955), *Time for the Stars* (1956), and *Double Star* (1956), are all, Erisman argues, powered by this contemporary debate about civil rights.

The Star Beast has its inevitable all-knowing all-competent Heinlein father figure; he is the Right Hon. Henry Gladstone Kiku, a Kenyan. His main problem, as a diplomat, is to deal with an alien race, yet he has an irrational hostility toward the alien ambassador: "He knew that he should not harbor race prejudice, not in this job. He was aware intellectually that he himself was relatively safe from persecution that could arise from differences of skin and hair and facial contour for the one reason that weird creatures such as Dr Ftaemi had made the differences between breeds of men seem less important" (83). The alien, interestingly, understands the problem: all races everywhere have this in-built hostility: "All languages carry within them a portrait of their users, and the idioms of every language say over and over again, 'He is a stranger and therefore a barbarian'" (113). Racial prejudices are natural, therefore, but have to be recognized as illogical and harmful.

The symbol of competence in *Tunnel in the Sky* is not only black but female: Caroline Mshiyeni. She becomes city manager; her sister is an assault captain in the Amazons. Alfred McNeil ("Uncle" or "Unc"), in *Time for the Stars*, on the other hand, is, outwardly, Uncle Tom reborn. Yet he too is shown to be intelligent, a good manager of people, and a model of humanity. Heinlein used Kiku, Mshiyeni, and Unc to demonstrate that "if a society is to endure, it must look to what a person is and can do rather than to that person's color or sex" (Erisman 219).

The last novel of the quartet was not intended, as the others were, as a juvenile. *Double Star* was serialized in the leading SF magazine of the day, *Astounding* (serialized, as Erisman noted, during the turmoil following the admission of the first black into the University of Alabama), and won the year's leading award, the Hugo for best novel. And from the point of view of Heinlein's message, it is much more subtle and effective than the other three. Its protagonist, Lawrence Smith, a down-at-heel actor known professionally as the Great Lorenzo, is egotistical, immoral, and a racial bigot. He cannot stand Martians—their smell, their sexual habits, their looks. "Nobody could accuse me of race prejudice. I didn't care what a man's color, race, or religion was. But men were men, whereas Martians were things. They weren't even animals to my way of thinking. Permitting them in restaurants and bars used by men struck me as outrageous" (7). But Lorenzo is employed as the double of the kidnapped statesman Joseph Bonforte, and as he lives himself into the role, he gradually takes on the ideals and beliefs of his model. Bonforte aims to bring humans and Martians together: "He kept harping on the notion that the human race must never again make the mistakes that the white subrace had made in Africa and Asia" (84) (back in "the late Dark Ages" [68]). His enemy is the Humanity Party, who believe humans "have a God-given mandate to spread enlightenment through the stars, dispensing their own brand of Civilization to the savages. This is the Uncle Remus school of sociology— the good dahkies singin' spirituals and Ole Massa lubbin' every one of dem! It is a beautiful picture, but the frame is too small; it fails to show the whip, the slave block—and the counting-house!" (85).

At the end of the book, Lorenzo actually meets Bonforte and experiences "that warm, almost holy, shock one feels when first coming into sight of that great statue of Abraham Lincoln" (119). *Double Star* has traced the personal and logical transformation of a bigot into a man who realized the importance of tolerance as a basic feature of the American way of life; it is a powerful message yet conveyed quite subtly beneath the fast-moving action. (It is also the story of a professional actor who, thanks to excellent coaching by his aides, manages to become president; quite implausible, really.)

The message of the later novel *Farnham's Freehold* (1964) is more complex in that it depicts a future (into which Hugh Farnham and his household have been involuntarily thrown) ruled by vicious slave-owning African blacks. But Heinlein's point is that an evil system is not the result of race but of circumstance: "Color does not matter to me. I want to know other things about a man. Is his work good? Does he meet his obligations? Does he do honest work? Is he brave? Does he stand up and be counted?" (95). The survival of the individual is perhaps even more important than his own sense of honor. Thus Joe, their black houseboy, joins the future black establishment despite its evil nature. When his former employer objects that he had once been a decently treated employee, not a slave, Joe replies, "Have you ever made a bus trip through Alabama. As a 'nigger'?" (206). Hugh recalled an area of Pernambuco he had seen while in the navy, a place where rich plantation owners, dignified, polished, educated in France, were black, while their servants and field hands—giggling, shuffling, shiftless knuckleheads, "obviously incapable of better things"—were mostly white men. He had stopped telling this anecdote in the States; it was never really believed, and it was almost always resented—even by those whites who made a big thing of how anxious they were to "help the American Negro improve himself." Hugh had formed the opinion that almost all of those bleeding hearts wanted the Negro's lot improved until it was almost as high as their own—and no longer on their consciences—but the idea that the tables could ever be turned was one they rejected emotionally (226).

As the civil rights struggle reached its climax came the only SF anthology, to my knowledge, actually devoted to the problems of racial intolerance: Allen DeGraeff's *Humans and Other Beings* (1963). It is a powerful set of sixteen stories, many of them anthologized before or since, ranging in publication date from 1949 to 1961 but coming mostly from the mid-fifties. The earliest is also the bitterest and most powerful: "The NRACP," by George P. Elliott (an author who has done little or nothing else in the SF field). The "National Relocation Authority: Colored Persons" is "relocating" American blacks on reservations. The story comprises letters written from an NRACP bureaucrat to a friend outside, as he slowly learns the secret. "Remember, back in the simple days of the Spanish Civil War, when Guernica was bombed, we speculated all one evening what the worst thing in the world could be? This is the worst thing in the world, Herb, I tell you, the worst. After this, nothing" (172). Elliott's story is, of course, a response to the experience of German concentration camps, but the NRACP (the fictional mirror reversal of the NAACP) is sending trainloads of blacks not just to slaughter but to meat canneries. The bleak message, I presume, is: It can happen here, too.

The other stories in DeGraeff's collection are more traditional science fiction, and all by well-known authors. Several concern mixed marriages. Richard Wilson's "Love" and its sequel "Honor" are about a Martian and his human bride; she is an outcast from Earth society because of her marriage—the couple live near the Earth colony on Mars, which humans called Spidertown, until his scientific discovery, which opens the way for his acceptance on Earth. J. T. McIntosh's "Made in U.S.A." is about the prejudice experienced by an android girl—indistinguishable from white Americans apart from the small mark "Made in U.S.A." stamped on her navel. "Dark Interlude," by Fredric Brown and Mack Reynolds, tells how a traveler from the future comes to rural America and marries a local girl. He gets on well with the locals despite his dubious origins until one day he gets discussing race with the girl's brother.

> He said that by his time—starting after the war of something-or-other, I forget its name—all the races had blended into one. That the whites and the yellows had mostly killed one another off, and then all the races had begun to blend into one by colonization and intermarriage and that by his time the process was

complete. I just stared at him and asked him, "You mean you got nigger blood in you?" and he said, just like it didn't mean anything, "At least one-fourth." I just saw red. He'd married Sis; he was sleeping with her. I was so crazy-mad I don't even remember getting my gun.

"Well, don't worry about it, boy" [said the sheriff]. "You did right." (22)[10]

Another story in the collection deals with the same cultural absurdity from another viewpoint: Robert Sheckley's "Holdout," in which a space-traveling southerner from Georgia has conquered all racial prejudices except that cultural taboo which prevents him from working with another white Georgian. His determination not to work on the spaceship with another Georgian dissolves once he discovers that the newcomer is not all-white.

"I'm one-eighth Cherokee on my mother's side."

"They should a told me in the first place you was a Cherokee. Come on, I'll show you your bunk."

When the incident was reported to Captain Sven, several hours after blast off, he was completely perplexed. How, he asked himself, could one-eighth Cherokee blood make a man a Cherokee? Wasn't the other seven-eighths more indicative?

He decided he didn't understand American Southerners at all. (299)

The story by Eric Frank Russell (an English author who published largely in American magazines and who fairly effectively disguised his English-ness from American readers) was "Test Piece," which also imagines a future in which racial prejudice will have disappeared without trace. An Earthman comes to an alien planet and is treated virtually like a god. Before he dies, he orders his followers to show any arriving Earthman his statue and portrait and to kill them if they utter the two words which he makes the aliens memorize. The Earthmen look at this gray-haired, black-skinned space scout's likenesses and, nonplussed, ask the aliens what the two words were. "Two simple words of two syllables each"—the reader is left to surmise that they are something like "fucking nigger"—but the offending words are simply gabble to the Earthmen. They have passed the test.

A more serious point is made in Leigh Brackett's "All the Colors of the Rainbow," about the fear that lies behind hatred and prejudice. A green alien comes with his wife to a rural backwater (the urban SF writer is often happy to find prejudice in the country) and lashes out at those who are persecuting him—"a nigger, even if he is a green one": "'Yes, we have white folks out there, about one in every ten thousand, and they don't think anything of it, and neither do we. You can't hide from the universe. You're going to be trampled under with color—all the colors of the rainbow!' And he understood then that that was exactly what they feared" (235). The result was corruption; the alien learned hatred: "The physical outrage and the pain were soon over, but the other things were harder to eradicate—the sense of injustice, the rankling fury, the blind hatred of all men whose faces were white" (240). Hatred is also the theme of Frederik Pohl and Cyril Kornbluth's "The World of Myrion Flowers," in which Flowers, a well-to-do and complacent Harlem black, tries on a device which he is told would render him telepathic.

> "It didn't stop. It's not like a radio. You can't turn it off. Now I can hear—every-body! Every mind for miles around is *pouring into my head* WHAT IT THINKS ABOUT ME—ABOUT ME—ABOUT US!"
>
> . . . The machine . . . was maddening and dizzying, and the man who wore the helmet would be harmed in any world; but only in the world of Myrion Flowers would he be hated to death. (247–48)

DeGraeff's collection shows that, for him, stories about blacks, aliens, robots, and androids are equally valid ways of commenting upon racial prejudice in contemporary society. However, there is a real methodological problem faced by anyone who wants to investigate changing ideas about race and, specifically, race relations in the United States: to distinguish those stories which actually are about race from those which are not and, secondarily perhaps, to separate those stories which are consciously about race from those which are not. The field is very wide, for one of the most ubiquitous themes in science fiction is Contact with the Other: there are potentially a huge number of stories which might "really" be about race. The problem of deciding whether the Other—an alien, a robot, an android—is actually intended as a metaphor for the racial Other is a crucial problem if we want to understand the role played by race in SF.

We may start by looking at the approach taken to this question by one of the general introductions to SF which appeared in the 1970s, that written by the Swedish author and critic Sam J. Lundwall. He argues that "the android functions as sf's contribution to the race debate. It is guilt for the Negroes, the Indians, the Jews, the Vietnamese, the peoples of South America and mankind's rape of weaker individuals that comes back in the android" (166). Androids, Lundwall argues, are quite different from other stock representatives of the Other in SF. Androids are created by mankind and so are technically secondary or inferior, but they have their own individuality and constantly strive toward equality with man. "The robots pose no problem, because they just obey, and the extraterrestrials are so different from us that some kind of understanding must be found in the end" (167). Lundwall takes Algis Budrys's story, "Dream of Victory," as a typical example of one common use of the android in American SF. A nuclear war has killed most humans; androids form the bulk of the postholocaust population and are largely responsible for the survival of civilization. As the human birth rate grows, the androids are gradually eased out. The story is seen from the viewpoint of one android, who is replaced as office boss by a human being and turns to alcoholism and eventually murder. When he murders his (human) mistress, it unleashes a campaign of hatred aimed at the androids. The reference to the white male perception of the black as a threat to white jobs and to white women is clear. However, we shall have to think whether Lundwall's neat distinction between androids on the one hand and robots, aliens, and the like on the other stands up in practice. Alongside Budrys's androids, for instance, can be placed Asimov's robots, which, as several critics have pointed out, seem to function as the equivalent of blacks. *The Caves of Steel* (1954), for instance, "begins with the bitter musings of the protagonist upon the dismissal of an office boy who has been replaced by a humanoid robot"—a robot who "shuffles his feet," with a vacuous grin on his face, in clear parody of the stereotypical black (Portelli 151). The protagonist, Lije Baley, is an antirobot extremist; his partner, R. Daneel Olivaw, represents the constant fear of the racist—the light-skinned black who might pass for white. Even so, the Three Laws restrain robots, just as the slave owner expected (or hoped) that his black slaves would be restrained by custom, fear, and conditioning to obey his every order. The dangers come when the conditioning is somehow overcome (a theme of a number of the classic early robot stories, collected as *I, Robot*) or when a slave/robot is misused by another slave owner (the explanation of the murder in both the Daneel Olivaw whodunits, *The Caves of Steel* and *The Naked Sun* [1957]). Gary K. Wolfe points to Asimov's well-known story, "Little Lost Robot," as providing "discomfiting support to the assertion made by some critics that robots provide science fiction with a means of dealing with racism" (162). Susan Calvin repeatedly refers to her robots as "boys" when she interrogates them to find out which robot's First Law programming was not working properly; the story is designed to find this "boy" and to deal with him. "To make the analogy stronger, the means Nestor uses to hide from the humans—mixing anonymously with a group of sixty-two identical robots—calls to mind the legend of Spartacus and his rebellious slaves"—not improbably a conscious analogy, given Asimov's wide reading in ancient history and mythology. However, there are problems. Slaves, obviously, are not necessarily racially separate, particularly for someone who (as in *Foundation*) drew so widely on ancient history. And there may well be other messages in the author's mind. Asimov himself describes how he wrote his robot stories as a conscious reaction against what, in the stories themselves, he called "the Frankenstein complex": the obsession with the idea that robots might destroy their creators. "My robots were machines designed by engineers, not pseudo-men created by blasphemers" (*Rest* 14). Portelli plausibly argues that this set Asimov up in a contradiction. His robots were machines, which inevitably tend to put people out of work and hence create resentment in the workforce. This causes men to treat the robots as slaves, as "boys"; this, however, creates sympathy in the reader, above all when we get humanoid robots, like Daneel Olivaw, who are seen to be the victims of blind prejudice. Asimov "cannot support the comparatively respectable cause of racial integration without at the same time supporting the more controversial cause of automation and unemployment" (Portelli 152). (But again we do not have to make that leap from "slave" to "black.") At the same time, despite his profession of faith, Asimov is setting up the robots as Frankenstein monsters, with the help of his link character, Susan Calvin. The efforts of the Society for Humanity to halt the robots will come to nothing. Robots, a superior breed, will triumph; humanity can only continue and can only achieve happiness through the Machine. When a character complains that mankind "*has* lost its own say in its future," Calvin replied, "it never had any, really" (*I, Robot* 271). The Machine will bring control to human society, and

> "The Machine cannot, *must* not, make us unhappy."
>
> "How horrible!"
>
> "Perhaps how wonderful! Think, that for all time, all conflicts are finally evitable. Only the Machines, from now on, are inevitable!"
>
> And the fire behind the quartz went out and only a curl of smoke was left to indicate its place. (271–72)

Those words, which conclude "The Evitable Conflict" (1950), the last story of *I, Robot*, are taken by Wolfe to represent the coming of a "cheerfully totalitarian Utopia": "the dying of the flame also carries a more ominous meaning that one assumes Asimov was aware of" (163). I don't think Wolfe's cynicism about Asimov's choice of words is called for; it is surely not intended as a presaging of a "cheerfully totalitarian Utopia" but an expression of uncertainty and unease about a Machine-led future. More important, however, it has little to do with the robot as American black, even if aspects of the black's position in American society might be mirrored in the position of the robot. Much more important in the early robot stories is the robot as representative of the ominous potentialities of man-made technology; the "Frankenstein complex" lies in the background, even if it is frequently denied. As the last passage quoted suggests, we are not intended to be fooled into uncritical sympathy with Susan Calvin's fanaticism.

Much later in the robot series, by the time of the third anthology, *The Bicentennial Man* (1976), the "Frankenstein complex" had indeed vanished (as Asimov claimed he had intended all along), and robots appear much more obviously as beings searching for equality with humans. Here perhaps, as Portelli argues, we are getting closer to the parallel with the blacks. But Asimov's main concern is to ponder the problems of what distinguishes the machine from the human. In the title story of the collection, "The Bicentennial Man," he relates the story of Andrew, a perfectly loyal household robot. It is different from other robots in that it has an artistic gift, which it uses to make money for its owner and, at its owner's request (although no one was sure it was legal) for its own private bank account. It, or perhaps he (Asimov uses "he" throughout), uses the money to make technical improvements to his body; eventually he decides to use the money to buy his freedom. The judge and the World Court eventually decided that "there is no right to deny freedom to any object with a mind advanced enough to grasp the concept and desire the state" (136). An incident in which two robot-hating men order Andrew to dismember himself leads eventually to a law forbidding robot-harming orders; decades more struggle lead him, finally, to be instrumental in procuring a law declaring humans and robots equal. In the meantime, technology has advanced to the point that he himself is humanoid—a proto–Daneel Olivaw; indeed, so desperate is his will to be human that he arranges for his own dying. The final decision for legal equality comes to a world in which medicine and technology are so far advanced that humans are themselves able to consist of a large number of artificial parts—androids, like Andrew. Portelli, arguing that the story is a more deliberate discussion of racial themes than the earlier robot stories, sees this merging of human and machine as "a skilful treatment of miscegenation" (152). But as cultural historians we have to ask (and I say this in full realization that most literary critics would deny the possibility of such a question) whether this was in Asimov's mind. Asimov may have written the scene where Andrew is baited by the robot haters while thinking of similar scenes produced by racial tensions, but it is hardly a clear or profound comment on those racial tensions (particularly when we note that it is written in the 1970s rather than the 1950s). But for the rest, he seems concerned only with a logical extrapolation about ideas of artificial intelligence, which was probably much in his mind in the mid-1970s, after he had become better acquainted with Marvin Minsky, the best known AI expert (and one of two people Asimov acknowledges as brighter than he is [*Joy* 302]). The robopsychologist of "The Bicentennial Man" is called Merton Mansky. That Asimov was rather more interested in the logical problems of robots and the Three Laws of Robotics than in anything that is happening in the wider contemporary world is suggested by his comments on "That Thou Art Mindful of Him!" in Ferman and Malzberg's anthology *Final Stage* (115–17). He points out that the deepest ambiguity inherent in the question of robot-human relations is the definition of *human*. Discussions with his former editor, John W. Campbell Jr., convinced him that if he dug too deeply into that question, the Three Laws would be totally upset. But with Campbell dead and the Three Laws thirty-four years old, Asimov decided to start digging. He has two robots work out for themselves not only that should they be regarded as human beings but that logic demanded that they also be treated as superior human beings: "Those that followed in their shape and kind must dominate" (115). Frankenstein's monsters rebel. And in the process, Asimov suggests that race was not something that preoccupied him at all.

The case of Asimov is a useful illustration of the problems there are in defining whether a particular SF story or novel is "about" race. Where there are clear statements placed in the mouth of narrator or character—as in the Heinlein novels quoted above—there is little problem. But when it is the case that the message has to be inferred by the reader from the treatment of the plot, then it is much more difficult. It seems to me—an impression based on over thirty years' reading, rather than the proper exhaustive survey and analysis of hundreds or thousands of stories—that there is a historical progression in the treatment of the Other. In the 1950s and early '60s, there is a constant treatment of the theme of a unified humanity; in the later '60s and early '70s, the alien, in particular, became the oppressed colonial (and Vietnam Wars devastated planet after planet); and in the '80s, the concerns have been primarily environmental. But also by the 1980s, SF had very largely lost the sense of being the educational tool that SF writers had, in the 1950s, espoused with sometimes almost missionary zeal.

Such an impression clearly ought to be backed up by statistics. But here I do no more than offer a relatively random sample of science fiction stories, published respectively in 1990 and 1960. My present-day sample comes from the two monthly magazines published by Davis Inc., the two most popular SF magazines, *Analog* and *Isaac Asimov's Science Fiction Magazine* for the first four months of 1990.[11] *Asimov's*, in those four issues (an average of 5–6 stories per issue) had precisely one story about aliens and none about androids or robots. This can be partly explained by the nature of *Asimov's*: not given to traditional themes and inclined to publish stories which are pure fantasy (ghosts, werewolves) as well as science fiction. The lone alien appears in Deborah Wessell's "Joyride" (Feb. 1990); he offers sexual satisfaction to the two women in the story—he is accepted as an exotic and interesting novelty, and if the story is making any serious point (which I doubt), it is that racial difference adds spice to life.

Analog, the sole "hard-science" SF magazine around now, has a very different tally: both February and April 1990 have two stories each featuring aliens, March 1990 has three, and January 1990 has one story about aliens and one about androids. (No robots in either magazine: computers have to a large extent replaced robots in SF iconography, and computers never seem to lend themselves to racial metaphor.) The January aliens (Michael F. Flynn's "The Feeders") are merely a conceit, concerning (among other things) the possible explanation for the Angels of Mons. One of the February aliens is concerned entirely with the problems of communication and of learning whether or not a species is intelligent (Ray Brown's "Tongues in Trees"). In the other, "Curlew's Choice," by British academic Ian Stewart, the intelligent aliens are very much offstage, having been totally wiped out before the action starts in an ecologically disastrous attempt to exploit the economic resources of a planet; the message is green rather than antiracist. Of the March stories, Joe Haldeman's "Passages" is merely a hunting story on an alien planet; Deborah D. Ross's "Expression of the Past" is another warning about messing with the ecology. The third March story, on the other hand, W. R. Thompson's "Backlash," is very reminiscent of some of the tales collected in Allen DeGraeff's anthology. There is a member of an alien embassy in New York, attacked in Central Park by muggers who, it is discovered, have been hired by the Human Brotherhood—an organization we have met before in various guises: a racist group determined to keep the human race pure and on top. In addition, we have a human society in which some people are, before birth, "gengineered"—genetically improved into a kind of superbeing. The Human Brotherhood is against them, too, and we witness a good deal of popular prejudice against them. The primary message, however, is that politics is complex and dirty. It emerges that the Human Brotherhood and some aliens are being manipulated by people, in alliance with another group of aliens who want power for themselves. If it is a comment on racism, as it must be, it is a much more cynical comment than we found in the 1950s: racists are fools whose unthinking prejudices are manipulated by power-seeking politicians. Neither of the April alien stories carries such a message. Michael F. Flynn's "The Common Goal of Nature" speculates on alien psychology, while Lou Grinzo's "Childhood's Confession" reworks an ancient SF theme (which, in its origins, goes back to the Book of Genesis): that aliens will come to observe humanity and judge it lacking. Finally, there is that one story about androids: D. M. Vidrine's "Lifer," in the January 1990 *Analog*. We have, very briefly, the obligatory sign of human prejudice against androids—in this case, against the beautiful female android in charge of the rehabilitation of a retired spaceman. But her function seems to be a means of comparing machine obsolescence with human aging and retirement rather than any sustained comment on prejudice against the Other.

Let us compare these eight issues with eight comparable issues, chosen equally randomly, from thirty years ago. *Asimov's* was not in existence then, but *Galaxy* makes a reasonable substitute; *Analog* was there, under its original name of *Astounding*. I have taken the first four issues of *Astounding* for 1960 (Jan.–Apr.) and the last four issues of the bimonthly *Galaxy* to appear in the British edition (end of 1959–Apr. 1960).[12] Only one of these issues features robots. Charles Satterfield's "Way Up Yonder" (*Galaxy* 76) is fairly undistinguished, even if it does have the memorable image of dancing robots. Humans run plantations; the robot workers have tribal dances and voodoo beliefs, all largely unknown to their owners. The historical parallel is fairly basic and obvious, but the story does not seem to be making any clear point about it. Aliens, however, figure quite largely in these issues—nine stories in *Galaxy* and six in *Astounding*, although four of those are in one issue, January 1960. Two of the *Galaxy* stories about aliens are by Clifford D. Simak, probably the greatest purveyor in the 1950s of the message that human beings will have to learn to live with the Other.[13] But only one of the stories in *Galaxy* seems to me to use aliens in any way as a comment on contemporary racial problems: Christopher Grimm's "Someone to Watch over Me" (*Galaxy* 76), in which the hero learns to realize that appearance means nothing—the horrific aliens are at root "human"—even if his alliance with them is viewed with great suspicion by more prejudiced humans.

The January issue of *Astounding*, however, has a number of interesting messages for its readers. The cover story, "The Aliens," by Murray Leinster, repeats the conclusion of his famous story "First Contact": that the Other should be met with caution but with friendliness—xenophobia is unnecessary and inefficient. In Randall Garrett's "Dead Giveaway," space explorers find a huge alien city, empty of inhabitants, which they recognize to be a screening device for humanity: to see whether humans can learn from a superior people and survive (like, a character says, the Mexicans and Peruvians) or whether they will refuse to learn and perish (as he says, like the Amerindians). The next story, whether by design or poor editing, is on a similar theme: A. Bertram Chandler's "The Outsiders" also offers an alien test of mankind—a test, perhaps, to see whether humanity can bear to face some unutterably alien Otherness:

It's an ingenious test, and amazingly simple. It's . . . a mirror that's held up to you, in which you see everything. Yes, *everything*. Things that you've forgotten and things that you've wished for years that you could forget. After all, a man can meet any alien monster without fear, without hate, without panic-motivated aggression, after he has met and faced that most horrible monster of all. . . .
        Himself.

The final story in the issue was George Whitley's "Familiar Pattern," effectively illustrated by just three pictures scattered through the text: a Polynesian war canoe in action; the same Polynesian war canoe rotting on a beach; the same canoe in a museum, in the room next to the dinosaurs. The story runs through that pattern, with commentary supplied by a Polynesian, Tom. An alien ship comes to Earth; quarrels result in a race riot; Melbourne is destroyed in retaliation. "'The familiar pattern . . . The chance contact—The Trader—The Missionary—The incident—And the gunboat—' 'And after the gunboat?' asked Lessing. 'We learned the answer to that many years ago,' said Tom. 'Now it's your turn.'"

The stories, as we see, reflect a number of ideas about meetings with other peoples, including a clear concept of the mistakes that have been made or crimes committed in the past when "superior" races came across "inferior" ones. And inherent in most of the stories from 1960 is the message that humanity is one race, which has emerged from an unhappy past of racial misunderstandings and conflicts. That message carried across clear in the American science fiction of the 1950s; it seems much less regarded in 1990. We may trust that that is a hopeful sign.

Notes

1. Freeman later publicly claimed it was a joke and said that the only people who really complained were those who would not be able to get domestic servants without the Negroes and Irish. But privately he confessed, "I feel a creep when I think that one of those great black apes may (in theory) be President" (Gossett 109–10).

2. The whole sorry story is well described in Gould.

3. I have been unable to find this passage in my copy. The hero is Johnny Rico, apparently Puerto Rican in origin but clearly from a rich and privileged family.

4. To a large extent I am here following Clareson 69–78. I have unfortunately not been able to consult Wu.

5. These tales mirror the contemporary spate of English tales of German invasion (Clarke) or Ulster tales of Irish wars (James).

6. Hugo Gernsback to Henrik Dahl June, 23 Jan. 1930, cited by Moskowitz 25.

7. McDermott discusses all the political assumptions in Heinlein's *The Day after Tomorrow*; she deals with racism on 264–66. The novel was originally serialized as "Sixth Column" in *Astounding*, Jan.–Mar. 1941 (as by Anson McDonald) and was expanded into book form in 1949.

8. The chief weapons of the American resistance were air balls, referred to by Nowlan as "our balls": such delights have been surgically removed from later texts. See Kalish et al. 312.

9. Christine Morris and Mary S. Weinkauf have both, separately, looked at the often patronizing way in which American Indians are treated in American SF.

10. The editor of *Galaxy*, H. L. Gold, noted in an editorial in May 1951 that some readers had thought that this story was in favor of racial prejudice (Carter 139).

11. Leaving out the extra stories printed in the sixtieth anniversary issue of *Analog*, Jan. 1990, which were reprints of some classic stories from the previous sixty years.

12. The four issues of *Astounding* are the British reprints (which continued to Aug. 1963): Jan.–Apr. 1960 (British ed.) are reprints of Aug. 1959, Nov. 1959, Dec. 1959, and Jan. 1960 (Sept. and Oct. were never reprinted in the United Kingdom). The four issues of *Galaxy* are 76–79, British ed., released one month later than in the United States. No. 80 was the first U.S. edition to be distributed in the United Kingdom, in June 1960.

13. On Simak's treatment of aliens, see Pringle.

Works Cited

Aliens. Dir. James Cameron. Twentieth Century Fox, 1986. Print.

Asimov, Isaac. "The Bicentennial Man." 1976. *The 1977 Annual World's Best SF*. Ed. Donald A. Wollheim. New York: DAW, 1977. 127–65. Print.

———. *The Bicentennial Man*. New York: Ballantine, 1976. Print.

———. *The Caves of Steel*. New York: Doubleday, 1954. Print.

———. "The Evitable Conflict." 1950. *I, Robot*. New York: Bantam Spectra, 1991. 240–72. Print.

———. *I, Robot*. 1950. New York: Bantam Spectra, 1991. Print.

———. *In Joy Still Felt: The Autobiography of Isaac Asimov, 1954–1978*. New York: Avon, 1981. Print.

———. "Little Lost Robot." 1947. *I, Robot*. New York: Bantam Spectra, 1991. 136–73. Print.

———. *The Naked Sun*. New York: Doubleday, 1957. Print.

———. *The Rest of the Robots*. 1964. London: Panther, 1968. Print.

———. "That Thou Art Mindful of Him!" 1974. *Final Stage*. Eds. Edward L. Ferman and Barry N. Malzberg. New York: Penguin, 1975. 91–117. Print.

Bellamy, Edward. *Looking Backward, 2000 to 1887*. 1888. New York: Oxford UP, 2007. Print.

Bonner, Frances. "Difference and Desire, Slavery and Seduction: Octavia Butler's *Xenogenesis*." *Foundation* 48 (1990): 50–61. Print.

Brackett, Leigh. "All the Colors of the Rainbow." 1957. *Humans and Other Beings*. Ed. Allen DeGraeff. New York: Collier, 1963. 219–40. Print.

Bradbury, Ray. "Way in the Middle of the Air." 1950. *The Martian Chronicles*. New York: Bantam, 1950. 89–102. Print.

Brown, Frederic, and Mack Reynolds. "Dark Interlude." 1951. *Humans and Other Beings*. Ed. Allen DeGraeff. New York: Collier, 1963. 15–22. Print.

Budrys, Algis. "Dream of Victory." 1953. *The Furious Future*. London: Panther, 1966. 128–54. Print.

Burroughs, Edgar R. *The Gods of Mars*. 1913. London: Four Square, 1961. Print.

———. *A Princess of Mars*. 1912. London: Four Square, 1961. Print.

———. *The Warlord of Mars*. 1913–14. London: Four Square, 1961. Print.

Card, Orson Scott. *Ender's Game*. New York: Tor, 1985. Print.

———. *Speaker for the Dead*. New York: Tor, 1986. Print.

Carter, Paul A. *The Creation of Tomorrow: Fifty Years of Magazine Science Fiction*. New York: Columbia UP, 1977. Print.

Clareson, Thomas D. *Some Kind of Paradise: The Emergence of American Science Fiction*. Westport: Greenwood, 1985. Print.

Clarke, I. F. *Voices Prophesying War, 1763–1984*. Oxford: Oxford UP, 1966. Print.

DeGraeff, Allen, ed. *Humans and Other Beings*. New York: Collier, 1963. Print.

Dick, Philip K. *The Man in the High Castle*. 1962. New York: Vintage, 1992. Print.

Dooner, Pierton W. *Last Days of the Republic*. 1880. Whitefish: Kessinger, 2010. Print.

Elliott, George P. "The NRACP." 1949. *Humans and Other Beings*. Ed. Allen DeGraeff. New York: Collier, 1963. 141–72. Print.

Erisman, Fred. "Robert Heinlein's Case for Racial Tolerance, 1954–1956." *Extrapolation* 29.3 (1988): 216–26. Print.

Giesy, J. U. *All for His Country*. New York: Macaulay, 1915. Print.

Gibbons, Floyd. *The Red Napoleon*. New York: Cape and Smith, 1929. Print.

Gossett, Thomas F. *Race: The History of an Idea in America*. Dallas: Southern Methodist UP, 1963. Print.

Gould, Stephen J. *The Mismeasure of Man*. New York: Norton, 1981. Print.

Heinlein, Robert A. "The Black Pits of Luna." 1948. *The Green Hills of Earth*. Chicago: Shasta, 1951. Print.

———. *The Day after Tomorrow*. New York: Gnome, 1949. Print.

———. *Double Star*. 1956. London: Panther, 1960. Print.

———. *Farnham's Freehold*. 1964. London: Corgi, 1967. Print.

———. *Space Cadet*. New York: Scribner's, 1948. Print.

———. *The Star Beast*. 1954. New York: Ace, 1970. Print.

———. *Starship Troopers*. 1959. Four Square: London, 1961. Print.

———. *Time for the Stars*. New York: Scribner's, 1956. Print.

———. *Tunnel in the Sky*. New York: Scribner's, 1955. Print.

Hjortsberg, William. *Gray Matters*. New York: Simon and Schuster, 1971. Print

James, Edward. "1886: Past Views of Ireland's Future." *Foundation* 36 (1986): 21–30. Print.

Kalish, Alan, et al. "'For Our Balls Were Sheathed in Inertron': Textual Variants in 'The Seminal Novel of Buck Rogers.'" *Extrapolation* 29.4 (1988): 303–18. Print.

Lawson, Benjamin S. "The Time and Place of Edgar Rice Burroughs's Early Martian Trilogy." *Extrapolation* 27.3 (1986): 208–20. Print.

Le Guin, Ursula K. *The Left Hand of Darkness*. New York: Ace, 1969. Print.

Leinster, Murray. "The Aliens." *Astounding Stories*. Aug. 1959. 9–40. Print.

———. "First Contact." 1945. *The Science Fiction Hall of Fame*. Vol. 1, 1929–64. Ed. Robert Silverberg. New York: Orb, 2005. 252–80.

Littlefield, Emerson. "The Mythologies of Race and Science in Samuel Delany's *The Einstein Intersection* and *Nova*." *Extrapolation* 23.3 (1982): 235–42. Print.

Lundwall, Sam J. *Science Fiction: What It's All About*. New York: Ace, 1971. Print.

Manson, Marsden. *The Yellow Peril in Action*. San Francisco: Britton and Rey, 1907. Print.

McDermott, K. A. "Ideology and Narrative: The Cold War and Robert Heinlein." *Extrapolation* 23.3 (1982): 254–69. Print.

McIntosh, J. T. "Made in U.S.A." 1953. *Humans and Other Beings*. Ed. Allen DeGraeff. New York: Collier, 1963. 107–38. Print.

Morris, Christine. "Indians and Other Aliens: A Native American View of Science Fiction." *Extrapolation* 20.4 (1979): 301–7. Print.

Moskowitz, Sam. "Henrik Dahl Juve and the Second Gernsback Dynasty." *Extrapolation* 30.1 (1989): 5–52. Print.

Pohl, Frederik. *Black Star Rising*. New York: Ballantine, 1985. Print.

Pohl, Frederik, and Cyril Kornbluth. "The World of Myrion Flowers." 1961. *Humans and Other Beings*. Ed. Allen DeGraeff. New York: Collier, 1963. 243–48. Print.

Portelli, Alessandro. "The Three Laws of Robotics: Laws of the Text, Laws of Production, Laws of Society." *Science Fiction Studies* 7.2 (1980): 150–56. Print.

Pringle, David. "Aliens for Neighbours: A Reassessment of Clifford D. Simak." *Foundation* 11 (1977): 15–29. Print.

Rabkin, Eric S., and Robert Scholes. *Science Fiction. History—Science—Vision*. New York: Oxford UP, 1977. Print.

Russell, Eric Frank, "Test Piece." 1951. *Humans and Other Beings*. Ed. Allen DeGraeff. New York: Collier, 1963. 303–19. Print.

Salvaggio, Ruth. "Octavia Butler and the Black Science Fiction Heroine." *Black American Literature Forum* 18.2 (1984): 78–81. Print.

Schachner, Nat. "Ancestral Voices." *Astounding Stories*, Dec. 1933, 70–82. Print.

———. "Pulp Writers Have a Job to Do." *Writer* 58 (Aug. 1945): 243–44. Print.

Sheckley, Robert. "Holdout." 1957. *Humans and Other Beings*. Ed. Allen DeGraeff. New York: Collier, 1963. 289–99. Print.

Shiel, M. P. *The Yellow Danger*. London: Richards, 1898. Print.

Spinrad, Norman. "A Thing of Beauty." 1973. *No Direction Home*. London: Fontana, 1977. 63–77. Print.

Stephensen-Payne, P. Review of *Armageddon 2419 AD*. *Vector* 7374 (1976): 16–17. Print.

Vinton, Arthur D. *Looking Further Backward*. 1890. New York: Arno, 1971. Print.

Wallace, King. *The Next War: A Prediction*. 1892. Washington, DC: Martyn, 1892. Print.

Weinbaum, Stanley G. *A Martian Odyssey and Others*. Reading: Fantasy, 1949. Print.

Weinkauf, Mary, S. "The Indian in Science Fiction." *Extrapolation* 20.4 (1979): 308–20. Print.

Wells, H. G. *The War of the Worlds*. 1897. London: Heinemann, 1898. Print.

Wilson, Richard. "Honor." 1953. *Humans and Other Beings*. Ed. Allen DeGraeff. New York: Collier, 1963. 35–44. Print.

———. "Love." 1952. *Humans and Other Beings.* Ed. Allen DeGraeff. New York: Collier, 1963. 25–31. Print.

Wolfe, Gary K. *The Known and the Unknown: The Iconography of Science Fiction.* Kent: Kent State UP, 1979. Print.

Woltor, Robert. *A Short and Truthful History of the Taking of California and Oregon by the Chinese in the Year A.D. 1899.* San Francisco: Bancroft, 1882. Print.

Wu, William F. *The Yellow Peril: Chinese Americans in American Fiction, 1850–1940.* Hamden: Archon, 1982. Print.

CODA

"THE WILD UNICORN HERD CHECK-IN"

The Politics of Race in Science Fiction Fandom

■ ■ ■

ROBIN ANNE REID

In 1998, Samuel R. Delany published an article, "Racism and Science Fiction" in *The New York Review of Science Fiction*; the article was later reprinted in Sheree R. Thomas's anthology, *Dark Matter: A Century of Speculative Fiction from the African Diaspora* (2000).[1] Delany's article inspired the formation of the Carl Brandon Society, announced at the 1999 WisCon, the oldest and only feminist science fiction convention. The group named itself after "Carl Joshua Brandon," a 1950s fictional black fan invented by Terry Carr and Peter Graham whose hoax existence was maintained for two years. The Carl Brandon Society's mission is "to increase racial and ethnic diversity in the production of and audience for speculative fiction," and its vision is "a world in which speculative fiction, about complex and diverse cultures from writers of all backgrounds, is used to understand the present and model possible futures; and where people of color are full citizens in the community of imagination and progress."

Eleven years after the founding of the Carl Brandon Society, fans of color participated in a communal calling out of the extent to which the white SF community still remained ignorant of their existence in the "community of imagination and progress" (Delux_Vivens). The callout, "The Wild Unicorn Herd Check-In," took place in the LiveJournal community, Deadbrowalking, and lasted from 11 May to 8 July 2009, with the final post in 2012. The event began when Delux_Vivens, a community moderator, posted a request for "POC/nonwhite people/native/aboriginal/first nations/ndn, whether members of the community or not, who watch or read science fiction and fantasy (genre fiction)," to identify themselves in the thread. The post was a response to claims by a white SF author, Lois McMaster Bujold, that "Readers of Color" (her term) were new to SF.

Bujold made these claims in a response to a 9 May 2009, LiveJournal post by Fiction_Theory that provided a number of links to online discussions about the problematic nature of Patricia C. Wrede's novel, *Thirteenth Child* (2010). Wrede's alternate history fantasy novel was based on the premise that the indigenous peoples of the Americas had never existed and that European settlers came to an unpeopled continent, Columbia, that was full of magical animals.[2] Fiction_Theory identifies herself as a historian and analyzes the cultural context of Wrede's novel, a context in which erasure of entire cultures based on racism exists, as do erasures of women and queer people. This historical and cultural context has shaped both academic and popular knowledge of "history" and was perpetuated in Wrede's novel. One of the authors that Fiction_Theory references in her discussion is Bujold. Bujold posted a signed response in Fiction_Theory's discussion thread that includes an acknowledgment of white privilege but claims that there is hope in the online conflicts taking place regarding Wrede's novel:

> The other and more hopeful point is that never before have so many Readers of Color existed to *have* the conversation, or been able to communicate with each other to do so. When I went to my first midwestern convention in 1968, there was exactly one black fan, male; it's only in late years that I've had cause to wonder how brave he must have been to venture in. Octavia Butler, at a library program, once described a young black reader meeting her as a black SCIENCE FICTION writer, and saying in some wonder, "I didn't know we *did* that!" As far as I can tell, the biggest single factor driving the current shift and growth in diversity in genre readers has been the invention of the Internet. This is the first occasion I know of that a book out of the former tradition has intersected the new audience. (Fiction_Theory)

This apparent expression of hope (that there are more "Readers of Color") implies that they did not exist during or before the 1960s; thus, they were not able to communicate with white people or each other before the invention of the Internet. Bujold's claim and assumption generated a range of responses from fans of color and white allies that included personal and historical information about the years (and generations) of SF and fantasy reading by people of color. As well as providing specifics from their own experiences, people posted multiple links to published material by African American SF authors who discussed race and racism in SF. The respondents critiqued the ways in which Bujold generalized from her experience to make a falsely universal claim about the demographics of SF fandom—that is, her experience in attending SF cons, which leads her to identify SF fans as those who attend cons. Bujold's claim, like Wrede's novel, was read by many as another example of erasure. That is, while it may have been accurate to talk about the smaller numbers of fans of color attending SF cons, especially in some regions of the United States (the Midwest, in Bujold's case), assuming that her limited regional experience was universal was problematic. Also frustrating to some of the fans responding to Bujold was her assumption that white-authored SF was not read by fans of color when in fact many of them had been fans/readers of her books as well as the works of other white authors for decades (as had their parents and, in some cases, their grandparents). Fiction_Theory notes the direct parallels between Wrede's novel and the larger systemic issues of erasure and marginalization in the national histories of the United States, and the example of a white SF author erasing people of color from the communities and histories of SF is related to those systemic erasures.

The response to Bujold's comments in Fiction_Theory's journal led to the posting of the "Wild Unicorn Check-In Post" at Deadbrowalking, which garnered more than a thousand comments, mostly by fans of color, although a few were made by white people who did not respect the request to limit responses to "POC/nonwhite people" and to "native/aboriginal/first nations/ndn" people, especially outside the United States. The comments testified to the multiple generations of people of color who were actively reading and viewing and participating in all media and genres of "science fiction" and who were creating many fandom activities, often in their own communities. Not only are the posters claiming "science fiction" (in the narrow definition of an American and British English-language popular genre) for themselves, but they are also creating a space to include multiple national folklores and mythologies and current popular genres in languages other than English as part of "science fiction." The Wild Unicorn Herd shows how SF (broadly defined) is a global phenomenon that, while dominated by English-language authors, is not limited to them. The "Check-In" embodies the point Fiction_Theory makes in one of her responses to Bujold, an analysis of the posts and advice to Bujold: "It's like you said, 'Well, before when there weren't as many planets...'" The "you" in this case is directed at Bujold but can stand for many white readers of SF, the ones who simply did not see all the planets (black and brown and many other colors) that exist and have existed, independent of white observers, and those who assume, in their ignorance, that what they do not see does not exist. The post at Deadbrowalking appeared two days after Fiction_Theory's post and was referenced in the discussion there, with recommendations to Bujold, and by extension other white readers, to read to expand their horizons by learning about the histories and universes that have been erased from the spaces in white-dominated SF culture.

The erasure of fans of color parallels and overlaps with the historical erasure of white women fans in SF fandom: recent ethnographies and cultural histories of SF by Justine Larbalestier and Helen Merrick have addressed the perception that SF fandom is (white) male only, arguing that focusing solely on the literary texts of SF does not do justice to the feminist and gender theory and praxis done by some within the SF community. Defining SF as not just a genre but as a community, Larbalestier and Merrick foreground women's erased historical and contemporary work against gender discrimination in the SF community, ranging from letters to the editors during the pulp fiction era to the founding of WisCon, as well as the work done by women writing SF.

In the same way, the real work being done on critical race and intersectional issues in theory and praxis in SF communities is being done by people of color in a number of fandom communities, online and offline, some public and some closed to or invisible to white members of the SF communities.[3] Fans of color have established communities in all the iterations of the web, including blogs and social networking sites dedicated to antiracist activism, education, and support. They have been working online for at least the past fifteen years to challenge the perceived whiteness of SF. The efforts include organized, nonprofit groups such as the Carl Brandon Society as well as more informal groups dedicated to activism in changing the "production of and audience for speculative fiction" (Carl Brandon Society). Fans run interventions in fandom communities and activities; host carnivals and festivals focusing on creating and celebrating stories, videos, and art featuring characters of color; create online support communities for each other (often locked down and heavily moderated to ensure the creation of safe spaces); and maintain archives for creative work by and about people of color in SF.[4]

In this essay, which is a part of a larger digital humanities project on which I am working with colleagues in linguistics and psychology, I offer a descriptive reading of the taxonomies of terminologies relating to identities, primarily involving race and ethnicity, that the Wild Unicorn Herd used in the "Check-In" post. By descriptive, I mean that while I report the results quantitatively, I am not doing any sort of inductive or inferential statistical analysis of the data: my goal is to chart the terminologies and categories that appear in the discussion thread. The categories I develop from this analysis will become part of an ontology for a larger project that involves analyzing a work on a corpus of natural language materials gathered from the Internet. The larger project will involve work with Lucy Pickering, a corpus linguist, and Christian Hempelmann, a computational linguist whose specialty is ontology, a term that has a different meaning in computational linguistics than it does in philosophy.[5] My aim is that the ontology (computational linguistics) that is eventually created will serve a goal that is best described by the philosophical ontological scholarship.

In philosophical ontological work such as that by Linda Martín Alcoff and Lisa Nakamura, one purpose is to analyze and critique simplistic ontologies of race and ethnicity, often created and maintained by intuitional authorities such as the U.S. Census, which has changed racial categories on a regular basis, responding to the changing ideologies in science and politics. Jennifer L. Hochschild and Brenna M. Powell argue that the development of the U.S. Census was marked by a period of extreme experimentations from 1850 to 1930, with a jumble of categories mixing racial, national, and religious terminologies, followed by a period of stability that lasted until the end of the twentieth century. As part of the current destabilization, Alcoff and others work to create social ontologies, using sociological and ethnographic lenses, with the goals of education and social change. The work of creating social ontologies can be done with traditional ethnographic methodologies or it can be done on the Internet, as Nakamura's work on cyberidentities proves. Analysis of Internet sites and communities (which can include commercial sites, individual blogs, discussion forum chat rooms, and gaming sites) does not rely on the ethnographic methodologies of questionnaires or interviews. Instead, the methodology draws on the analysis of natural language texts generated by users. In this project, I focus on the posts in one community on one social network site (LiveJournal), a focus often used in this sort of project.[6] An ontology, in the field of computational linguistics, is a complex object that identifies word meanings in terms of underlying concepts, which are also linked to related concepts in a hierarchical relationship. My work in identifying taxonomic categories can be considered a very low level, or beginning level, of the ontology that will take place as a part of the larger corpus project.

The importance of looking at the work being done in online social justice communities (which include not only communities relating to race but also those relating to other equality and civil rights movements by marginalized groups) is that the Internet allows access to larger and more diverse discourses created by global populations. Previous scholarship on Internet activity relating to minority communities has tended to be minimal and, as David Parker and Miri Song argue, related to topics such as the digital divide or the practice of white people who attempt to pass as members of minority communities. In "New Ethnicities Online: Reflexive Racialisation and the Internet" (2006), Parker and Song challenge the gaps and limits in the earlier scholarship by analyzing the discourse on two websites, a South Asian British and a Chinese British site. Parker and Song coin the term *reflexive racialization* to explain how the sites are redefining collective identities (in opposition to erasure online). Furthermore, they argue that such forums can allow community members to share their experiences of racism and to build oppositional social perspectives in response to the experiences of oppression and marginalizations (from micro- to macro-aggressions) the members relate from their lives on- and offline. Parker and Song's research focused on a different type of website, including discussion forums, than does mine, and on specifically identified communities in Britain, but their findings can apply to the Deadbrowalking site (and others) that I consider. Parker and Song's work supports Wendy Chun's argument regarding the changing nature and perceptions of the Internet.

In *Control and Freedom: Power and Paranoia in the Age of Internet Optics*, Chun argues that discourses created around the topic of the Internet in the 1990s promised a race-free utopia in this new virtual world. Fans of color, however, realize that as Chun argues, what occurs is not truly freedom from discrimination but the chance, if one wishes, to pass as an unmarked white male. Such a chance results in erasure both of individuals and of minority groups. The 1990s claim that marked bodies are not "seen" (are invisible) in a text-only environment (which lasted for only a short time as visual and graphic programs appeared and grew in popularity) is based on the essentialist theory that difference is carried only by and on the body, as a physical sign, as opposed to a sociolinguistic theory that culture is created and "embodied" in part through language and in communities. The extent to which the "race-free" theory of the early Internet is related to white people's failure to "see" people of color in online spaces, such as fandom, is exemplified by the surprise Bujold expressed. However, such surprise is not unique to her, to fandom, or even to online spaces: commenters in the Wild Unicorn Herd Check-In report experiencing (and being tired of) expressions of surprise about their SF fannishness and activities by white people in SF fandom years before the Internet became an additional gathering space for fans. These fandom issues are directly connected to the larger cultural ones, such as the ones Alcoff considers in "Comparative Race, Comparative Racisms," an analysis of the issue of how affirmative action policies draw on problematic racial categories. In this project, I use her suggested methodology of social ethnography: "Given that ethnicity and race *only* figure as *social* kinds of entities, I suggest that we can learn about *what* they are from *how* they operate in communities and *what effects* they have on practice. In other words, given that their only locus of existence is the social realm, which includes practices, structures, and beliefs, we must look to find them here, and not in an imagined pre-social realm through intuition or conceptual analysis. Empirical based analysis may not yield an exhaustive or completely adequate account, but it is indispensable in order to draw out important aspects of the social ontology of race, ethnicity, and their interrelations."

Wild Unicorn Herd Taxonomies

The data used in this chapter were collected on 20 July 2012 by expanding all the responses to Delux_Vivens's post to what LiveJournal calls "flat view." The flat view gives easy access to the full text of all the responses as well as the original post and organizes them in chronological order. The view does lose the threaded format, which is the LiveJournal default. However, in this project, I am not looking at the different discussions between individual posters that the threaded view foregrounds, so that loss is not a problem. The content was copied and pasted to my hard drive, creating two files: an html version (with all the images and the formatting in LiveJournal), and a text version. Then I went through the text version manually and deleted all but the top-level responses (the responses to the original post); this editing left me with 785 responses by unique posters. Individual responses ranged in length from one word ("Me.") to several hundred (the longest one was 404 words). The total word count in the text file is 34,680 (including usernames and time stamps as well as the text of the posts). Then, using a combination of the "find" command in Word and reading and hand marking the printed-out document, I compiled lists of various kinds of identifiers used in the responses. My complete tables are in the following categories: Ethnicity/Nationality; Race; Intersectional; New Coinages; and Geographical Location Identifiers. Within the body of each table, the terms are arranged alphabetically. I then broke the larger tables into smaller ones, reflecting categories developed from the patterns I saw in the data. All the terms in the tables reflect the original users' spelling and punctuation except that I capitalized the first letters of words and keywords in phrases.

Table 1 lists the single-term identifiers; by *single-term*, I mean mostly one word or a phrase that is a name for a single location (Costa Rican). These terms are based on national, regional, or continental identifiers such as German, Caribbean, African. Terms clearly used as geographical locations (whether born in, living in, immigrated to) are in table 11. While many of these terms are similar to governmental and institutional taxonomies, there are others where the fans are members of indigenous cultures that have their own status as nations (Aboriginal, First Nations, Native). In this taxonomy, Aboriginal, Aztec, and Cherokee are equivalent to Chinese, German, and so forth.

Table 2 also contains single-term identifiers that are one word long, but I placed them in a different category for several reasons. They are recent coinages, mostly from vernacular and slang. Some originated in derogatory usage by colonizers and were reclaimed by some in the culture, such as Desi; others came from other languages but have not yet achieved the status of borrowed

Table 1. Single-Term National, Regional, and Continental Identifiers

Identifier	Count	Identifier	Count
Aboriginal	1	Jamaican	5
African	6	Japanese	16
Aztec	1	Korean	5
Barbadian	2	Kyrgyz	1
Cantonese	1	Latino	4
Caribbean	19	Malaysian	3
Cherokee	4	Navajo	1
Chicana	3	Mestizo	2
Chinese	93	Mexican	4
Eurasian	1	Native	20
Costa Rican	2	Pakistani	1
East Indian	6	Paraguayan	1
Egyptian	1	Singaporean	7
First Nations	2	Puerto Rican	10
German	4	Sami in Norway	1
Greek	1	Sri Lankan	2
Filipina	5	Swedish	3
Filipino	12	Taiwanese	1
Finnish	1	Torres Strait Islander	3
Hispanic	19	Trinidadian	2
Indonesian	4	Vietnamese	1

Table 2. Single-Term Vernacular and Recently Coined Identifiers

Identifier	Count	Description
Afro	5	Vernacular, for African American, can form compounds (see two words below). Earliest compound 1831.
Desi	10	Earliest use was derogatory (1885), a British term coined for the colonized natives in the Anglo Indian dialect. Starting in mid-twentieth century, became more descriptive. Outside South Asia used to identify South Asian origin. Derogatory still, for rustic, so obviously a reclaiming.
Pinoy	1	British origin, meaning an immigrant from the Philippines. Earliest written usage 1924.
Estadounidense	1	Mexican Spanish term for person from or born in the United States.
Ndn	3	Abbreviation/vernacular/slang for Indian (American Indian).
SpanaRican	1	Personal usages (MySpace, blogs, twitter) seem to indicate a blend of "Spanish" and "American."*
Trinis	16	Colloquial for Trinidadian. 1973.
Tsalagi	1	Cherokee in Cherokee (Iroquoian language spoken by the Cherokee).*

*Does not appear in *Oxford English Dictionary*

Table 3. Hyphenated National, Regional, and Continental Identifiers

African American	10	Guatemalan/Basque	1
African American and part Cherokee	1	Haitian/Dominican	1
African-Bermudan	1	Indian(/British)	1
African-Trinidadian	1	Indo-Caribbean	1
Afro-Caribbean	2	Indonesian Javanese	1
Afro-Caucasian	1	Iranian-American	1
American but not white	1	Jamaican-American	1
American Indian	1	Jamaican-Canadian	1
American Indian (Owingeh Pueblo) and African American	1	Jewish and Chinese	1
Anglo Indian	1	Jewish Hispanic	1
Arab American	3	Jewish-American	1
AsAm	1	Korean + more	1
Australian Peruvian	1	Korean American	6
Bengali Canadian	1	Korean Canadian	2
British Asian	2	Korean-American	5
British Filipino	1	Malaysian Chinese	4
British Indian	2	Malaysian Eurasian	1
British Nigerian	1	Malaysian Malay	2
Chinese and Canadian	1	Mauritian/English	1
Chinese Australian	1	Metis-Cree	1
Chinese Canadian	2	Mex-Am	6
Chinese/Czech	1	Nigerian-American	1
Chinese-Filipino	2	Persian/Pacific Islander	1
Cree and Cherokee	1	Peruvian-American	1
Cuban-American	2	Russian Jew	1
East Asian British 2nd generation	1	Seaconke Wampanoag/White	1
East Indian–West Indian	1	Singapore Chinese	3
Eritrean Canadian	1	Sinhalese with a dash of Dutch Burgher	1
Filipina American	2	Somali-American	1
Filipina-Canadian	1	South Asian	2
Filipino American	5	South Asian–American	6
Filipino-Chinese	2	Southeast Asian and French	1
First Nations Cree	1	Taiwanese American	2
French Canadian	2	Vietnamese-American	1
Guatemalan/Latina	1	West Indian	1

Table 4. Triple-Term National and Regional Identifiers	
American Hispanic (Mexican Spanish)	1
American of Cuban and Middle Eastern descent	1
Anglo-Burmese Brit	2
Canadian-Filipina-Portuguese	1
Caucasian, Afro-Caribbean, Amerindian (Arawak/Lokono)	1
Chinese Spanish Filipina	1
Chinese-Filipina-American	1
Choctaw, Cherokee, and Scottish	3
Cuban/Irish/??? native Floridian	1
Jamaican/Trini/American mix up of Black Chinese South Asian and so on	1
Korean American TCK	1
Malaysian Eurasian (mainly Chinese + faint traces of Portuguese blood)	1
Malaysian of Javanese-Arabic=Malay-Thai-mysterious	1
Mexican-American Texan	1
Mexican-American/Hispanic	1
Scottish Italian Aztec	1

Table 5. Quadruple-Term Continental and Immigrant Identifiers	
Choctaw/Irish/English/Black (dabs of almost everything else)	1
Irish, French, German, African-Bermudan and English, and African-American descent	1
Scots/Irish/German/Cherokee	1

words into mainstream English (Estadounidense and Tsalagi). Still others blend languages and nationalities (SpanaRican). Etymological information was taken from the *Oxford English Dictionary* when an entry existed; in other cases, Internet searches supplies the usage and definitions.

Table 3 lists what are sometimes (in the United States) called hyphenated identities. Originally a derogatory term for certain immigrant groups, the idea of hyphenated identities has been reclaimed by some members of immigrant groups. These pairs use terms that appear in table 1, usually signifying past colonialist histories, including diasporas and forced immigrations. Individual typographies (such as the uses of slashes, parentheses, the plus sign) have not been edited, though I have capitalized all words.

Table 6. Blended Racial and Ethnic Identifiers	
Biracial Zapotex Indian and White	1
Black Jamaican-Canadian	1
Black, but I'm also Chinese, English, East Indian, and Spanish	1
Black, Canadian, Caribbean	1
Black, Trinidadian	1
Black/Choctaw	1

Table 7. Half-and-half Racial or Ethnic Identifiers	
American, half-Korean	1
Half Caucasian half Bengali	1
Half Korean/Half white	1
Half-mestizo half white (Greek extraction)	1
Half-Australian, Half-Chinese	1
Half-Ghanaian Canadian	1
Half-Iranian Kurdish, half-white	1
Half-white American (German extraction), half Sri Lankan	1
Luk Khrueng* half-Thai half-Austrian	1

*Luk Khrueng ("child half") is a colloquial term meaning mixed Thai and white ancestry

Table 8. Mixed and Hybrid National or Racial Identifiers	
American of mixed heritage, mostly identifying as Hispanic but aware of my Ojibwe forebears	1
Caribbean Afro-mix	1
Chinese-Caucasian mixed	1
Desi/Irish hybrid	1
Jamaican/Trini/American mix up of Black, Chinese, South Asian	1
Mixed (African, Indian, European) from the Caribbean	1
Mixed heritage	1
Mixed-race Indigenous Australian	1
Mixed-Race, Puerto Rican, European	1
Mixed Race (South East Asian/Portuguesey/Welshish—Yeah it's complicated)	1

Table 9. Immigrant or Born to Immigrant Identifiers	
African-Trinidadian descended Canadian	1
African-American, Moroccan born	1
Australian-born Chinese/Scottish	1
Canadian-Born Chinese ancestry	1
French (of Indian/African descent) My parents were born in the French West Indies (Guadeloupe)	1
Korean-born Canadian	1
North Indian background	1
Panama-born Latina	1
US born Korean	1

Table 4 contains identifiers that are phrases using three terms (some with hyphens, parentheses, slash marks, or multiple punctuation marks). These are similar to the ones in table 3, but the additional terminology provides even more complex heritages/ancestries as identifiers. Most are still drawing on national or regional identifiers, but some use racial terminology, and there are also new coinages (TCK [third culture kids] are children who grow up outside their passport country, perhaps in multiple countries/cultures, because of their parents' professions). Some people use "???" to indicate gaps in their knowledge. This table and table 5 reflect identifiers that have more specificity and complexity than the terms in table 1.

Table 5 has identifiers drawing on four or more terms. These identifiers involve multiple continents and immigrant patterns and contain a mix of European, American, and First Nations terminologies. These are a relatively small group, but larger data sets may reveal more information about the usage of complex identifiers.

Tables 6–8 blend terminologies from racialized discourses ("black" and "Caucasian") with ethnic terminologies; in some cases, the identifiers pair concepts of "mixed" or "half" with national terminologies. Table 6 has examples that range from two to five identifiers in a phrase: they are grouped together because of the common pattern of starting with biracial/black and following with other national and ethnic identifiers. Table 7 contains those identifiers that use "half," often as the first word in the phrase (in all but two cases). Table 8 contains all those identifiers that use "mixed" (either in terms of heritage, national identities, or race) and "hybrid."

Table 9 contains the identifiers that all contain the word *born* in them, often identifying as born to immigrant parents. Sixteen posters identified

Table 10. Intersectional Identifiers	
18-Year-Old Mixed Race (Black and Irish) American Female	1
Afghan-American Muslim and Not a Unicorn	1
Bangladeshi British Born and Raised in a Muslim Family	1
Canadian native Woman	1
Ceylonese Mixed Chinese Girl Living in Singapore	1
Ethnic Chinese Singaporean Female Queer	1
Female Jewish Mestiza Mutt	1
Half Mexicana Who Loooooves That Foxy Foxy Seven of Nine	1
Hawai'i-Born Mixed-Blood Enrolled Seneca	1
Indian Girl from Canada	1
Indian Bombay-Born Bred and -Resident Brown on the Outside Aquamarine on the Inside	1
Iranian American Woman	1
Malaysian Malay Muslim	1
Native Alaskan/Filipina/White American Gal Here Sci-Fi Till I Die!	1
POC/Queer/Female	1
Queer Jewish Biracial Latin@	1
South Asian Chick	1
WOC	4

themselves as immigrants or the children of immigrants. These posters tended toward more use of hyphens, blending national/regional identities. The one user who specified "background" is also included here, though that may change when more data are analyzed.

Table 10 uses intersectional identifiers. By *intersectional*, I mean terminologies for identity that contain language reflecting two or more axes of identity: race or ethnicity plus gender, sexuality, religion, age, nationality, geographical location, or fandom-specific identifiers that were part of the phrases (as opposed to appearing in different clauses or phrases).

There were two new coinages relating to the title of the post ("Wild Unicorn Herd Check-In): twelve posters identified themselves as "unicorns" and five as "dinocorns." This usage seems related back to the premise of Wrede's novel (which removed indigenous cultures, replacing them with magical, fabulous beasts).

Table 11. Geographic Locations			
Alberta, Canada	1	Miami	1
Anishnabe	1	Middle East	4
Appalachia	1	Minneapolis	1
Austin, Texas	1	Minneapolis/St. Paul	1
Australia	9	Mississippi	1
Austria	1	Montreal, Canada	2
Belize	1	New Zealand	4
Brooklyn	2	Northeast USA	1
Bumblefuck, Texas	1	Northern Virginia	1
California	5	Norway	1
Caribbean	19	Oklahoma	2
Chicago	6	Peru	2
Costa Rica	2	Philippines	8
Delhi, India	1	Portland	1
Ecuador	1	Quebec	2
England	9	Queens	1
Finland	1	Rhode Island	1
Germany	1	S. Kitts	1
Hawaii	1	Saudi Arabia	1
Hawai'i	1	Seattle	4
Hong Kong	7	Seneca	1
India	12	Seoul	1
Indonesia	1	Shanghai	2
Italy	1	Singapore	13
Jamaica	12	South Africa	2
Japan	5	Southeast Asia	2
Lagos State	1	Southern United States	1
Latin America	3	Switzerland	1
London	2	Taiwan	2
Maine	1	Tampa (Ybor City)	1
Malaysia	2	Texas	2
Malaysia East Side	1	Tokyo	3
Massachusetts	2	UK	17
Md (Maryland)	1	US Deep South	1
Mexico	1	Venezuela	1
Mexico City	1	Whitefish Lank Band	1

Table 11 contains all the geographical locations (city, region, state, nation) given by the posters. At this point, I have ranked all the locations as equal (rather than breaking them into different categories). Further work needs to be done in identifying whether posters are giving birthplaces, current places of residence, or previous places of residence. But even a cursory reading reinforces the global nature of SF fandom on the Internet, even in this small and self-selected group.

These taxonomies, limited as they are, provide the beginning of categories that complicate the overly simplified and essentialist constructions of "race" that have existed, historically and currently, in the United States as well as the constructions of "race" in other countries. The complicated identifiers used by fans in a single community on a social network site show the possibilities for changing perceptions of racial identifiers by means of historicizing racial identifiers; incorporating terminologies from the vernacular; coining new terms; and layering, mixing, and remixing multiple terminologies from a variety categories. This ontological sociological work was all done in the context of making the "dark matter" (Thomas's term) of the universe more visible to the white SF community, meaning that SF identifiers are incorporated into the taxonomies of identity.

Notes

1. This anthology, the first of two groundbreaking collections of African American science fiction and fantasy, won the World Fantasy Award.

2. I suspect that the references to "magical animals" inhabiting the human-free continent played at least a part in the call for "wild unicorns" to check in.

3. My larger project, of which this essay is one part, is done entirely with public material on the Internet. I have not applied to become a member of any of the closed communities, though I do read public posts.

4. One reason for the fans' strong response to Bujold's comment was that it was made just two months after the demise of RaceFail '09, a lengthy, intense, and conflicted debate about cultural appropriation, race, and racisms in the SF communities that ran from Jan. to Mar. 2009 (Rydra_Wong).

5. Additional members of the multidisciplinary research team include Dr. Salvatore Attardo, Dr. Sarah Gatson, and Dr. Stephen Reysen. All of the team, except for Dr. Gatson, work at Texas A&M University–Commerce; Dr. Gatson is at College Station, the flagship campus of Texas A&M.

6. The need to consider the larger patterns of discourse across multiple Internet sites— for example, the one thousand posts in the RaceFail '09 debate, each containing multiple comments (some as many as five hundred) is why I have begun exploring digital humanities methodologies.

Works Cited

Alcoff, Linda. "Comparative Race, Comparative Racisms." *Race or Ethnicity: On Black and Latino Identity*. Ed. Jorge J. E. Gracia. Ithaca: Cornell UP, 2007. 170–88. www.alcoff.com/content/comprace.html. Web. 21 Oct. 2012.

The Carl Brandon Society Homepage. http://www.carlbrandon.org/about.html. Web. 25 June 2011.

Chun, Wendy H. K. *Control and Freedom: Power and Paranoia in the Age of Fiber Optics*. *Cambridge*: MIT P, 2007. Print.

Deadbrowalking. "The People of Color Deathwatch." http://deadbrowalking.livejournal.com/357066.html. Web. 25 June 2011.

Delany, Samuel R. "Racism and Science Fiction." *Dark Matter: A Century of Speculative Fiction from the African Diaspora*. Ed. Sherree R. Thomas. New York: Warner, 2000. 383–97. Print.

Delux_Vivens. "Wild Unicorn Herd Check In." Deadbrowalking. 11 May 2009. Web. 25 June 2011.

Fiction_Theory. "You're Hurting My Head Again, SF/F." Livejournal.com. 9 May 2009. http://fiction-theory.livejournal.com/116708.html?thread=288996#t288996. Web. 25 June 2011.

Hochschild, Jennifer L., and Brenna M. Powell. "Racial Reorganization and the United States Census, 1850–1930: Mulattoes, Half-Breeds, Mixed Parentage, Hindoos, and the Mexican Race." *Studies in American Political Development* 22.1 (2008): 59–96. Print.

Larbalestier, Justine. *The Battle of the Sexes in Science Fiction*. Middletown: Wesleyan UP, 2002. Print.

Merrick, Helen. *The Secret Feminist Cabal: A Cultural History of Science Fiction Feminisms*. Seattle: Aqueduct, 2009. Print.

Nakamura, Lisa. *Cybertypes: Race, Ethnicity, and Identity on the Internet*. New York: Routledge, 2002. Print.

———. *Digitizing Race: Visual Cultures of the Internet*. Minneapolis: U of Minnesota P, 2008. Print.

Parker, David, and Miri Song. "New Ethnicities Online: Reflexive Racialisation and the Internet." *Sociological Review* 54.3 (2006): 575–94. Print.

Rydra_Wong. 2009. "RaceFail '09. The Internet Is My Prosthetic Brain." 4 Feb. 2002. Web. 10 Ap. 2011. http://rydra-wong.dreamwidth.org/148996.html.

Thomas, Sheree R., ed. *Dark Matter: A Century of Speculative Fiction from the African Diaspora*. New York: Warner/Aspect, 2000. Print.

Wrede, Patricia C. *Thirteenth Child*. New York: Scholastic, 2010. Print.

Contributors

Marleen S. Barr is known for her pioneering work in feminist science fiction and teaches English at the City University of New York. She has won the Science Fiction Research Association Pilgrim Award for lifetime achievement in science fiction criticism (1997). Barr is the author of *Alien to Femininity: Speculative Fiction and Feminist Theory, Lost in Space: Probing Feminist Science Fiction and Beyond, Feminist Fabulation: Space/Postmodern Fiction,* and *Genre Fission: A New Discourse Practice for Cultural Studies.* Barr has edited many anthologies and coedited the science fiction issue of *PMLA* with Carl Freedman. She is the author of the humorous campus novel *Oy Pioneer!*

Gerry Canavan is an assistant professor of twentieth- and twenty-first-century literature in the Department of English at Marquette University. He is a coeditor of recent special issues of *Polygraph* and *American Literature* as well as of two forthcoming collections, *Green Planets: Ecology and Science Fiction* and *The Cambridge Companion to American Science Fiction.* He is currently at work on two books: one on SF, critical theory, and totality and the second on Octavia Butler.

Grace L. Dillon (Anishinaabe) is an associate professor in the Indigenous Nations Studies Program at Portland State University, where she teaches undergraduate and graduate courses on a range of interests including Native American and indigenous studies, science fiction, indigenous cinema, popular culture, race and social justice, and early modern literature. She is the editor of *Walking the Clouds: An Anthology of Indigenous Science Fiction* and *Hive of Dreams: Contemporary Science Fiction from the Pacific Northwest.* Her science fiction scholarship has appeared in *Science Fiction Film and Television, Foundation, Extrapolation,* and *The Journal of the Fantastic in the Arts.*

M. Elizabeth Ginway is an associate professor of Portuguese and Brazilian literature in the Department of Spanish and Portuguese Studies at the University of Florida. She is author of *Brazilian Science Fiction: Cultural Myths and Nationhood in the Land of the Future* and *Visão alienígena* and coeditor of *Latin American Science Fiction: Theory and Practice* (J. Andrew Brown). She has published articles related to science fiction in *Foundation, Extrapolation*, and *Science Fiction Studies*.

Matthew Goodwin recently completed his doctorate in comparative literature at the University of Massachusetts, Amherst. His research is centered on migration, which he examines through genres such as science fiction and digital culture. He is currently preparing to publish his dissertation, "The Fusion of Migration and Science Fiction in Mexico, Puerto Rico, and the United States."

Edward James is an emeritus professor of medieval history at University College Dublin. Between 1986 and 2001, he served as editor of *Foundation: The International Review of Science Fiction*. He received the Eaton Award for *Science Fiction in the Twentieth Century* (1994), and the Hugo Award (2005) for *The Cambridge Companion to Science Fiction* (coedited with Farah Mendlesohn). He also received the Science Fiction Research Association Pilgrim Award for lifetime achievement in science fiction criticism (2004). With Farah Mendlesohn, he coauthored *A Short History of Fantasy* and coedited *The Cambridge Companion to Fantasy Literature*. His next book will be on Lois McMaster Bujold. He currently serves as chair of the Science Fiction Foundation.

De Witt Douglas Kilgore is an associate professor of English at Indiana University. He is the author of *Astrofuturism: Science, Race, and Visions of Utopia in Space*. Recent publications include articles on scientific utopianism in Kim Stanley Robinson's fiction and Afrofuturism. He is a past recipient of the Science Fiction Research Association's Pioneer Award for best critical essay (2001).

Malisa Kurtz is a doctoral candidate in the interdisciplinary humanities program at Brock University. Her dissertation focuses on the intersections of postcoloniality, globalization, and technoculture in twentieth-century science fiction. She has forthcoming publications in the journals *Paradoxa* and *Science Fiction Studies*.

Isiah Lavender III is an assistant professor of English at Louisiana State University, where he researches and teaches race in American literature and science fiction.

In addition to *Race in American Science Fiction*, his publications on science fiction include essays and reviews in *Extrapolation*, *Journal of the Fantastic in the Arts*, and *Science Fiction Studies*. He is presently at work on a book project investigating the limits of Afrofuturism.

Robin Anne Reid is a professor of literature and languages at Texas A&M University–Commerce. Her teaching areas are creative writing, critical theory (critical race feminism, gender/queer theories, and sociolinguistics), and new media, especially how the Internet is changing the creation, production, and circulation of content. She has edited the first encyclopedia on women in science fiction *Women in Science Fiction and Fantasy* and has authored essays on feminisms in sf, *The Lord of the Rings* (novels and films), and fan fiction. Her current scholarship falls under the area of digital humanities and corpus stylistics, both in fan studies and Tolkien studies.

Lysa M. Rivera is an associate professor of English at Western Washington University, where she teaches courses in Chicano/a and African American literature and American cultural studies. Her current research interests involve the science fiction of multicultural America. Her critical work has appeared in *MELUS*, *Aztlán*, and *Science Fiction Studies*. She is a past recipient of the Science Fiction Research Association's Pioneer Award for best critical essay (2013).

Patrick B. Sharp is a professor and chair of liberal studies at California State University, Los Angeles. He is the author of *Savage Perils: Racial Frontiers and Nuclear Apocalypse in American Culture* and the editor of *Darwin in Atlantic Cultures: Evolutionary Visions of Race, Gender, and Sexuality*. He has also published articles on nuclear narratives, gender, race, and science fiction in *Twentieth Century Literature* and *Science Fiction Film and Television*.

Lisa Yaszek is a professor in the School of Literature, Media, and Communication at Georgia Tech, where she researches and teaches science fiction, critical gender and race studies, and science and technology studies. Her essays on science fiction as a global language crossing centuries, cultures and continents have appeared in *Extrapolation*, *NWSA Journal*, and *Rethinking History*. Yaszek is the author of *Galactic Suburbia: Recovering Women's Science Fiction* and editor of *Practicing Science Fiction: Critical Essays on Writing, Reading, and Teaching the Genre*. She is a past recipient of the Science Fiction Research Association's Pioneer Award for best critical essay (2005).

Index

CPSIA information can be obtained at www.ICGtesting.com
Printed in the USA
BVOW02*1654040914

365237BV00002B/5/P

9 781628 461237